Rethinking Contexts for Learning and Teaching

Now that learning is seen as lifelong and lifewide, what specifically makes a learning context? What are the resultant consequences for teaching practices when working in specific contexts? Drawing upon a variety of academic disciplines, *Rethinking Contexts for Learning and Teaching* explores some of the different means of understanding teaching and learning, both in and across contexts, the issues they raise and their implications for pedagogy and research. It specifically addresses:

- What constitutes a context for learning?
- How do we engage the full resources of learners for learning?
- What are the relationships between different learning contexts?
- What forms of teaching can most effectively mobilise learning across contexts?
- How do we methodologically and theoretically conceptualise contexts for learning?

Drawing upon practical examples and the UK's TLRP, this book brings together a number of leading researchers to examine the assumptions about context embedded within specific teaching and learning practices. It considers how they might be developed to extend opportunity by drawing upon learning from a range of contexts, including schools, colleges, universities and workplaces.

Richard Edwards is Professor of Education at the Stirling Institute of Education, University of Stirling, UK.

Gert Biesta is Professor of Education at the Stirling Institute of Education, University of Stirling, UK and Visiting Professor at Örebro University and Mälardalen University, Sweden.

Mary Thorpe is Professor of Educational Technology in the Open University Institute of Educational Technology, UK.

Rethinking Contexts for Learning and Teaching

Communities, activities and networks

Edited by
Richard Edwards, Gert Biesta and
Mary Thorpe

 Routledge
Taylor & Francis Group

LONDON AND NEW YORK

First published 2009
by Routledge
2 Park Square, Milton Park, Abingdon, Oxon, OX14 4RN

Simultaneously published in the USA and Canada
by Routledge
270 Madison Ave, New York, NY 10016

*Routledge is an imprint of the Taylor & Francis Group,
an informa business*

© 2009 Richard Edwards, Gert Biesta, Mary Thorpe

Typeset in Garamond by Keyword Group Ltd
Printed and bound in Great Britain by TJ International Ltd, Padstow,
Cornwall

British Library Cataloguing in Publication Data
A catalogue record for this book is available from the British Library

Library of Congress Cataloging-in-Publication Data
Rethinking contexts for learning and teaching / [edited by] Richard
Edwards, Gert Biesta, Mary Thorpe.
      p. cm.
    1. Learning—Philosophy. 2. Adult learning. I. Edwards, Richard, 1956
July 2- II. Biesta, Gert. III. Thorpe, Mary.
    LB1060.R448 2009
    370.15'23—dc22   2008036518

ISBN 13: 978-0-415-46775-9 (hardback)
ISBN 13: 978-0-415-46776-6 (paperback)
ISBN 13: 978-0-203-88175-0 (ebook)

ISBN 10: 0-415-46775-6 (hardback)
ISBN 10: 0-415-46776-4 (paperback)
ISBN 10: 0-203-88175-3 (ebook)

Contents

Figures

Contributors

Gert Biesta (www.gertbiesta.com) is Professor of Education at The Stirling Institute of Education, University of Stirling, UK and Visiting Professor at Örebro University and Mälardalen University, Sweden. He conducts theoretical and empirical research with a particular focus on the relationships between education, democracy and democratization. Recent books include: *Derrida and Education* (2001, co-edited with Denise Egéa-Kuehne); *Pragmatism and Educational Research* (2003, co-authored with Nicholas C. Burbules); *Beyond Learning: Democratic Education for a Human Future* (2006); *Improving Learning Cultures in Further Education* (2007, co-edited with David James); *Democracy, Education and the Moral Life* (2008, co-edited with Michael Katz and Susan Verducci).

Beth Crossan worked as a researcher in the field of lifelong learning for over ten years, based in the Centre for Research in Lifelong Learning (CRLL), Glasgow Caledonian University. During this time she researched many areas of lifelong learning, including policy making and implementation within the devolved Scotland, the development of the Scottish Credit and Qualifications Framework and community-based further education. Recently Beth moved from CRLL to take on a student-focused role, providing academic support and guidance within Glasgow Caledonian University.

Richard Edwards is Professor of Education at the The Stirling Institute of Education, University of Stirling. His research focuses on further and adult education and lifelong learning, with a particular interest in post-structural framings. Recent books include: *Globalization and Pedagogy: Space, Place and Identity* (2008, co-authored with Robin Usher), *Lifelong Learning – Signs, Discourses and Practices* (2007, co-authored with Robin Usher) and *Learning Outside the Academy* (2006, co-edited with Jim Gallacher and Susan Whittaker).

Alan Felstead is Research Professor at the Cardiff School of Social Sciences, Cardiff University. His research focuses on training, skills and learning, non-standard forms of employment and the spaces and places of work. He has completed over 30 funded research projects (including seven funded by the ESRC), produced five books and written over 100 journal articles, book chapters and research reports.

Steve Fox is Professor of Social and Management Learning, Department of Management Learning and Leadership, Lancaster University, UK. He researches in the area of practical action and social learning theory as applied to management and organization studies and education studies. Drawing upon ethnomethodology and actor-network theory, he undertakes studies of and critiques of situated learning and community of practice theory in management learning and education and in organization studies. This work sits in the interstices of management, education and sociology and he has published extensively in these areas.

Alison Fuller is Professor of Education and Work and Head of the Post Compulsory Education and Training Research Centre at the School of Education, University of Southampton. Her main research and publishing interests are in the fields of education – work transitions; vocational education, training and apprenticeship; workplace learning; and patterns of adult participation in education and training.

Jim Gallacher is Professor of Lifelong Learning and Co-director, Centre for Research in Lifelong Learning, Glasgow Caledonian University. Recent and current research interests include the work of further education colleges; links between further and higher education; widening access to further and higher education; work-related higher education; work-based learning; and credit and qualifications frameworks. He has managed a wide range of research projects on these topics, and published numerous articles, reports and books on the basis of this work. He is a member of the Scottish Funding Council for Further and Higher Education, where he chairs the Access and Inclusion Committee. He was an adviser to the Scottish Parliament's Enterprise and Lifelong Learning Committee for their Inquiry into Lifelong Learning.

Tamsin Haggis is Lecturer in Lifelong Learning at The Stirling Institute of Education, University of Stirling, Scotland. Her research focuses on the different ways that learning is defined, researched and theorized, particularly within the field of higher education. More generally, she is exploring the possibilities of complexity and dynamic systems theories in relation to theory, epistemology and method in educational research.

Roz Ivanič worked in the Literacy Research Centre, Lancaster University, UK. Her main research interests are pedagogy in adult literacy provision and how it relates to learners' lives and purposes for learning; academic literacy practices; the learning and teaching of writing; the discoursal construction of identity in writing; the multimodality of literacy practices; and integrating research with practice. She has written extensively on these topics. Between 2004 and 2007, she was Director of the ESRC TLRP funded project, Literacies for Learning in Further Education.

Carey Jewitt is a Reader in Education and Technology at the London Knowledge Laboratory, Institute of Education, University of London. Her research investigates the relationships between representation, technologies and pedagogy with a focus on visual and multimodal research methods and theory. Carey is co-editor of the journal *Visual Communication* and her books include *Technology, Literacy, Learning: A Multimodality Approach* (2006); *English in Urban Classrooms* (2005, with G. Kress and colleagues); *Multimodal Literacy*, (2003, edited with G. Kress) and *A Handbook of Visual Analysis* (2001, with T. van Leeuwen). She is currently editing *The Routledge Handbook of Multimodal Analysis* (forthcoming, 2009).

Nick Jewson is an Honorary Research Fellow at the Cardiff School of Social Sciences, Cardiff University, His research interests include the changing spaces and places of work, equal opportunities policies and practices, and processes of learning, education and training in employment relations.

Terry Mayes is an Emeritus Professor at Glasgow Caledonian University where he was Head of Academic Practice until 2006. He currently leads the evaluation and dissemination team for the Higher Education Academy's e-learning benchmarking and pathfinder programme. He is also advisor to the Scottish enhancement theme for the first year experience. In the first part of his career Terry taught cognitive psychology at the University of Strathclyde. He moved into full-time research in 1986, and in 1990 became Director of Research in the new Institute for Computer-based Learning at Heriot-Watt. Terry has a broad theoretical interest in learning and has been largely responsible for the modern awakening of interest in vicarious learning.

Kate Miller is a Researcher at The Stirling Institute of Education, University of Stirling, Scotland. She conducts research in teaching and learning and curriculum making with a particular interest in literacy and language. She was a researcher on the *Literacies for Learning in Further Education* project, funded through the Teaching and Learning Research Programme (TLRP) and was also the researcher for the *Contexts, Communities and Networks* TLRP Thematic Seminar Series. She is currently researching curriculum-making practices across Further Education and School contexts in an ESRC funded project.

David R. Russell is Professor of English at Iowa State University, where he teaches in the PhD program in Rhetoric and Professional Communication. His research interests are in writing across the curriculum, international writing instruction, online education and Cultural-historical Activity Theory. His book, *Writing in the Academic Disciplines: A Curricular History*, now in its second edition, examines the history of American writing instruction outside of composition courses. He has also co-edited four books, including *Writing and Learning in Cross-national Perspective*, with David Foster, and, with Charles Bazerman, *Writing Selves, Writing Societies*, a free online collection on activity theory and writing.

Candice Satchwell is a Research Associate at the Lancaster University Literacy Research Centre. From 2004 to 2007 she worked on the *Literacies for Learning in Further Education* research project funded by ESRC Teaching and Learning Research Programme, and then on a project on homelessness and educational needs and provision, funded by the National Research and Development Centre for Adult Literacy and Numeracy. She is also a Lecturer at Blackpool and The Fylde College on the BA (Hons) English programme. She has published work on children's concepts of punctuation, and has recent and forthcoming papers in the *Journal of Vocational Education and Training, The Teacher Trainer, Journal of Applied Linguistics,* and *Pedagogy, Culture and Society.*

Mary Thorpe is Professor of Educational Technology in the Open University Institute of Educational Technology, UK, where she was Director from 1995 to 2003. She is also one of the Principals in the Centre of Excellence in Practice-based Professional Learning. She has published and authored course materials in learner support, conceptualizations of open and distance learning and technology-enhanced learning. Her research focuses on three areas – the impact of computer-mediated interaction; the experience of learners in using ICT for practice learning; the potential of social networking tools for the development of practice learning. She was a member of the ESRC/TLRP Thematic Seminar Series: *Contexts, Communities and Networks.*

Lorna Unwin is Professor of Vocational Education and Deputy Director of the ESRC-funded Centre for Learning and Life Chances in Knowledge Economies and Societies (LLAKES) at the Institute of Education, University of London. Her research interests are in: the creation and use of vocational knowledge and skills; the role of work in people's lives and societies; apprenticeship as a model of skill formation (past and present); and the role of vocational education in a changing world.

Foreword

This book showcases findings from projects within the ESRC's Teaching and Learning Research Programme (TLRP) – the UK's largest-ever coordinated educational research initiative.

This edited collection comes from a thematic seminar series, organized by the editors, within the TLRP's portfolio, to follow up on themes that had arisen from a number of individual research projects. The seminar series was explicitly designed to support the work of the individual projects in providing 'evidence-informed' decisions in educational practice and policy-making. These projects, and the thematic seminars, combined rigorous social and educational science with high awareness of the theoretical and philosophical significance of the issues being researched.

Working closely with agencies, organizations and practitioners covering all educational phases, the programme has supported many of the UK's best researchers to work on the direct improvement of policy and practice to support learning. Over 60 projects have been supported, covering many issues across the lifecourse. In addition, there have been over 12 seminar series, developing cross-cutting themes from across the programme.

This supplementary book provides a concise, accessible and definitive overview of innovative findings and themes from across TLRP investments. If more advanced information is required, the book may be used as a gateway to academic journals, monographs, websites, etc. On the other hand, shorter summaries and *Research Briefings* on key findings from the individual projects are also available via the programme's website: www.tlrp.org.

We hope that you will find the analysis presented in this edited collection helpful to you in your work on improving outcomes for learners.

Miriam David,
Associate Director, TLRP,
Institute of Education,
University of London

Chapter 1

Introduction

Life as a learning context?

Richard Edwards

> Research on everyday practices typically focuses on the activities of persons
> acting, although there is agreement that such phenomena cannot be ana-
> lyzed in isolation from the socially material world of that activity. But less
> attention has been given to the difficult task of conceptualizing *relations*
> between persons acting and the social world. Nor has there been sufficient
> attention to rethinking the 'social world of activity' in relational terms.
> Together, these constitute the problem of context.
>
> (Lave 1996: 5, emphasis in original)

Introduction

Questions of context are not new, but are brought into particularly stark relief
by developments promoted through a discourse of lifelong learning. If learning
is lifelong and lifewide, what specifically then is a learning context? Are living
and learning collapsed into each other? Under the sign of lifelong learning
and following work on situated learning (e.g. Lave and Wenger 1991), a great
deal of attention is being given to those strata outside educational institutions
and other structured learning opportunities wherein people are held to learn.
The workplace, the home and the community can all be held to be strata of
learning, within which there are specific situations. In this sense, there are
learning contexts distributed across the associational order and embedded in
practices to such an extent that this order is itself already a learning context,
and potentially learning becomes undifferentiated as a practice from other
practices. Here the associational order becomes, by definition, a learning order
and all contexts are learning contexts.

Insofar as we expand our concept of learning to embrace apparently all
strata of life, we might be said to start to lose the conceptual basis for talking
specifically of a learning context. This raises important questions.

- What is specific to a learning context which is not to be found in other
  contexts?

- What characterizes a specifically learning context?
- What is the relationship between learning and context?
- Who names these contexts as learning contexts?

The latter is particularly important insofar as the discourses of educators, policy makers and researchers are not necessarily shared by those who are engaging in practices within the stratum identified as contexts of learning. Thus, for instance, doing family history may be considered a leisure activity by those who are engaging in it, when for many educators this could be considered a form of learning. The meaning and significance of practices can therefore be scaled in various ways. Insofar as people do not identify themselves as learning in different strata, they may not draw upon the artefacts and relationships available to them for learning in other strata. Here it is a question of what can be ascribed as learning by whom, rather than uncovering what is learnt. Learning is a discursive achievement, an effect.

However, insofar as learning is identified as taking place in a range of strata and the learners themselves move in and between them, then issues of *transfer* are raised, the presumed movement of learning from one activity to another. This may be from task to task within a single stratum or between strata, signifying different *distances* between contexts. However, even here we have to be cautious, as that notion of learning being transferred from one activity to another already assumes a certain view of learning and context, where learning is taken from one box and put into another. Here learning can be viewed metaphorically as a parcel moving from one mail box to another, an educational version of pass the parcel!

The question then emerges about how we understand a learning context, when the learning is not necessarily bound by a specific set of institutional relationships and structures. Pedagogic approaches may seek to bound the learning and the learner as belonging to a learning context, but there is also the sense in which there is a desire for learning to be mobile, to be for a purpose. This is exemplified, for instance, in the discourses of transferability and transferable skills and those of the recognition of prior experiential learning. In this sense, a context may be considered a bounded container within which the learning takes place or a more fluid and relational set of practices. In the former, there is a sense in which there is closure to contain or structure the learning, which once acquired may, in principle, be poured from one container to another.

> In all commonsense uses of the term, context refers to an empty slot, a container, into which other things are placed. It is the 'con' that contains the 'text', the bowl that contains the soup. As such, it shapes the contours of its contents: it has its effects only at the borders of the phenomenon under analysis ... A static sense of context delivers a stable world.
>
> (McDermott, quoted in Lave 1996: 22–3)

The relational framings find expression in theories of learning that emphasize activity and draw upon concepts of communities and networks rather than those of context. Here, rather than a thing, context is an outcome of activity or is itself a set of practices – contextualizing rather than context becomes that upon which we focus (Nespor 2003). Practices are not bounded by context but emerge relationally and are polycontextual, i.e. have the potential to be realized in a range of strata and situations based upon participation in multiple settings (Tuomi-Grohn et al. 2003). Here learning is a specific effect of practices of contextualization rather than simply emerging within a context. To understand context in static and/or relational terms has effects on how we conceptualize the mobilizing of learning across strata and associated pedagogic practices. To reject the notion of context in favour of that of activity or situated practice is one strategy. To change the understanding of context is another. It is the latter that largely informs the chapters in this book.

Framing contexts

Once we look beyond the context of conventional situations for education and training, such as schools, colleges and universities, allowing learning contexts to be extended into the dimension of relationships between people, artefacts and variously defined others mediated through a range of social, organizational and technological factors, then the limitations of much conventional pedagogy comes into sharp focus. Pedagogy has for some been defined as contained within the 'spaces of enclosure' of the classroom, the book and the curriculum (Lankshear et al. 1996). Here learners move from one classroom to another, one curriculum area to another, one institution to another in a linear step-by-step way. Learning is linear and cumulative. Identifying pedagogy in specific sites and strata across the life course, however, may require different conceptual framings where, for instance, there is no teacher as such, or teaching is embedded in texts of various sorts or in the peer support of the team.

The interest in lifelong learning has expanded the strata in which learning is now a concern for practitioners and the range of people who might be considered to have an educational role. It is not simply educators or teachers who have an educational role, but, for instance, supervisors, mentors, software designers or architects. Learning and pedagogy therefore have become in principle a part of many if not all aspects of social life. At least potentially, the whole of life becomes pedagogized. This is particularly the case when we take into account the growth of the consumer market in learning opportunities (Field 1996) and the structured, if distributed, opportunities and self-structuring practices provided by the Internet and other technologies (Lea and Nicoll 2002). The growth of e-learning and borderless education (Cunningham et al. 1997) raises significant questions regarding the relationships it can foster across cultures with implications regarding the different cultures of teaching and learning in different contexts and the value placed on different forms of learning. It also raises questions about how the use of computers in one strata – e.g. home, workplace – might be drawn into learning within education.

The relationship between learning in different strata is often framed by notions of informal, non-formal and formal learning and how to mobilize the full resources – e.g. funds of knowledge, literacy practices, experiential learning – of learners within specific situations. From a search of the literature, it is possible to locate a number of areas of debate and conceptual framings relevant to the question of context in the fields of:

- socio-cultural psychology (e.g. Tochon 2000; Edwards 2001);
- applied linguistics (e.g. Barton and Hamilton 1998; Barton *et al.* 2000, Maybin 2000; Russell and Yáñez 2003);
- social anthropology (e.g. Lave and Wenger 1991);
- social studies of science (e.g. Bowker and Star 2000); and
- organizational studies (e.g. Boreham *et al.* 2002).

These complement and contribute to existing work in education on areas such as

- informal and community-based learning;
- learning in the home;
- workplace learning (e.g. Eraut 2004);
- experiential and vicarious learning e.g. (Mayes *et al.* 2001);
- vertical and horizontal discourse (e.g. Bernstein 1999); and
- tacit knowledge (e.g. Eraut 2000).

There is thus a large multi-disciplinary range of conceptual resources upon which to pull in order to explore questions of learning and context. Some of this work focuses on strata other than educational institutions, e.g. the workplace, some on the relationship between stratum, e.g. home–school relationships, some on the relationships between people and other groups, and some on the transferability of learning from one stratum to another (e.g. Oates 1992; Eraut 2004). This area is enmeshed or rhizomatic in terms of the conceptual borrowings, entwinings and offshoots, which one can follow and that pop up all over the place. It is not a tidy arena or context of debate, thereby reflexively demonstrating the very complexity it is seeking to illuminate. It is thus the case that in bringing together a collection to explore the issue of learning and context, we have not sought to produce a tidy, singular view of the issues, but to illustrate the diversity of conceptual framing available.

What is perhaps significant is that much of the literature on learning is framed within a set of binaries, which separate strata from one another. Thus, broadly within the arena of cultural psychology, there is a distinction made between everyday and formal/scientific learning (see contributions to

Murphy and Ivinson 2003). In the realm of applied linguistics, the focus is on vernacular/contextualized and formal/decontextualized literacy practices (Barton and Hamilton 1998) framed within the everyday and educational experiences of learners. In educational research, the debate has become focused around either informal or experiential learning and formal learning.

Each of these binaries identifies that learning is occurring across a range of strata and situations, but that this learning is in some senses situated or contextualized. The range of learning contexts may therefore be extended and what can be identified as learning. However, their very situatedness and pedagogical approaches that assume domains to be discrete – we leave parts of ourselves at the metaphorical door of the classroom – mean that learning from one situation is not necessarily realized in other situations by either teachers or learners. Logically also, if learning occurs in particular situations, why should or how can it be relevant to other contexts?

This is the situation to which each of the areas of research addresses itself. There is the identification of a gap and exploration of how that comes to be and how these gaps might be overcome. This is sometimes in order that learners' resources can be realized in formal educational sites, but also vice versa, especially where the concern is for the transfer of learning from education to the workplace (Tuomi-Grohn and Engeström 2003a). Certain aspects of these debates might be perceived as a push-pull effect within research. Within the discourses of *education* there is tendency to centre the learning context within certain institutional sites, while within the discourses of *learning* there is a decentring of learning contexts, within which there is an identification of diverse but separate strata, e.g. workplace, home, etc.

Learning in different contexts may involve different types of learning, the learning of different somethings, and for different purposes, the value of which might be variable. We might therefore need to question the extent to which, as educational researchers and pedagogic practitioners, we should try to overcome the gaps between learning in different strata. Some practices may best be left where they emerge. Learners themselves might not want to overcome these gaps and may not even identify their practices as learning. It also involves the learning of something particular to each context, even if that something is a form of abstract, generalized knowledge as in parts of the curriculum of education (Lave 1996). Given the contemporary interest in notions of situated learning (Lave and Wenger 1991), there is of course the issue whether that overcoming might be possible at all. The educational rationale for such an approach is often that education is not recognizing or developing the full potential of learners by not mobilizing their full resources in formal sites, or that what is learnt is not relevant to the 'real world'. However, this has a centring logic to it, which tends also to deny conflict and difference in and through learning. It assumes the inherent worthwhileness and benignness of education that denies the very struggles in and around it, where some people seek to keep a gap between their lives and what is educationally available. Some might argue that education and pedagogy can and should change to be more inclusive, as though inclusion can overcome all gaps and struggles. However, this is to ignore that inclusions can only occur on the basis of exclusions and the constant play of difference (Edwards *et al.* 2001).

A concern is that in starting with these binaries, a whole discourse is produced as a result that sends us down particular pathways, looking at certain things in certain ways. As a result, we may realize only certain pedagogical issues and, perhaps more importantly, we may frame issues in educational terms when more appropriately they should be framed in other ways. With the above theories, there is a tendency for a slippage from framing literacy/learning/knowledge as practices, regardless of place, to framing them as spatially located practices in particular ways. As a result, we end up with discourses and practices about the inside and outside, with metaphors of scaffolding, boundary zones, boundary objects and border crossings discourses of parity of esteem and practices such as attempts at the accreditation of prior experiential learning and the production of all-encompassing credit frameworks. Similarly, simulations and boundary zones (Beach 2003, Tuomi-Grohn *et al.* 2003b) are formulated as mediators between strata within which pedagogy may seek to mobilize a fuller range of resources for learning than in the formal domain of education.

The discussion of informal and formal learning also often ignores the informality of learning in educational institutions and the formality of some learning in other organizations (Coffield 2000). Billett (2002) has argued that the informal/formal learning debate is a waste of time and that either people are learning or they are not. Colley *et al.* (2003) have argued somewhat differently that attributes of formality and informality can be found in all learning situations. These suggest that sites of learning are more complex and relational, as to produce the formal there must be a realization of that which is informal and vice versa. In other words, learning contexts are practically and discursively performed and performative. They co-emerge with the activities by which they are shaped and vice versa. Indeed Van Oers (1998), like Nespor (2003), suggests dropping the notion of contexts altogether to focus on contextualizing as a set of practices.

Conceptualizing learning contexts

In education, concepts of:

* communities of practice (Lave and Wenger 1991; Wenger 1998; Swales 1998);
* networks (Nespor 1994; Fox 2000; Poell *et al.* 2000);
* activity systems (Engeström *et al.* 1999); and
* complexity (Haggis 2007).

have come to the fore to help frame our understanding of pedagogy and address some of the perceived weaknesses of more conventional cognitive approaches to learning. Situated learning, activity theory and actor-network theory have been drawn upon in different ways by a range of writers to help conceptualize learning that is not confined to educational institutions. Metaphorically and analytically each attempts to frame learning in alternative ways to that of the context as container. There is a paradox in some of this, as the arguments are often that learning is only meaningful within the specific situation or context, but also that the latter is not itself absolutely distinct from other contexts. Thus the significance of notions of practice, activity and polycontextuality.

Conventionally we might focus on what occurs in one context to the exclusion of others. What is suggested here is that this is only an effective pedagogic strategy if we assume context as a container and as a result contain learning. This is something which is central to the notion of education as a curricular practice and it is perhaps noticeable that the discourse of learning has come to the fore through the backgrounding of questions of curriculum. When we start to question that, the interesting pedagogic space is that in-between arena of polycontextual practices, where 'elements from both sides are always present in the boundary zone' (Tuomi-Grohn et al. 2003b: 5). These are not closed spaces but networked and mediated strata, which give rise to alternative framings and metaphors, where context is an effect and not pre-existing the practices that give rise to it.

We can begin to explore these processes by drawing upon concepts derived from actor-network theory (Latour 1993), which focuses on the people and artefacts that are networked through the practices of purification – separating out – and translation – relating together. What results is a naturalizing of certain practices as an emergent part of learning-in-context, rather than context as a bounded, pre-existing container for them. Naturalizing is itself a set of practices – of folding and purification – through which a context emerges, one form of which might be as a bounded container. Here different networking practices make different contexts, meaning that the same objects may be part of different purifications, by being networked differently. Learning therefore relies on the purification practices in play of all actors and the power and hierarchies of value that make certain naturalizations more likely than others. Purification entails work to naturalize certain practices as learning in specific forms of situatedness, which are then taken for granted. Such views tend to view curricula as 'trajectories' rather than bodies of knowledge to be conveyed. 'Schooling works by moving people and things along trajectories that ultimately situate them in spatial and temporal orders where only certain meanings, identities, and lines of action can be easily sustained' (Nespor 2003: 98).

Different purifications and translations may bring forth different interactions or foldings in the learning of different knowledges, skills and communication practices. A question then arises whether we seek to relate different learning practices across strata within the current regime of purification or to change the regime. The former is framed within the logic of an existing semiotic landscape of situated contexts, while the latter arises in and from a more scrumpled geography in which the possibilities for purified geologies are thrown into question and a new regime for purification emerges which contains within it the desire for multiplicity and difference negotiated as a constant tension within the pedagogic (en)counter. These are not systems, nor communities of practice, each of which can be read as a series of containers, between which people, objects, practices, meanings move. Here we point to the significance of folding by contrast with notions of crossing borders or boundaries from one context to another. Folding entails work and can take multiple different forms signifying creolization and hybridity in purification practices. It also has the possibility of unfolding, which means that learning is insecure, the work to keep it contextualized and naturalized needs to be sustained if those practices are to continue.

Simple dichotomies or binaries, therefore, such as informal/formal, vernacular/formal, contextualized/decontextualized, participation/acquisition and purification/translation prove inadequate for investigating learning in and across different strata. This points to the limitations of a border crossing metaphor in conceptualizing the possible foldings between strata, despite its popularity among some as an alternative to notions of transfer (Tuomi-Grohn and Engeström, 2003b). I do not see these processes as simple border-crossings therefore, but as complex reorientations or changes in foldings, translations, purification and naturalization, which are likely to entail effort, awareness-raising, creativity and identity work on the part of the all concerned.

Boundary objects

What role might we identify here for boundary objects in and between learning contexts? The notion of boundary objects was developed in actor-network theory (ANT) (Star 1989), but has also been taken up by Wenger (1998) in his conceptualization of communities of practice. It is also to be found in activity theory. For Wenger (1998: 107) boundary objects work at the edges of communities of practice mediating their external relationships; 'they enable coordination, but they can do so without actually creating a bridge between the perspectives and the meanings of various communities'. However, some caution is necessary against a simple uptake of Wenger's view of boundary object, as these sit at the boundary of communities. In ANT, boundary objects sit within the middle of a network. The latter is more in keeping with the theoretical position suggested here, as the former still seems to indicate the notion of context as container rather than the more relational understandings which we are exploring in this book.

In ANT, boundary objects are

> both plastic enough to adapt to local needs and constraints of the several parties employing them, yet robust enough to maintain a common identity across sites. Like the blackboard, a boundary object 'sits in the middle' of a group of actors with divergent viewpoints.
>
> (Star 1989: 46).

They are

> plastic enough to adapt to local needs and the constraints of the several parties employing them, yet robust enough to maintain a common identity across sites. [...] They have different meanings in different social worlds but their structure is common enough to more than one world to make them recognizable, a means of translation. The creation and maintenance of boundary objects is a key process in developing and maintaining coherence across intersecting social worlds.
>
> (Star and Griesemer 1989: 393)

Such objects are not merely material; they can be 'stuff and things, tools, artefacts and techniques, and ideas, stories and memories' (Bowker and Star 2000: 298). They are objects which are not contained nor containable by context, but can be folded or crumpled between differing stratum, dependent on the various affordances at play and the work entailed in naturalizing them differently.

> Objects exist, with respect to a community, along a trajectory of naturalization. This trajectory has elements of both ambiguity and duration. It is not predetermined whether an object will become naturalised, or how long it will remains so, rather practice-activity is required to make it so and keep it so.
>
> (Bowker and Star 2000: 299)

Boundary objects do not sit between the borders of different contexts, at the edge, but express a relationship between strata brought together through the practices of folding, creolization, purification, translation and naturalization. These can be based upon pedagogic performances which seek to make certain connections rather than deny them, because they are the tokens through which people relate their practices between one stratum to another. They do not pre-exist practices, but rely on those practices to make them into boundary objects. This suggests that the 'normal' condition for practices is as a boundary object with multiple possibilities or stablizations. Rather than think of boundary objects as stable things that can be related to different contexts, we might rather think of them as fluid and capable of being stabilized within different networks.

There are more questions that answers

I cannot begin to fully embrace the conceptual sophistication of all the positions upon which we have drawn above in this book, but we try and make a start. The question of context is large and many debates in different disciplines are relevant. In the strata of research and practice, therefore, there are significant issues to be addressed and tensions in approaches to practice and descriptions and explanation of pedagogy. How such framings constitute a learning context and their implications for learning and teaching across the life course requires closer attention therefore. It is to an exploration of some of the possibilities and issues that the chapters in this book are addressed. There are three broad questions which we try to address:

1. What are the assumptions about learning and context underpinning pedagogical practices?
2. What are the pedagogical implications of understanding learning and context in particular ways?
3. How can we best understand learning and context in order to mobilize learners' resources and relationships across domains and should we?

It is with such questions that the chapters in Part II of the book attempt to engage, whether exploring the question of learning and context in the classroom (Jewitt), the learning relationships in community-based college provision (Crossan and Gallacher), the mobilizing of literacy practices from the everyday to the formal curriculum (Satchwell and Ivanic), the mediations of different levels of context in the workplace (Unwin and her colleagues), or the networked mediations in online learning (Thorpe). Each chapter explores specific pedagogical cases and highlights some of the issues and illustrates some of the conceptual framings through which we can explore issues of learning and context. Most draw to varying degrees upon conceptual framings which are introduced in Part I of the book, whether these are from activity theory and genre studies (Russell), actor-network theory (Fox), complexity theory (Haggis) or pragmatism (Biesta). While many of the chapters in Part II of the book draw primarily upon social–cultural understandings of learning and context, associated with activity theory and situated learning, the perspectives provided by Fox, Haggis and Biesta seek to challenge some aspects of emerging orthodoxy. Part III of the book draws upon what has gone before to explore the implications for pedagogy (Mayes and Thorpe) and research (Miller).

The collection as a whole does not and is not intended to suggest definitive ways of settling debates in this area. It is intended as a stimulus to further debate on a set of issues and questions which are implicit in the daily practices of pedagogy, but which are not always surfaced. It is to the exploration of the taken for grantedness of the notion of a learning context that this book is addressed as a means to build theoretical capacity in research for the future.

Note

The ideas explored in this chapter have been rehearsed on a number of occasions since 2005. I would like to thank the many people who have engaged on the issues raised and the formulations put forward. The chapter and those in the rest of the book are based upon work funded by the ESRC's Teaching and Learning Research Programme (ref: RES-139-25-0174) for which we express our gratitude. The chapters in this book have all been refereed by the editors.

References

Barton, D. and Hamilton, M. (1998) *Local Literacies*. London: Routledge.

Barton, D., Hamilton, M. and Ivanic, R. (eds) (2000) *Situated Literacies*. London: Routledge.

Beach, K. (2003) 'Consequential transitions: a developmental view of knowledge propagation through social organisations', in T. Tuomi-Grohn and Y. Engeström (eds) *Between Work and School: New Perspectives on Transfer and Boundary-crossing*. London: Pergamon.

Bernstein, B. (1999) 'Vertical and horizontal discourse: An essay', *British Journal of Sociology of Education*, 20, 2: 157–73.

Billett, S. (2002) 'Critiquing workplace learning discourses: Participation and continuity at work', *Studies in the Education of Adults*, 34, 1: 65–7.

Boreham, N., Samurcay, R. and Fischer, M. (eds) (2002) *Work Process Knowledge*. London: Routledge.

Bowker, G. and Star, S. (2000) *Sorting Things Out: Classification and its Consequences*. Cambridge, MA: MIT Press.

Coffield, F. (2000) 'Introduction: The structure below the surface: Reassessing the significance of informal learning', in F. Coffield (ed.) *The Necessity of Informal Learning*. Bristol: Policy Press.

Colley, H., Hodkinson, P. and Malcolm, J. (2003) *Informality and Formality in Learning*. London: LSDA.

Cunningham, S., Tapsall, S., Ryan, Y., Stedman, L., Bagdon, K. and Flew, T. (1997) *New Media and Borderless Education: A Review of the Convergence Between Global Media Networks and Higher Education Provision*. Canberra: Department of Employment, Education, Training and Youth Affairs.

Edwards, A. (2001) 'Researching pedagogy: A sociocultural agenda', *Pedagogy, Culture, Society*, 9, 2: 161–86.

Edwards, R., Armstrong, P. and Miller, N. (2001) 'Include me out: Critical readings of social exclusion, social inclusion and lifelong learning', *International Journal of Lifelong Education*, 20, 5: 417–28.

Engeström, Y., Miettinen, R. and Punamaki, R.-L. (eds) (1999) *Perspectives on Activity Theory*. Cambridge: Cambridge University Press.

Eraut, M. (2000) 'Non-formal learning, implicit learning and tacit knowledge in professional work', in F. Coffield (ed.) *The Necessity of Informal Learning*. Bristol: Policy Press.

Eraut, M. (2004) 'Informal learning in the workplace', *Studies in Continuing Education*, 26, 2: 247–74.

Field, J. (1996) 'Open learning and consumer culture', in P. Raggatt, R. Edwards and N. Small (eds) *The Learning Society: Trends and Issues*. London: Routledge.

Fox, S. (2000) 'Communities of practice, Foucault and actor-network theory', *Journal of Management Studies*, 37, 6: 853–67.

Haggis, T. (2007) 'Conceptualizing the case in adult and higher education research: A dynamic systems view', in J. Bogg and R. Geyer (eds) *Complexity, Science and Society*. Oxford: Radcliff.

Lankshear, C., Peters, M. and Knobel, M. (1996) 'Critical pedagogy and cyberspace', in H. Giroux, C. Lankshear, P. McLaren and M. Peters (eds) *Counternarratives*. London: Routledge.

Latour, B. (1993) *We Have Never Been Modern*. Harlow: Harvester Wheatcheaf.

Lave, J. (1996) 'The practice of learning', in S. Chaiklin and J. Lave (eds) *Understanding Practice: Perspectives on Activity and Context*. Cambridge: Cambridge University Press.

Lave, J. and Wenger, E. (1991) *Situated Learning*. Cambridge: Cambridge University Press.

Lea, M. and Nicoll, K. (eds) (2002) *Distributed Learning*. London: Routledge.

Maybin, J. (2000) 'The new literacy studies: Context, intertextuality and discourse', in D. Barton, M. Hamilton and R. Ivanic (eds) *Situated Literacies: Reading and Writing in Context*. London: Routledge.

Mayes, J.T., Dineen, F., McKendree, J. and Lee, J. (2001) 'Learning from watching others learn', in C. Steeples and C. Jones (eds) *Networked Learning: Perspectives and Issues*. London: Springer.

Murphy, P. and Ivinson, G. (2003) 'Pedagogy and cultural knowledge', special issue of *Pedagogy, Culture and Society*, 11, 1.

Nespor, J. (1994) *Knowledge in Motion*. London: Falmer.

Nespor, J. (2003) 'Undergraduate curricula as networks and trajectories', in R. Edwards and R. Usher (eds) *Space, Curriculum and Learning*. Greenwich: IAP.

Oates, T. (1992) 'Core skills and transfer: Aiming high', *Educational Technology and Training International*, 29, 3.

Poell, R., Chivers, G., Van der Krogt, F. and Wildemeersch, D. (2000) 'Learning-network theory', *Management Learning*, 31, 1: 25–49.

Russell, D. and Yanez, A. (2003) ' "Big picture people rarely become historians": Genre systems and the contradictions of general education', available at http://wac.colostate.edu/books/selves_societies/ (accessed 25 March 2004).

Star, S.L. (1989) 'The structure of ill-structured solutions: Boundary objects and heterogeneous distributed problem solving', in L. Gasser and M. Huhns (eds) *Distributed Artificial Intelligence*, Vol. II. London: Pitman.

Star, S. and Griesemer, J. (1989) 'Institutional ecology, "translations" and boundary objects: Amateurs and professionals in Berkeley's Museum of Vertebrate Zoology', *Social Studies of Science*, 19: 387–420.

Swales, J. (1998) *Other Floors, Other Voices: A Textography of a Small University Building*. Mahwah, NJ: Lawrence Earlbaum.

Tochon, F. (2000) 'When authentic experiences are "enminded" into disciplinary genres: Crossing biographic and situated knowledge', *Learning and Instruction*, 10: 331–59.

Tuomi-Grohn, T. and Engeström, Y. (eds) (2003a) *Between Work and School: New Perspectives on Transfer and Boundary-crossing*. London: Pergamon.

Tuomi-Grohn, T. and Engeström, Y. (2003b) 'Conceptualizing transfer: From standard notions to developmental notions', in T. Tuomi-Grohn and Y. Engeström (eds) *Between Work and School: New Perspectives on Transfer and Boundary-crossing*. London: Pergamon.

Tuomi-Grohn, T., Engestrom, Y. and Young, M. (2003) 'From transfer to boundary-crossing between school and work as a tool for developing vocational education: An introduction', in T. Tuomi-Grohn and Y. Engestrom (eds) *Between Work and School: New Perspectives on Transfer and Boundary-crossing*. London: Pergamon.

Van Oers, B. (1998) 'From context to contextualizing', *Learning and Instruction*, 8, 6: 473–88.

Wenger, E. (1998) *Communities of Practice*. Cambridge: Cambridge University Press.

Part I

Conceptualizing contexts of learning

Chapter 2

Texts in contexts

Theorizing learning by looking at genre and activity

David R. Russell

Written texts are central to formal education. The reading (consumption) and writing (production) of texts constitutes a great deal of the activity of students and teachers, and usually forms the basis for assessment and sorting. For this reason, a whole range of fields have taken up the problem of 'literacy' (or rather literacies) in formal schooling, not only applied linguistics, rhetoric and education, but also sociology, semiotics, psychology, social psychology, socio-linguistics, linguistic anthropology, communication studies and so on. Similarly, learning in workplace and civic contexts is also highly dependent on literacy, and the relations between formal schooling and other contexts for learning are also mediated by alphanumeric texts.

Yet the relationship between texts and the contexts of education has not typically been a central concern of education, either in its practice or in educational theory, until rather recently. Reading and writing tend to be viewed, at least in modern western culture, in dualist terms, through metaphors of conduit and container. Texts are seen as mere conduits for thought or meaning or ideas or 'content', and largely thought of as independent of social context. Similarly, contexts tend to be viewed as containers for communication, as Richard Edwards points out in his chapter in this book, quoting McDermott:

> In all commonsense uses of the term, context refers to an empty slot, a container, into which other things are placed. It is the 'con' that contains the 'text', the bowl that contains the soup. As such, it shapes the contours of its contents: it has its effects only at the borders of the phenomenon under analysis ... A static sense of context delivers a stable world.
> (McDermott, quoted in Lave 1996: 22–3)

In viewing texts as conduits and their contexts as containers, the production, circulation, reception and use of texts tends to disappear from conscious attention, and instead one attends to the ideas, etc. they 'transmit' or 'contain'. Writing disappears, as Derrida (see Neel 1988) argues. The process of education becomes a question of transmission through the transparent conduit of language, and social practices involved with reading and writing are bracketed off, in this dualistic view, as the containers of thought or 'content'. For much educational research, this has also been true. Lea and Street (1998) have characterized this conduit and container view as the 'autonomous model' of literacy. It makes 'universal claims for literacy which are related to beliefs in fundamental cognitive differences between literate and non-literate groups in society, and ... relates becoming literate to the development of logical thought and abstraction' (Lea 1998). Learning to read and write become in this view a single, generalizable set of skills, usually learned at an early age, and the rest is remediation of a deficit. Indeed, the deficit model is nowhere more powerful than in literacy education.

From container/conduit to network/activity approaches: New literacy studies and the new rhetoric

In reaction against the dualist conduit/container approach and the autonomous model of literacy, traditions of research have grown up in the last 35 years that theorize educational contexts in relation to language. One of these, North American genre theory, begun in the 1980s (Russell 1997b; Bazerman and Russell 2003), grows out of US traditions of rhetorical analysis applied to texts, particularly the concept of genre as social action (Miller 1984), with deep roots in Schutz's phenomenological analysis of typification (Schutz and Luckmann 1973). It is often combined with Vygotskian cultural-historical activity theory, in various versions. It views texts as material tools that are shared among people in dynamic social practices, tools that mediate their interactions, including reading and writing, speaking and listening, viewing and designing – literacy. This tradition systematically takes into account the contexts of communication. Indeed, it does not separate reading and writing, etc. from the contexts and practices which they mediate.

As Figure 2.1 suggests, transmission models of education and communication, such as behaviourism and information-processing cognitive psychology, generally see transmission between individual minds (or brains) as the focus, and lump everything else together as context (the left side of Figure 2.2). Social context is what contains the interaction and transmission models tend to view literacy as autonomous, transparent, uninteresting, because the emphasis in the analysis is on what is contained (in the container or the conduit of language).

Cultural-historical activity theory approaches to literacy often take the 'network' as their metaphor for context. People and their tools (including especially those tools called symbols) form complex networks of interactions, stabilized-for-now in literacy practices. These models, which I have called 'shared tool models' (the right side of Figure 2.2) see context as a weaving together of people and their tools in culture. The network *is* the context. Etymologically, context (con-text) is from the Greek term for weaving, as in

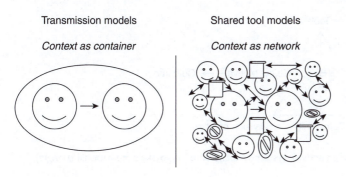

Figure 2.1 'Context' as container or network.

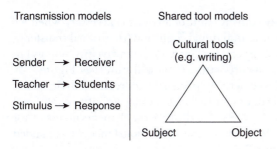

Figure 2.2 Transmission v. shared tool models of communication.

textile, or texture. In this sense, context is what is 'woven together with' (Cole 1996). These linguistic approaches view the diagram on the right of Figure 2.1 – the messy one – as a much more accurate picture of what instructors and researchers face when they try to understand what is happening with a student or a classroom. Students' interactions, past, present, and (hoped for) future, all play a part in their (and the instructor's) learning. The problem is that it is hard to know what to focus on in our analysis. How can we do justice to the complexity while still coming up with a useful analysis?

Activity theory and the new rhetoric: Learning by expanding

Activity theory is a development of Vygotsky's (1978) theories of tool mediation and zone of proximal development, Activity theory tries to make sense of the messy networks of human interactions by looking at people and their tools

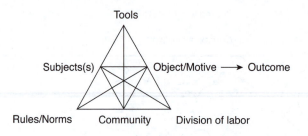

Figure 2.3 Model of an activity system (expansion of Vygotsky's mediational triangle).

as they engage in particular activities. Activity theory calls these networks and theorizes context in terms of activity systems (Leont'ev 1981; Cole and Engeström 1993).

This broad (some would say squishy) unit of analysis is necessary when we go beyond transmission models of individual cognition (traditional transfer of skills or cognitive apprenticeship) or a specific task (cognitive psychology) to take a shared tool approach that incorporates a range of features (see Figure 2.2).

Vygotsky's theory of mediated activity primarily addressed individuals or dyads. It was broadened by Leont'ev in the 1940s to an activity system, and elaborated by Cole and Engeström (1993) to theorize the elements necessary for understanding social activity. Vygotsky's basic mediational model is expanded in the triangles shown in Figure 2.3.

In a course in higher education, for example, there are the people involved, the students and teacher. These are the subjects, with their identities, their subjectivities; and one can use this flexible triangular lens to zoom in and out: to one student, to several or all the participants, or to the whole institution or discipline, depending on the research questions one is asking.

In a course in formal schooling there are a range of tools. There are desks, chalkboard, and so on, but also other material tools: spoken, written and visual symbols (sounds in the air and marks on surfaces) which can be analyzed as belonging to various genres: syllabus, lectures, discussions, readings, writing assignments, grade books, grade report forms, diplomas. These literacy tools are shared among the participants as part of ongoing and 'stabilized-for-now' practices, though the literacy tools and practices are interpreted in different ways, used in different ways.

A course also has an object (the content or object of the discipline) and motive, though here we get into difficulties because the teacher and the students sometimes have very different – even contradictory – motives. There are the official motives, the 'compentencies,' and so on; but students and teachers may have their 'own' motives as well. So we have a potential contradiction in motives.

There is a division of labour. The teacher does certain things and the students do other things. One has more power than the others. There is a community in the classroom, though the kind of community differs in different classrooms. There are rules, both official rules and unofficial, unwritten rules or norms. Some of these rules or norms are conventions for using writing in the university or in the discipline or in other systems of activity beyond schooling. Finally, the activity system produces outcomes. People are potentially different when they leave, one way or another, individually and perhaps collectively. Learning (a kind of change) went on – though not always in ways that the teacher, much less the students, had in mind.

Activity theory, then, sees human activity (including communication and learning) in broader – and messier – terms than transmission models. Higher-order learning (unlike rote learning or mere imitation) is not viewed as the process of passing something from sender to receiver, teacher to student, and transfer is not viewed as knowledge or know-how (skills) carried from one context to another. Rather, learning is viewed as change resulting from expanding involvement with others over time, developmentally, in a system of social activity (activity system), mediated by tools, including texts, and practices. This is what Cole and Engeström (1993) call *learning by expanding*.

Similarly, transfer is viewed in terms of expanding involvement across contexts – horizontal as well as vertical development. Learning is viewed in both individual and collective terms. Individuals expand their knowledge and know-how through involvement with others, but collectives (whether members of the class, an organization or discipline, an institution) may expand their involvements and reorganize their activity as well.

However, to theorize expansion through different contexts, one must theorize the relations of all these elements in *multiple* activity systems, what Engeström *et al.* call polycontextuality, the 'third stage' of activity theory (Engeström, Engeström and Kärkkäinen 1997). Participants within one activity system, one context, come from various contexts, and will enter various contexts. To understand the various ways participants interpret and use the tools, object, motive, rules/norms, etc. of an activity system, it is often necessary to analyze the relations among various contexts.

Figure 2.4, for example, is a diagram of a university course in Irish history we recently analyzed (Russell and Yañez 2003), showing some of the activity systems that participants mentioned as affecting their behaviour in the course.

All of the students in the university Irish history course had learned history in secondary school, but none of them were planning to become academic historians. They interpreted the activity system and literacy practices of the course differently, in light of the activity systems in which they had previously been participants, or the activity systems they would enter, and/or the activity systems in which they would continue to be participants: the university, or careers (journalism for some) or hobbies (a love of things Irish), or critical citizenship (the then-current political controversies in Ireland). So students saw the tools,

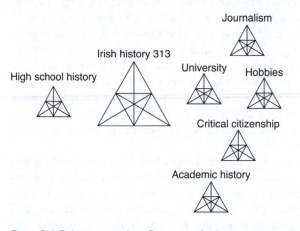

Figure 2.4 Polycontextuality: Diagram of salient activity systems of an HE Irish history course.

object and motive in different ways and read and wrote differently than the teacher expected.

The direction or motive of an activity system and its object are contested, as individuals bring many motives to a collective interaction. Indeed, the division of labour in the system itself guarantees diversity. Dissensus, resistance, conflicts and deep contradictions are constantly produced in activity systems. These differences in participants' perceptions of the object and motive, within and among activity systems, means that people are often at cross-purposes. The object and motive of the activity system are inevitably resisted, contested, and/or negotiated. Similarly, the tools, rules, community and division of labour are often perceived differently, and thus also resisted, contested and/or negotiated – overtly or tacitly, consciously or unconsciously.

In Engeström's version of AT, these tensions within and among activity systems are viewed as symptoms of deeper dialectical contradictions, 'historically accumulating structural tensions within and between activity systems' (Engeström 2001: 137). All human activity is contradictory at a very basic level. Human actions are at once individual and social. In each culture and each activity system specific contradictions arise out of the division of labour. These contradictions are the source of discoordinations, tensions and conflicts. In complex activities with fragmented division of labour, the participants themselves have great difficulties in constructing a connection between the goals of their individual actions and the object and motive of their collective activity. Within these contradictions, the identities of the participants are also formed and negotiated.

Engeström argues that the fundamental contradiction of educational activity in capitalist societies is that of exchange value versus use value (socialist education has its own contradictions, which require a different analysis). This contradiction, he says, produces alienation, as in many other activity systems in capitalist societies. Are students just 'doing school', doing it 'for the grade', which will be exchanged or cashed out later? (The motive of a grade within the activity system of the university.) Or are they doing something for which they can see some use value in their lives, now or in the future? (Activity systems of hobby, career, citizenship, etc).

These various interpretations of the activity may give rise to alienation (Engeström 1999), but contradictions also present a constant potential for change in people and tools (including writing) – for transforming – re-mediating – activity systems. Thus, there is always potential for expansive learning, both individual and social, for becoming a changed person and changed collectives, with new identities, new possibilities – often opened up (or closed down) through reading and writing in various genres. These deep dialectical contradictions within and among activity systems profoundly condition (but never finally determine) what individual teachers and students do (and do not do) – and what they learn (and do not learn).

Research on reading and writing practices have for almost twenty years now found that people have great difficulty coming to write and speak in the specialized ways demanded by the complex division of labour, within or across activity systems (McCarthy 1987, Dias *et al.* 1999). This is true even of highly placed insiders in an activity system who are called on to write or speak in new ways, as in Smart's (2000b) study of a Canadian central bank manager forced to write a new genre. Not much seems to 'transfer' (a finding as old as Judd) (Tuomi-Grohn *et al.* 2003) and this has led some (Dias *et al.* 1999) to argue that formal education, because of its different social motives and organization, simply cannot prepare people for new workplace literacies – that only situated learning or apprenticeships (learning by doing) can provide the specific knowledge and know-how necessary for specialized literacy in the workplace.

Yet there are perhaps ways of analyzing the textual relationships among activity systems that would allow for restructuring (re-mediating) formal education to facilitate learning by expanding in more or less formal ways. One useful theoretical concept is that of boundary objects, material or conceptual tools that bridge the chasm and provide pathways to mediate expanding involvement (Star 1989). One sort of boundary object that has been fruitful in some research is texts, and particularly texts in systems of genres.

North American genre theory: Systems of genre/activity

One way that researchers in North America have tried to systematically understand learning across contexts is through genre. In North American genre theory (Freedman and Medway 1994a, 1994b; Russell 1997a), genres are understood not merely as formal textual features, textual conventions. Genres are also seen as expected ways of using words to get things done in certain recurring situations – literacy practices in and among activity systems. This brings into genre analysis questions of social motive and identity – the why and who of genre. For genre expectations enact the division of labour, define roles, and, in Miller's (1984) phrase 'signal what intentions we may have'.

To analyze the ways texts mediate activity, one must go beyond the conventional notion of genre as a set of formally definable text features that certain texts have in common across various contexts, however defined, and consider genre in relation to social action and social motives in specific contexts, specific literacy practices. North American genre theory defines genres, following Miller (1984), as typified ways of purposefully *interacting* in and among some activity system(s). Genres are not merely texts that share some formal features; they are shared expectations among some group(s) of people. Genres are ways of recognizing and predicting how certain tools, in certain *typified* – typical, reoccurring – conditions, may be used to help participants act together purposefully. In this sense, genres, as Bazerman (1994) says, are not best described as textual forms, but as 'forms of life', ways of being, frames for social action. They are environments for learning and teaching. As 'forms of life', genres and the activity systems they operationalize are (temporarily) regularized, stabilized, through routinized tool-use within and among groups. Thus, 'context' is an ongoing accomplishment, not a container for actions or texts. The behaviour of individual writers/subjects is constantly recreated through the specific actions of people together; and thus, genres are always only 'stabilized-for-now', in Schryer's apt phrase (1994), from the point of view of the group or groups involved.

This more dynamic and situated theory of genre has been developed to see the relationships among genres, in and across contexts, as knowledge and know-how (as well as structures of power) are re-inscribed in new genres. Bazerman's genre systems theory (1994) (or Spinuzzi's [2003] related genre ecologies theory) analyze the ways genres form systems that follow and mediate the work pathways within and among activity systems. Systems of genres realize social motives, focusing attention and coordinating action, and they shape (and are shaped by) the identities of participants. In a hospital, for example, medical records in a huge range of genres are all intertextually linked (now on computer): medical histories, test results, prescriptions, insurance forms and so on coordinate the work and shape the identities of patients, nurses, technicians, bureaucrats, researchers, advocacy groups and so on (Bawarshi 2003). To take another example, in a university, assignments produce student writing, comments on papers, etc. Grades are entered on grade forms and then transcripts and eventually produce diplomas, one hopes, and resumes and so on, each linked intertextually.

Learning to function in some workplace is to know how discourse circulates in genre systems, where one stands in relation to the literacy practices, and how to realize the motives, individual and/or collective, through reading and writing in certain ways, as well as acting in certain ways – and being able to negotiate the conflicts and changes with the 'stabilized-for-now' structure.

Moreover, the genres of workplace practices are intertextually linked to the genres of formal schooling. The textbook representations of a field are related to those of research reports in the disciplines and professions. The genres' research reports written by professionals in workplaces are linked, intertextually, to classroom genres of research papers (as they are called in the US), the laboratory reports of lab technicians to the lab reports of students, through citations, allusions, references, organizational structures and so on. Similarly, the genres of workplace activity and formal education are intertextually linked to genres of mass communication (news reports on scientific findings, for example). The rhetorical life of information is one of continual textual transformation as it moves through various contexts in systems of genres. Sometimes these are regularized formally or even legally (e.g. food labels). Sometimes they are less formal (web blogs and other more personal genres), but these transformations, and powerful networks through which these systems function, can become resources for analyzing and changing teaching and learning (for example, by introducing into formal education genres other than the essay – and with it the essayist literacy practices so entrenched in higher education) (Scollon and Scollon 1981).

Through the boundary of classroom genre systems, one can construct a model of ways classroom writing that is linked to writing in wider social practices and rethink such issues as agency, task representation, learning and assessment (Russell 1997a). Genres and their systems help us make sense of what is happening. They allow participants to do certain kinds of work that are otherwise impossible (imagine a hospital without medical records). Of course they can also be constraining (there are expectations, rules, norms). Teachers and students may potentially follow these genre pathways to new ways of getting involved with others, new ways of living, new identities, as students come to read and write similarly to some and differently from others, expanding their involvement with some activity systems and perhaps restricting or resisting their involvement with others.

There have been many studies over the last 20 years of the reading and writing practices of organizations, of informal learning in workplaces (e.g. internships) and of transitions from formal education to workplaces that use genre theory, often combined with activity theory, situated learning or distributed cognition, to analyze the ways cognition in organizations is enacted, preserved, communicated and renegotiated through written texts, in systems of genres that mediate the routine actions (Russell 1997b). I do not have space here to recount them but I will conclude by mentioning some experiments that have grown out of research on activity and genre in the New Rhetoric.

The challenge: Re-mediating teaching and learning

The most difficult challenge for any theory of context is to restructure learning environments, formal or informal, based on theoretical analysis. From an AT perspective this restructuring might be thought of as *re-mediating* (Bolter and Grusin 2000) learning and teaching. Re-mediation, not in the sense of remediating a deficit, but rather finding new mediational tools, often new texts and genres, that will make the intertextual and genre connections within and among activity systems more evident, transparent and provide a critical space for negotiating the contradictions of education. The idea is to move from an autonomous to an ideological view of literacy, in Street's (1985) terms.

One approach is to systematically cycle the learning that students do on internships and work experiences into vocational and professional curricula and pedagogy. Teaching staff sit down with recent interns and alumni from the programme (and, sometimes, their workplace mentors) to explore the intertextual and genre links between reading/writing practices in the activity systems of the educational programme and the workplaces students from the programme have entered (or likely will enter). The idea is *not* that the workplace experiences of students or workplace practices should determine curriculum, but rather that the contradictions between school and work would be exposed and literacy practices critically examined in dialogue (Smart 2000a).

Another approach, called communication across the curriculum, is to have departments in higher education, working with a communications consultant, rethink their curriculum and pedagogy in terms of what they wish students to be able to *do* when they leave the programme (not simply what they want them to *know*), then examine the genres students read and write and the teaching and assessment practices associated, to re-mediate the textual tools used (Anson *et al.* 2003). These approaches are very similar to the *developmental work research* (DWR) Engeström has developed to work with participants to improve organizational learning in continuously changing, complex environments. However, these are focused more explicitly on literacy practices than in DWR.

Yet another approach is to critically examine some genre system of formal schooling in the light of qualitative research on literacy practices in higher education and in other linked activity systems (home, workplaces, etc.) then re-mediate learning environments using internet technology. The most demonstrably effective example is Labwrite, an online programme to teach students the processes of laboratory practice and lab report writing (Carter 2004). The lab report is a genre common in workplaces for scientists, engineers, and technicians, but a genre whose classroom version often degenerates into a cookbook or worksheet formulaic genre. Drawing on workplace studies of professionals writing lab reports, classroom/laboratory practices, and students' literacy practices in writing reports outside of classroom/

laboratory, the researchers developed a web-based learning environment that, in quasi-experimental quantitative studies, proved significantly better than traditional instruction in improving students' understanding of specific scientific concepts, understanding of the scientific method, and attitudes toward lab work.

My own research group (Fisher 2007; MyCase 2005) is developing and researching computer-mediated multimedia case studies that use a content management system (CMS) to model the circulation of documents within or among fictional organizations, represented by fictional internet and intranet sites. Students in professional curricula (business administration, biosystems engineering, genetics) role-play as they collaboratively engage in workplace-like activities using the sorts of tools and genres common in workplaces (databases, files of documents, meeting minutes, videoed meetings, synchronous and asynchronous communication, etc.). The computer-mediated case exists explicitly as a boundary object between two 'real' activity systems of school and workplace. The cases provide students with experiences that may be more closely aligned with their motive for being in school, but, at the same time, it is explicitly not work, it is playing at work. The social motive of schooling continues (epistemic learning). Students are also doing the sorts of reading and writing assignments that mediate formal schooling, along with the case assignments. Thus, the case study CMS exists in a space where students and teacher can critique both, potentially, and these spaces for critique are built into the learning environment to systematically exploit. the contradictions between school and work in order to encourage learning by expanding (Russell 2001).

Our research into students' attributions of their learning in the online case study environment, as compared with other parts of the courses that use more traditional CMS learning environments (e.g. Blackboard) and face-to-face instruction, suggests that students in professional curricula attribute extra-classroom significance to the activities they undertake in the classroom when those actions are mediated by a tool in which workplace, rather than school practices, seem to be crystallized, such as the case study CMS. (Attribution research in social psychology, brought to our attention by Simon Pardoe's work [2000] at Lancaster, has proved useful for gauging students' potential for 'transfer' or expansive learning).

Our activity theory analysis suggests that these attributions result, in part, from the shaping of, in the case of individual activity, classroom actions by the way the mediating tool (CMS) is configured (i.e. with its representation of workplace genres, its dynamically circulating texts and its affordances for participation in workplace-like activity). At the same time, these attributions seem to be shaped by the changes in classroom rules, division of labour and community that the case study CMS affords. For example, in our engineering and business case study CMSs, students draw freely from each other's work as it is posted to a shared file space, and from the work published in the case study.

This literacy practice is extremely unusual in classroom settings (traditionally governed by rules for academic quotation/citation and individual assessment) but is extremely common in the workplace, where people often draw from a common pool of documents and where documents cycle through multiple readers in the division of labour. Students saw this feature of the class as something unique in their school experience and many felt that such activity would be something they would need to know how to do in their careers. Thus, several suggested that assignment sharing was a feature that made them feel as if the simulation were a realistic representation of workplace practices.

Conclusion

I have tried here to suggest the importance and usefulness of literacy approaches for theorizing context in post-compulsory education, particularly activity theory and genre. The units of analysis that activity theory and genre construct are 'squishy', but they have proved helpful in approaching the complexities of 'transfer', which is enormously difficult to analyze. These approaches offer space to accommodate insights from other theoretical approaches, such as distributed cognition, constructivism, social constructionism, sociology of science, Bakhtinian dialogism and situated learning. Also, they offer a principled way for researchers to bring texts, literacy practices and genres into analyses of teaching and learning, while providing a basis for practical change efforts.

References

Anson, C.M., Carter, M., Dannels, D. and Rust, J. (2003) 'Mutual support: CAC programs and institutional improvement in undergraduate education', *Journal of Language and Learning Across the Disciplines*, 6: 26–38.

Bawarshi, A. (2003) *Genre and the Invention of the Writer: Reconsidering the Place of Invention in Composition*. Logan, UT: Utah State University Press.

Bazerman, C. (1994) 'Systems of genres and the enactment of social intentions', in A. Freedman and P. Medway (eds) *Genre and the New Rhetoric*. London: Taylor and Francis.

Bazerman, C. and Russell, D.R. (eds) (2003) *Writing Selves/Writing Societies: Research from Activity Perspectives*. Fort Collins, CO: The WAC Clearinghouse.

Bolter, J.D. and Grusin, R. (2000) *Remediation*. Cambridge, MA: MIT Press.

Carter, M. (2004) 'Teaching genre to English first-language adults: A study of the laboratory report', *Research in the Teaching of English*, 38: 395–413.

Cole, M. and Engeström, Y. (1993) 'A cultural-historical approach to distributed cognition', in G. Salomon (ed.) *Distributed Cognitions: Psychological and Educational Considerations*. New York: Cambridge University Press.

Dias, P., Freedman, A., Medway, P. and Paré, A. (1999) *Worlds Apart: Acting and Writing in Academic and Workplace Contexts*. Mahwah, NJ: Lawrence Erlbaum Associates.

Engeström, Y. (1999) 'Communication, discourse and activity,' *Communication Review*, 3: 165–85.

Engeström, Y. (2001) 'Expansive learning at work: Toward an activity theoretical reconceptualization', *Journal of Education and Work*, 14: 133–57.

Engeström, Y., Engeström, R. and Kärkkäinen, M. (1997) 'The emerging horizontal dimension of practical intelligence: Polycontextuality and boundary crossing in complex work activities', in R.J. Sternberg and E. Grigorenko (eds) *Intelligence: Heredity and Environment*. Cambridge: Cambridge University Press.

Fisher, D. (2007) 'CMS-based simulations in the writing classroom: Evoking genre through game play', *Computers and Composition*, 24: 179–97.

Freedman, A. and Medway, P. (eds) (1994a) *Genre and the New Rhetoric*. London: Taylor and Francis.

Freedman, A. and Medway, P. (eds) (1994b) *Learning and Teaching Genre*. Portsmouth, NH: Boynton/Cook Heinemann.

Lave, J. (1996) 'The practice of learning', in S. Chaiklin and J. Lave (eds) *Understanding Practice: Perspectives on Activity and Context*. Cambridge: Cambridge University Press.

Lea, M. (1998) 'Academic literacies and learning in higher education: Constructing knowledge through texts and experience', *Studies in the Education of Adults*, 30: 156–71.

Lea, M. and Street, B. (1998) 'Student writing in higher education: An academic literacies approach', *Studies in Higher Education*, 23: 157–72.

Leont'ev, A.N. (1981) 'The problem of activity in psychology', in J.V. Wertsch (ed.) *The Concept of Activity in Soviet Psychology*. Armonk, NY: M.E. Sharpe.

McCarthy, L. (1987) 'A stranger in strange lands: A college student writing across the curriculum', *Research in the Teaching of English*, 21: 233–65.

Miller, C.R. (1984) 'Genre as social action', *Quarterly Journal of Speech*, 70: 151–67.

MyCase (2005) http://mycase.engl.iastate.edu/.

Neel, J. (1988) *Plato, Derrida, and Writing*. Carbondale, IL: Southern Illinois UP.

Pardoe, S. (2000) 'A question of attribution: The indeterminacy of learning from experience', in M.R. Lea and B. Street (eds) *Student Writing in Higher Education: New Contexts*. Buckingham: Society for Research into Higher Education and Open University Press.

Russell, D.R. (1997a) 'Rethinking genre in school and society: An activity theory analysis', *Written Communication*, 14: 504–54.

Russell, D.R. (1997b) 'Writing and genre in higher education and workplaces: A review of studies that use cultural-historical activity theory', *Mind, Culture, and Activity*, 4: 224–37.

Russell, D.R. (2001) 'Looking beyond the interface: Activity theory and distributed learning', in M. Lea and K. Nicoll (eds) *Understanding Distributed Learning*. London: Routledge.

Russell, D.R. and Yañez, A. (2003) ' "Big picture people rarely become historians": Genre systems and the contradictions of general education', in C. Bazerman and D.R. Russell, (eds) *Writing Selves/Writing Societies: Research from Activity Perspectives*. http://wac.colostate.edu/books/writing_selves/.

Schryer, C.F. (1994) 'The lab vs. the clinic: Sites of competing genres', in A. Freedman and P. Medway (eds) *Genre and the New Rhetoric*. London: Taylor and Francis.

Schutz, A. and Luckmann, T. (1973) *The Structures of the Life-world*. Evanston, IL: Northwestern University Press.

Scollon, R. and Scollon, S.B. (1981) *Narrative, Literacy, and Face in Interethnic Communication*. Norwood, NJ: Ablex Publishing Corp.

Smart, G. (2000a) 'Collaborating with student interns and graduates in research that contributes to the development of programs in technical communication', *CPTSC Proceedings*. http://www.cptsc.org/conferences/conference2000/Smart.html

Smart, G. (2000b) 'Reinventing expertise: Experienced writers in the workplace encounter a new genre', in P. Dias and A. Paré (eds) *Transitions: Writing in Academic and Workplace Settings*. Cresskill, NJ: Hampton Press.

Spinuzzi, C. (2003) *Tracing Genres through Organizations*. Cambridge, MA: MIT Press.

Star, S.L. (1989) 'The structure of ill-structured solutions: Boundary objects and heterogeneous distributed problem solving', in L. Gasser and M. Huhns (eds) *Distributed Artificial Intelligence*, Vol. II. London: Pitman.

Street, B.V. (1985) *Literacy in Theory and Practice*. Cambridge University Press.

Tuomi-Grohn, T., Engeström, Y. and Young, M. (2003) 'From transfer to boundary-crossing between school and work as a tool for developing vocational education: An introduction', in T. Tuomi-Grohn and Y. Engeström (eds) *Between School and Work: New Perspectives on Transfer and Boundary-crossing*. Amsterdam, The Netherlands: Pergamon.

Vygotsky, L. (1978) *Mind in Society*. Cambridge, MA: Harvard University Press.

Chapter 3

Contexts of teaching and learning

An actor-network view of the classroom

Steve Fox

Introduction

Actor-network theory (ANT) is not a learning theory as such, nor is it a peda-gogy, but it is a theory of knowledge, agency and machines (Law 1992). In this chapter I will consider how this theory may nevertheless inform our under-standing of learning and teaching. It is an approach which aims to *analytically* treat humans and non-humans equally. By non-humans, ANT thinks mainly of technologies or machines, but can also think of other forms of materiality, for example, 'natural' materials. However, the 'natural–social' (Nature–Society) distinction is one which ANT challenges in a thorough-going way. As a theory of knowledge, agency and machines, ANT is 'a relational and process-oriented sociology that treats agents, organizations, and devices as interactive effects' (Law 1992: 389). 'Interaction' is a pivotal issue in that it necessitates an understanding of *process* and an acknowledgement that effects (desirable and undesirable) take time and depend upon interactional sequences which must be studied closely to understand how they produce effects.

When we apply ANT to an understanding of contexts for learning and teaching, we will necessarily be seeing 'the learner' and 'the learning process' in a distinctive way, consistent with ANT as a process-oriented sociology. The 'learner', like any other agent theorized by ANT, will not be reified as such but will be seen as a network-effect. The learner will be seen, not so much as an individual possessing typical cognitive capacities, but as a participant in networks of practices[1] (Latour 1993) which can only be unravelled empir-ically through research; and the 'learning process', as well as the learner, will also be understood as a network-effect, where the network in question will be understood as 'heterogeneous', comprised of bits and pieces of materials (technologies, texts, architectures, furnitures) as well as, and *in*, interaction with humans (students, pupils, teachers, principals) and human institutions (schools, language, social relations).

The chapter will first outline some key ideas in actor-network theory and raise issues for educational institutions and practices as important aspects of the context of learning and teaching, seen from an actor-network viewpoint. Second, it will summarize and draw upon a narrative account of one teacher/researcher's experience in teaching 'simple' practices of quantification and her theoretical reflections on this experience, which are in the light of actor-network theory (Verran 1999). Third, the chapter will pull together several implications for an understanding of contexts of learning and teaching which will suggest issues for consideration in the design of learning/teaching contexts.

Outline of actor-network theory

ANT emerged as one approach to science and technology studies (STS) within a wider field: the sociology of scientific knowledge (SSK). Although it has more recently been considered as making a contribution to studies of learning (Verran 1999; Fox 2000, 2001, 2005), this was not its original purpose. Its focus was not: how does an individual (scientist) *learn* from practical activity? but was: how are scientific facts produced? and: how do publicly warrantable scientific facts circulate and accumulate? (Callon and Law 1982; Latour 1988, 1990).

One may argue that this is a learning process, but it is not one which is primarily about an *individual* learner acquiring an abstract or situated body of knowledge and analytical skills in an *educational* context, rather it is a *collective or communal* learning process within a research and development context. As such it has similarities with that area which has become known as organizational learning and knowledge management (OLKM), which is especially concerned with the management of innovation (Brown and Duguid 1991). ANT, like much of the literature in the sociology of knowledge, does not refer to the psychology of learning as a cognitive process.

An illustration of this communal or collective learning process is Boyle's development of the 'air pump' (a piece of technology) which manifested his theories concerning the possibility of a vacuum and the 'springiness' of air (discussed at length in Shapin and Schaffer [1985], and in brief by Latour [1993] as an illustration of some general principles of ANT).

Shapin's and Shaffer's (1985) work juxtaposes two seventeenth-century thinkers, Thomas Hobbes and Robert Boyle, the former a political theorist and the latter a physicist. Surprisingly, for the non-historian, their historical investigation shows that Hobbes also produced scientific works and Boyle produced political theories. Thus they show that 'Boyle has a science and a political theory; Hobbes has a political theory and a science' (Latour 1993: 17). Latour's book, *We Have Never Been Modern* (Latour 1993) credits Shapin and Schaffer (1985) as the start of an anthropology that takes science seriously and notes several features of the interweaving of political and scientific ideas since the start of the modern period. This point is one that we will build on in considering Helen Verran's study in a later section.[2]

To promote his theory of the measurement of air-weight, Boyle sought to avoid taking sides with the 'plenists' and the 'vacuists' and 'refrained from talking about vacuum pumps'; his theories of air were prompted by the 'discovery of the Toricellian space at the top of a mercury tube inverted in a basin of the same substance' (Latour 1993: 17). He developed a prototype apparatus that could evacuate air from a transparent glass container and this piece of equipment was as costly in his day 'as any major piece of equipment in contemporary physics' (ibid.). The *transparency* of the apparatus became crucial to the dissemination of Boyle's ideas. As Latour (ibid.) tells us:

> The great advantage of Boyle's installations was that they made it possible to see inside the glass walls and to introduce or even manipulate samples, owing to a series of ingeniously constructed lock chambers and covers. The pistons of the pump, the thick glass containers and the gaskets were not of adequate quality, so Boyle had to push technological research far enough, for instance, to be able to carry out the experiment he cared about most: that of the vacuum within a vacuum.

Boyle then undertook dozens of experiments with his expensive equipment, seeking to disprove alternative explanations of the vacuum (e.g. that it was caused by wind). These experiments would become popular staples of 'eighteenth-century parlour physics' and over the centuries the price of the equipment needed fell, while its sophistication and standardization have increased, making it a routine part of any physics laboratory today.

In order to prove his theories, Boyle did not rely on logic or mathematics but as the English civil wars raged, he sought a modern political route to gaining the agreement of his peers. He brought together 'credible, trustworthy, well-to-do, witnesses' (Latour 1993: 18), people who knew a little science and were interested in the debate, and showed them the scene of the experimental action. He showed them his air pump *working* and 'invented the empirical style we still use today' (Latour 1993: 18, citing Shapin 1984). These reliable witnesses, his scientific colleagues, might have differed in terms of the theories to which they subscribed, but could agree on what they actually observed. The apparatus could be transported and Boyle could win over new audiences as he travelled. The popularization of his experiments, made possible by advances in the technology in the eighteenth and later centuries cemented 'Boyle's Laws' in the learned imagination. As Latour explains:

> Shapin and Shaffer pursue their discussion of objects, laboratories, capacities, and changes of scale to its extreme consequences. If science is based not on ideas but on practice, if it is located not outside but inside the transparent chamber of the air pump, and if it takes place within the private space of the experimental community, then how does it reach 'everywhere'?

How does it become as universal as 'Boyle's laws' or 'Newton's laws'? The answer is that it never becomes universal – not, at least, in the epistemologist's terms! Its network is extended and stabilized. ... By following the reproduction of each prototype air pump throughout Europe, and the progressive transformation of a piece of costly, not very reliable and quite cumbersome equipment, into a cheap black box that gradually becomes standard equipment in every laboratory, the authors [Shapin and Schaffer] bring *the universal application of a law of physics back within a network of standardized practices.* Unquestionably, Boyle's interpretation of the air's spring is propagated – but its speed of propagation is exactly equivalent to the rate at which the community of experimenters and their equipment develop. *No science can exit from the network of its practice.* The weight of air is always a universal, but a universal in a network. ... but universal in the old sense? Never.

(Latour 1993: 24, emphasis added)

In this example, we can see several key points of ANT illustrated: first, that scientific 'facts' are not only, or *even*, a matter of epistemology but they are definitely a matter of *social practices* which inherently depend upon *heterogeneous materials* networked together in and through technological devices and social practices. Second, that 'agency' is distributed between humans (such as Boyle) who design a new technology and the technical properties of the technology and materials from which it is constructed. Thick glass chambers are necessary, thin ones won't do. The properties of the glass play an active role (a form of *agency*) in the success of the experiment, which is the basis on which the network expands. Also the apparatus itself constitutes a *machine* that does something no other machine can do. Third, a specific audience is 'enrolled' by Boyle to act as an informed witness to his experiment. This 'community of experimenters' plays a role in validating the facts claimed for the equipment and experiments it alone permits. This experimental community *translates* for the wider world the facts and their import which they observe and allow Boyle to win an audience for his theory (Boyle's Laws). Fourth, his apparatus and the network which it brings together (Boyle and his audience) becomes an *obligatory passage point* for those who would in Boyle's, and future generations, seek to understand the nature of air; without this passage point, a proper scientific *knowledge* of air does not exist. Fifth, this apparatus – a specific machine for a specific purpose – does not remain the same but is improved upon through passing generations; the prototype is both reproduced and developed by successive generations networked through the reproduction of social practices.

Stepping back from the above points, we can see that although ANT is not itself a learning theory (at least not yet), it assumes that learning takes place between people and their technologies; that knowledge changes hands through interactions between people and their material technologies and is *embodied* in mechanical devices and in social practices which are networked together *acting* as one.

To take this a step further, we will draw upon an article by John Law to highlight and explain just two key aspects of ANT, illustrated above, which will become helpful in seeing how Helen Verran's study (1999) uses ANT to better understand classrooms within networks of socio-material practices which contextualize learning and teaching.

What does ANT help us explain?

First, we note that ANT is a materialist social theory which specializes in examining relations between the sorts of social and material entities which it calls 'actor-networks'. Hence John Law describes ANT as a relational materialist perspective but notes that:

> ... its *relational materialism* is quite distinctive ... the actor-network approach ... not only effaces the analytical divisions between agency and structure, and the micro-macro- and the micro-social, but it also asks us to treat different materials – people, machines, 'ideas', and all the rest – as interactional effects rather than primitive causes. The actor-network approach is thus a theory of agency, a theory of knowledge and a theory of machines. And, more importantly, it says that we should be exploring social effects, whatever their material form, if we want to answer the 'how' questions about social structure, power, and organization.
>
> (Law 1992: 389)

The theory has some common ground with Giddens' structuration thesis or Bourdieu's ideas of habitus in social reproduction, but it argues that society can only reproduce itself 'because it is materially heterogeneous' (ibid.). Applying this point to the theory of organizations in particular, and we may include here both scientific research communities and schools and other educational institutions, Law argues that ANT explores 'the precarious *mechanics* of organization' (Law 1992: 389). As Boyle's air pump illustrates, the social reproduction of a scientific community depends upon the physical reproduction of a certain network of material objects and technologies. When we examine Verran's study in the next section, we will see that if classroom learning is seen as one form of social reproduction, then the very process of learning here is also dependent upon a socio-material network, a composite of heterogeneous objects and living, yet changing, social practices. ANT thus provides a particular way of understanding contexts for learning and teaching which focuses on the relations between social practices and material objects networked together and seen as an actor-network.

Second, ANT argues that people, including learners, may be understood as effects of socio-material networks. For John Law, 'to say that there is no fundamental difference between people and objects is an analytical stance, not an ethical position' (Law 1992: 383). Expanding on this, he argues that ANT:

> insists that social agents are never located in bodies and bodies alone, but rather that an actor is a patterned network of heterogeneous relations, or an effect produced by such a network … Hence the term, actor-network – an actor is also, always, a network … a machine is also a heterogeneous network … So, too, is a text. All of these are networks which participate in the social. And the same is true for organizations and institutions.
>
> (Law 1992: 384)

As we turn our attention to the classroom practices for teaching quantification techniques in the following section, we will see that the student-teachers in Nigeria can only rise to the challenge of teaching western concepts of quantification by inventing specific (simple) devices which make it possible to translate one cultural understanding of number by use of social practices saturated with a different cultural understanding of number. This challenge required a new actor-network, a reflexively reorganized context for learning and teaching not dissimilar to Boyle's demonstrations with his air pump.

Quantification practices

Helen Verran who, under another name, has studied the teaching and learning of mathematics amongst English- and Yoruba-speaking children in Nigeria (Watson 1987, 1990; Watson et al. 1989), outlines one of the first applications of ANT to a formal educational context (Verran 1999). Like the discussion of Boyle' air pump above, her work manifests key ANT themes which concern agency, knowledge and technical devices and applies them to an understanding of learning. This understanding is formulated within a specific situated context and illustrates not only how mathematical knowledge may be taught and learnt but the socio-material networks that make this possible. Her work is focused on her 'disconcertment' with a particular approach to teaching how to calculate length, practised by one of her students, Mr Ojo, a teacher. Initially, although she could see *that* his approach worked, she could not see *how* it worked.

In Verran (1999) she supplies an illuminating ANT explanation which shows the extent to which even a simple lesson plan assumes and trades upon the presence of alternative and deeply cultural conceptions of number and demonstrates a form of learning that always makes her laugh (in a good way).

'Measuring Ourselves'

'Measuring Ourselves' was the title of a pamphlet produced by the African Primary Science Program, which was a 'large and prestigious USAID project which sponsored science and maths curriculum development with a focus on practical work in many African countries in the 1960s–70s' (Verran 1999: 137). Verran (then called Dr (Mrs) Watson-Verran; see Verran 1999: 138) was responsible for teaching a group of teachers in the laboratory of the Institute of Education at the University of Ife (now Obafemi Awolowo University). The aim was to modify the lesson plan in the pamphlet so that it would be suitable for teaching a typical class of some 50 or so Yoruba children in classrooms almost devoid of resources.

Mr Ojo was a one of Verran's students, a man her own age and with considerably more teaching experience in Yoruba classrooms. Like the other teaching students in her class at the university Institute, he had completed primary education, then attended 'teacher training college', which was a form of Nigerian secondary school, from which students such as he would take up posts as primary school teachers at the age of seventeen or eighteen. After at least ten years, they would then become eligible for two years 'retraining' at the university Institute, after which they would often go on to become a secondary school teacher. Verran herself was a teacher at the university Institute of Education providing a part of this 'retraining'. However, as she herself explains 'given my own gross inexperience when it came to Nigerian classrooms, this course in science education was, by necessity, very much a two-way programme of training. As a group, students and lecturer, we worked out a way of negotiating the curriculum we were developing. And the classrooms that these students taught in of necessity entered our negotiations' (Verran 1999: 137).

In her class at the Institute, Verran taught students such as Mr Ojo how to teach 'length', according to a lesson plan courtesy of the African Primary Science Program. She was well aware that on its own, this involved not only science but politics; a politics of colonialism and post-colonialism we might say these days. In the 1960s–70s she called these politics the 'African thought discourse'. Her task was to teach Yoruba-speaking student-teachers in English how to count and measure in the way that the African Primary Science Program required.

The lesson she taught Mr Ojo to teach 'Length in Our Bodies' required children to use string to record another child's height, leg length, arm length, etc. and then to use a one-metre rule to report the length in metric units. The children would have to use a length of string to demonstrate whether or not they had understood. The student-teachers were very nervous about adopting this approach as it meant that pupils would leave their desks and use other material resources other than pencils and exercise books; they would also have to talk with each other instead of in reply to the teacher and in response to what was on the blackboard. The student-teachers expected their pupils 'to become unruly and noisy at such a departure from the norm' which could cause problems in a small class with 50 pupils (Verran 1999: 138).

One student-teacher, Mrs Taiwo, had been an extremely well prepared and experienced teacher, who herself possessed a good grasp of quantification. She had paid, from her own money, a tin smith to make twenty 1-metre rulers and, using a ballpoint pen, she had marked 10 cm and 1 cm divisions on each of these 1-metre strips of tin. She had produced charts for the pupils to record their measurements, hand drawn using carbon copying as there were no photocopiers. However, her lesson turned into a disaster. Very few of her charts were filled out, most of the children 'lost the plot' and not a single one would volunteer to show the height of another. Mrs Taiwo was understandably disconcerted and 'she blamed the stupid children and the poor teaching of their regular teacher' (ibid.). Verran was less sure, as she had seen these very children doing mental calculations and handling number in Yoruba talk.

When Mr Ojo commenced his practice lesson, Verran was not expecting much, as he had taken an easier way out; in terms of preparation he had some 10cm-length cards and a chart on the blackboard, plus the string:

> Speaking in Yoruba, Mr Ojo demonstrated the procedure. He completely missed out the neat 'lecture' on length that we had collectively prepared back in the Institute laboratory. Mr Ojo called a boy to the front: end of string just under the boy's heel, he held his finger at the point on the string which matched the top of the boy's head. Tying a loose knot at this point, he took the other end of the string from under the boy's foot; holding this at one end of a card, he wound the length of string around until he came to the knot. Then he instructed: "Count the number of full lengths [i.e. 10 cm lengths] on the card, e.g. 9. Write down the number. Multiply by ten. How do we multiply by ten? ... ninety ... now add the bit of string left over ... Yes we have 96 cm."
>
> (Verran 1999: 139)

Verran 'was scandalized' because 'he was presenting multiplicity as constitutive of length. The notion of extension, so important for children to grasp as the "abstract" element of length had been rendered incidental, contingent upon the multiplicity' (Verran 1999: 139).

However, following the above demonstration, the children set to working in pairs and threes and had soon completed the entire exercise: 'The lesson could only be judged a complete success' (ibid.) though Verran was 'profoundly confused and puzzled'. As she puts this:

> I had glimpsed the lesson as both the same and different from the one we had prepared, but I was unable to say in exactly what way it was either the same or different. I was disconcerted and felt disempowered by being put out so. But this was no power play against the ... (white) lecturer on

Mr Ojo's part. As he saw it, the lesson was a triumph for our group, I was included as one of those who should feel proud at this little success.

(ibid.).

Before long all Verran's student-teachers were teaching the lesson in Mr Ojo's way, adopting the technology of 10 cm cards and string and using it with or without the lecture on length and the concept of *extension*.

Before applying ANT to understand the social process of this classroom exercise and its repercussions within the student-teacher community at the Institute, Verran sums up the experience in a way that captures her strange mixture of emotions and feelings:

> As I write about this episode, remembering my confused feelings of delight and suspicion, failure and success, I am shaking again with a sort of visceral laughter, the same sort of chuckling that often afflicted me as I watched my students teaching this lesson. The sort of laughter that grows from seeing a certainty disrupted to become a different sort of certainty: a certainty that sees itself. I felt as if I 'saw' length (that serious 'abstract' quality by which we organize so much of our modern lives) and 'saw through' it at the same time.
>
> (Verran 1999: 140).

She realized that this episode could be seen as a political story about institutional power relations, in which she was warranted to teach a canonical western account of length and had the right to pronounce whether her students got it right or wrong. In these terms the failure of her student-teachers could prevent generations of Yoruba-speaking children from learning western forms of quantification and continuing with 'primitive ways of quantifying' (Verran 1999: 141); but it could equally be seen as a story of Yoruba resistance against this 'western imposition', and these were the two explanations for her experience, that were characteristic of the 'African thought discourse' of the times. However, for Verran, 'to tell either of these stories would betray participants in the episode in unacceptable ways' (Verran 1999: 142).

Accounting for disconcernment

In our earlier example of Boyle's air pump apparatus, discussed by Latour (1993), we saw that rather than win his argument through logical argument and mathematical reasoning, Boyle simply showed his learned and well-to-do witnesses his apparatus working. The fact that it worked, that it could be replicated, the fact that the apparatus itself could be reproduced at declining units of cost, all meant that socio-material practices changed first and knowledge of the characteristics of air changed as a result, 'Boyle's Laws' becoming established knowledge in the process.

Mr Ojo's lesson can be looked at in directly comparable terms. His method of teaching the quantification of length relied upon a demonstration first, followed by a widespread change in his pupils' practices which enabled them to learn how to measure length and to learn new (group-work) ways of interacting in class, simultaneously. The easy repeatability of the demonstration and low cost of reproducing the apparatus or technology needed, allowed for widespread changes in the social practices of his pupils, the student-teachers just like himself and other Institute of education staff, like Helen Verran. His technology – in the way he used it – permitted a new way of knowing mathematical knowledge, and a new way of learning it, facilitating the emergence of a new network of practice spanning the university Institute, its teachers, their students and the latters' schools and their children. However, while this comparison clearly shows Mr Ojo's lesson plan as another actor-network analyzable in ANT terms as 'a network of heterogeneous, interacting, materials' (Law 1992: 383), an example of 'a relational and process-oriented sociology that treats agents, organizations and devices as interactive effects' (Law 1992: 389), at the same time it takes us further.

Helen Verran's disconcertment led her to examine orthodox number theory and compare it with vernacular practices of quantification as practised by Yoruba speakers. In Quine's (1960) foundationalist account, the world is just naturally comprised of bounded entities which possess spatial *extensions*, which endure over time. Butterfly wings and pebbles share this property even though one lasts longer than the other. In this logical positivist view 'the world really is an array of spatiotemporal entities, which are the given foundation for the symbolic practices of quantification' (Verran 1999: 145).

By Quine's account 'Mr Ojo is wrong to present an image to children where length is implicitly portrayed as a multiply divided bundle of string, whose multiplicity can be counted and manipulated to come up with a value for length' (Verran 1999: 145). However, an alternative foundationist account to Quine's universalist view is relativism, which instead of saying the world is really made up of entities with extension, says that different language communities have sets of social practices for referring to entities in the world, unitizing that material world and generating (recursively) numerals. Specifically, English speakers refer to 'spatiotemporal entities' while Yoruba speakers refer to the world as constituted by 'sortal entities' (Verran, 1999: 146). The latter are 'used in a further practice of abstracting', which involves sortal entities being 'rendered as the "mode of being collected" which represents the physical practices of unitizing the concrete world in the process of *ka* and *won*' (ibid). Simply put, what this means for the different practices of quantification familiar to Yoruba as opposed to English speakers is this:

> the repetitions when generating number names in English will focus up
> number making as beginning with the one finger and going one-by-one

along the fingers. It will keep the fingers there in front of us, not delete and hide this material symbolic embodiment of number. In contrast, the number making of Yoruba will be identified as beginning with the whole digital complement of a person with fingers and toes, while separating set by set will be understood as mimicked: twenty into tens, tens into fives and fives into ones.

(Verran 1999: 149)

Whereas in English the image of infinite extension comes first and order is then seen as a linear progression of equal divisions, in Yoruba the practice is to image a set of units comprising a whole, and to see order as a nesting of units within units. This explains Mr Ojo's practice of using *multiplication* as a way of calculating *extension*, to the chuckling disconcertment of Helen Verran.

Conclusion

Verran's case study (if I can call it that) uses ANT not simply to show that a classroom can be understood as 'a network of heterogeneous, interacting, materials' (Law 1992: 383), in much the same way as Latour interprets Boyle's air pump, but as an example of 'a relational and process-oriented sociology that treats agents, organizations and devices as interactive effects' (Law 1992: 389). Her case study shows how an ANT analysis can provide insights into the contexts of learning and teaching. One effect of her study is to problematize western, English-speaking conceptions of number and quantification on two levels. On the first level it shows that the apparent universalism of Quine's number theory is contingent upon a set of social practices which his theory simply assumes. Numbering and quantification can be done according to sortal entities rather than spatiotemporal entities.

On the second level, she shows that Mr Ojo's lesson works because it translates English-speaking practices of quantification into Yoruba-speaking practices, which reveal and trade upon these different starting assumptions about number whilst nonetheless teaching English-speaking ways of measuring length to Yoruba-speakers.

Verran's case graphically illustrates that agency, knowledge and simple mechanisms are effects of a heterogeneous network of specific languages' social practices of quantifying and devices which embody a Yoruba conception of number based on sortal entities, for translating an English language conception of number based on spatio-temporal entities. Through an actor-network of heterogeneous elements: string, cardboard, classes, the Yoruba language community, the Institute of Education within the university, an English-speaking teacher of student-teachers, hundreds of Yoruba children learned to measure themselves. Without the socio-material construction of such a network, which transformed the context for teaching and learning, it is doubtful they would have learned their lessons.

People, in tandem with material objects, are constantly transforming their social world and material environment, creating and learning new knowledge as they go. Actor-network theory provides a set of concepts and methodological principles for understanding *how*.

Notes

1 This is not to be equated with 'communities of practice' (Wenger 1998). See Fox (2000) for an account of the differences.
2 In some ways, Shapin and Schaffer repeat the slogan of the Edinburgh school of science studies that 'questions of epistemology are also questions of social order' and justice can be done to neither question if the two are separated out into departments of philosophy and sociology (Latour 1993: 15–16).

References

Brown, J.S. and Duguid, P. (1991) 'Organizational learning and communities of practice: Toward a unified view of working, learning and innovation', *Organization Science*, 2: 40–57.
Callon, M. and Law, J. (1982) 'On interests and their transformation: enrolment and counter-enrolment', *Social Studies of Science*, 12: 615–25.
Fox, S. (2000) 'Communities of practice, Foucault and actor-network theory', *Journal of Management Studies*, 37: 853–67.
Fox, S. (2001) 'Studying networked learning: Some implications from socially situated learning theory and actor network theory', in C. Steeples and C. Jones (eds) *Networked Learning: Perspectives and Issues*. London: Springer-Verlag.
Fox, S. (2005) 'An actor-network critique of community in higher education: implications for networked learning', *Studies in Higher Education*, 30: 95–110.
Latour, B. (1988) *The Pasteurization of France*. Cambridge, MA: Harvard University Press.
Latour, B. (1990) 'Drawing things together', in M. Lynch and S. Woolgar (eds) *Representations in Scientific Practice*. Cambridge, MA: MIT Press.
Latour, B. (1993) *We Have Never Been Modern*. New York: Harvester Wheatsheaf.
Law, J. (1987) 'Technology and heterogeneous engineering: The case of the Portuguese expansion', in W.E. Bijker, T.P. Hughes and T. Pinch (eds) *Social Construction of Technological Systems*. Cambridge, MA: MIT Press.
Law, J. (1992) 'Notes on the theory of the actor network: Ordering, strategy and heterogeneity', *Systems Practice*, 5: 379–93.
Quine, W. (1960) *Word and Object*, Cambridge: MIT Press and John Wiley.
Shapin, S. and Schaffer, S. (1985) *Leviathan and the Air-pump: Hobbes, Boyle and the Experimental Life*, Princeton: Princeton University Press.
Verran, H. (1999) 'Staying true to the laughter in Nigerian classrooms', in J. Law and J. Hassard (eds) *Actor Network Theory and After*. Oxford: Blackwell.
Watson, H. (1987) 'Learning to apply numbers to nature: A comparison of English speaking and Yoruba speaking children learning to quantify', *Educational Studies in Mathematics*, 18: 339–57.

Watson, H. (1990) 'Investigating the social foundations of mathematics: Natural number in culturally diverse forms of life', *Social Studies of Science*, 29: 283–312.

Watson, H, with Yolnga Community, Yirrkala and Chambers, D.W. (1989) *Singing the Land, Signing the Land*. Geelong: Deakin University Press.

Wenger, E. (1998) *Communities of Practice*. Cambridge: Cambridge University Press.

Chapter 4

Beyond 'mutual constitution'

Looking at learning and context from the perspective of complexity theory

Tamsin Haggis

> The field of education is greatly dispersed. It must be simultaneously attentive to issues and phenomena across many levels of organization.
>
> (Davis and Sumara 2006: 130)

The question of 'mobilizing learning across domains' seems to directly contradict the notion of learning as situated, and tied up with the particularities of context. The requirement to consider such different ideas together, however, signifies something of the range of competing agendas, theoretical concepts and divergent histories which characterize the state of contemporary learning theory. This chapter will argue that some of the conceptual difficulties involved in theorizing learning are the result of a clash between, on the one hand, a range of perspectives which have come to the conclusion that 'knowledge must be contextual' (Byrne 2005a) and, on the other, a prevailing ontology which declares that contextual knowledge can only ever be 'idiosyncratic' (Bassey, in Marsden 2007). Evolving interpretations of situated learning, activity theory and actor-network theory all attempt to deal with the difficulties that this creates. This chapter will explore how complexity theory, as a perspective which 'arises among' other discourses, rather than 'over them' (Davis and Sumara 2006: 8), offers a means of exploring some of the issues involved in contemporary articulations of knowledge, learning, cognition, and context in more detail.

Limitations and problems within sociocultural approaches

> A clearer understanding of human cognition would be achieved if studies were based on the concept that cognition is distributed among individuals, that knowledge is socially constructed through collaborative efforts to achieve shared objectives in cultural surroundings, and that information

is processed between individuals and tools and artefacts provided by the culture.

(Salomon, in Daniels 2001:70)

Sociocultural approaches to the study of learning represent a move away from the decontextualized, individualistic approach of certain types of cognitive psychology towards more collective, social and participatory types of framing. Whereas in the early days of psychology learning used to refer to the behavioural and cognitive processes of individuals, it is now more likely to be thought of as a characteristic of social practices and activities (Lave and Wenger 1991; Engeström 1987). Interestingly, however, despite the move towards participation and distributed notions of knowledge, the ideas of 'cognition' and 'learning' have not disappeared. Daniels, for example, suggests that sociocultural approaches investigate 'the *development of cognition* using non-deterministic, non-reductionist theories' (Daniels 2001: 70, emphasis added), and describes the focus of these theories as being 'the processes of the social formation of *mind*'. An extension of this approach is the idea that cognition itself is 'distributed' (e.g. Nespor 1994). What does it mean to talk of 'mind' and 'cognition', distributed or otherwise, within an overall framing of practice and participation?

Deep structure, underlying principles, categories

Despite the intentions of many theorists to develop non-deterministic, non-reductionist types of theory, the concepts and approaches used in current discussions about learning are usually strongly constrained by particular types of Anglophone/Euroamerican predisposition. These include certain epistemological and ontological assumptions, many of which reflect the early intentions of science 'to reveal the simple behind the complex' (Gare 2000). In education, this often translates into a desire to identify general principles[1] which can in some way meaningfully be said to 'underlie' (Briggs 2007) manifestations of difference and apparent unpredictability (see Haggis 2007, 2008). For example, whilst a theory such as situated learning might be expected to imply the impossibility of any general statements about learning (as learning is so specific to context), Lave and Wenger (1991) nonetheless formulate two general principles which apparently apply to *all* types of situated learning: 'community of practice' and 'legitimate peripheral participation'. Here, the epistemological imperative to create a general principle arguably merges with a perceived need to demonstrate progress in the 'accumulation of knowledge', resulting in an implicit striving to created the *best* and most *complete* approach or theory. In the case of situated learning, this results in general principles such as 'community of practice' being taken up across a range of different fields as if 'the' mechanism of learning has finally been identified. Here an explanatory category is taken up as a pedagogic technique.

Similarly, in the move away from trying to articulate underpinning structures[2] in relation to individuals, many forms of sociological/sociocultural research attempt instead to identify underpinning, explanatory structures of the social, which are then used to explain difference (e.g. division of labour, class, gender, social capital). These types of formulation can be immensely useful, particularly in trying to understand the ways in which people may be constrained and produced by larger social forces; but there are also limitations to investigating and explaining difference in terms of categories of the social. Methodologically, the 'underlying principle' imperative (which also appears as the requirement for qualitative studies to outline 'implications for other contexts') creates serious problems for the theorization and investigation of learning, in the sense that learning is arguably always local and particular. The assumption underlying this imperative (i.e. that everything in the world is amenable to description in terms of underlying principles) creates a conceptual impasse when it is applied to phenomena that might also be validly characterized in terms of their particularity. This, in turn, arguably results in an endless circularity of argument about the supposed impossibility of understanding dynamic, multi-factorial specificities.

Backwards and forwards across the binary: The social 'wins'

Whilst most perspectives will certainly discuss the idea that individual practices contribute to the emergence of the social, in many sociocultural framings there has been a demonstrable shift from a focus on 'the manner in which the individual constructs the world to the manner in which the world constructs the individual' (Davis and Sumara 2006: 117). In these types of framing, there is a sense that 'the social' is *the* ultimate deep structure:

> Briefly, a theory of social practice … claims that learning, thinking, and knowing are relations among people in activity, in, with, and arising from the socially and culturally structured world. This world is socially constituted: objective forms and systems of activity, on the one hand, and agents' subjective and intersubjective understandings of them, on the other, mutually constitute both the world and its experienced forms.
>
> (Lave and Wenger 1991: 50–1)

Many examples of educational theorizing seem only able to seesaw backwards and forwards across the individual/social binary, and in contemporary discourses this movement almost always ends up privileging the structuring forces of society. Historically, this stress on the social has been important in understanding the role of discourse and language forms, recognizing the effects of power, and surfacing the oppressive nature of many forms of social practice.[3] The focus on collectives in relation to learning has developed understandings of activity and practice which have radically changed the way that learning is understood. The privileging of the structuring forces of the social, however, has also made it increasingly difficult to talk about individual human agents. Although 'agency' and 'identity' acknowledge some aspects of human particularity in general terms, too much focus on this tends to be seen as a reactionary return to previous, decontextualized and 'individualistic' positions.

Social and collective orientations potentially provide new contexts within which to re-examine previous concerns differently. Instead, however, the 'deep structure'/generalization imperative, combined with the shift to the social end of the individual/social binary, often come together to produce particular kinds of theoretical limitation. Discussing how individual affects social, how social affects individual, or which of the two is the most influential, is relevant to some questions, but not others. For example, it seems relevant for anthropologists to talk about the need for human societies to *distribute* the 'tasks of learning, remembering, and transmitting cultural knowledge' (Hutchins, in Daniels 2001: 70), when the focus is on the maintenance and development of cultural knowledge, in the context of societies, but can this idea be transferred to all discussions about learning as this might be understood by educators?

Some of the problems discussed so far in relation to educational theorizing arguably arise because of a lack of clarity about the meaning of the term 'learning'. Far from being self-evident, as is often assumed, 'learning' covers a wide range of possible meanings. The idea of distributed knowledge or cognition has been generative in relation to understanding the largely 'unintentional' learning involved in different forms of vocational and professional learning, as these forms of learning are focused on the development of collective and culturally-based knowledge practices; but a perspective which is useful for understanding collective, unintentional forms of learning does not necessarily work particularly well for understanding how and why individuals within collectives *experience participatory practices differentially*. It also provides only one type of answer to the question of how and why people involved in intentional forms of collective learning activity (e.g. assessed learning in institutions) are *differentially engaged*, and produce *differential results* in terms of assessment outcomes.

Generalized notions of interdependence

Another challenge to current sociocultural framings is the difficulty of articulating the way that the complexities of the social work together. Many attempts to do this suggest that different elements are 'mutually constitutive', but the desire to express mutual co-specification can result in an extremely generalized articulation of 'things working together':

> ... context is not simply where action and learning are located, it is constructed in the course of social interaction as part of the meaning-making

processes, or learning, which inform action. The meanings are an integral part of the context. Thus, action and learning exist in a mutually constitutive relationship with context or situation.

(Bloomer and Hodkinson 2000: 589–90)

The weaving together of layers of context, histories and intentions, the dialectical construction of self and the shifting locations of individuals within different configurations does relate agency to context in a way that accounts for both individual agency and the take up of affordances. It is the embedding of agency in current interwoven and shifting contexts which distinguishes the sociocultural view of agency

(Edwards 2001: 173)

Both of these discussions try hard to articulate the immanence of 'context' in ideas of action, meaning, learning and agency. However, the attempt to create a sense of interrelatedness, dynamic construction and change through time arguably works to fragment each unit of analysis at the same time as it tries to create it, leaving only a vague sense of mutual co-specification. In one sense, context becomes expanded to incorporate everything, and could thus be said to refer to nothing. Valsiner (1998: 15) has suggested that conceiving of person and context as 'being in a "mutually constituted" or "seamless" relation' results in the researcher being 'left without the phenomena that had interested them'. Gee (2000) discusses the same idea in relation to discourse perspectives:

What is often left out in discussions of the mutually constitutive nature of words and contexts is the person who utters (writes) the words with (conscious and unconscious) personal, social, cultural and political goals and purposes. … the person as an actor engaged in an effort to achieve purposes and goals is left out as an embarrassing residue of our pre-social days.

(Gee 2000: 190)

There still seem to be problems with finding 'non-deterministic, non-reductionist' (Daniels 2001) ways to acknowledge and explore aspects of concrete particularity without resorting to the centring, essentializing tendencies of previous cognitive approaches.

Implicating, and avoiding, difference and particularity

It has been argued that the current focus on 'the social' has led to context largely being interpreted in terms of social and collective categories and structures, and also that the 'mutual constitution' framings employed by many sociocultural approaches can render both people and collectivities problematically vague. It has also been suggested that these problems are at

least partly the result of prevailing epistemological and ontological imperatives, which make it difficult to think about differentiated human beings in
non-deterministic, non-reductionist ways. Yet, at the same time, a recognition of 'difference', which extends quite clearly to the level of human
actors, is continually arising as a key issue in many different theoretical
areas (e.g. Law 2004). Difference, in this sense, is radical, irreducible and
inescapable; it cannot be captured by categories or laws. The reality of difference is recognized even in traditionally 'scientific' disciplinary areas such as
medicine:

> ... the 'truths' established by empirical observation of populations in
> randomized trials and cohort studies cannot be mechanistically applied to
> individual patients or episodes of illness, whose behaviour is irremediably
> contextual and (seemingly) idiosyncratic.
>
> (Greenhalgh and Hurwitz 1998: 251)

> Our exploration hints at the importance of understanding how individuals
> are functioning in terms of their dynamics, i.e. how people interact with
> their context, their social networks and their own bodies, and how this
> changes over time.
>
> (Griffiths *et al.* 2007: 43)

These interests create a need for ways to conceptualize and articulate the
local, the concrete and the particular, whether at the level of person, group, culture, or society. Dominant epistemologies, however, demand that particularity
be deliberately transcended, prescribing methodologies that work upwards
and out of specifics towards the identification of more abstract and general
principles. The conclusions of a great deal of research in the social sciences and
humanities (that 'knowledge must be contextual') thus stand in direct contradiction to the assumptions and mechanisms of many current epistemological/
methodological practices (Thomas 2002), particularly in the field of education. One way to address this problem is to tackle it at the level of underlying
ontology; to develop a wider range of ways of understanding both 'things
in the world' and the ways that such things come into being. This will be
returned to below in relation to possible ontologies implied by complexity
theory.

Learning: Collectivist confusions and exclusions

Lemke (in Daniels 2001: 71) suggests that situated learning portrays
people as:

> ... functioning in micro-ecologies, material environments endowed with
> cultural meanings; acting and being acted on directly or with the

mediation of physical-cultural tools and cultural-material systems of words, signs, and other symbolic values.

Though this kind of articulation has been very important for drawing attention to the importance of collective processes (or for conceptualizing processes collectively ...), the problem with the dominance of these types of frameworks is that they are often interpreted as implying that *the only things which are relevant to learning are collective*. Examination of the following example shows how this kind of understanding can arise:

> Analyses of distributed cognition focus on how humans working with instruments such as computers and how humans working in groups form integrated cognitive systems that cannot be understood by examining the elements of such systems taken separately (e.g. Hutchins 1995). Analyses of mediated action pursue this line of reasoning by assuming that virtually any human mental process is distributed. Even an individual thinking in seeming isolation typically employs one or another set of linguistic or other semiotic tools, the result being that the mediational means shape the performance at hand.
>
> (Daniels 2001: 83)

Here, it is suggested that the idea of distributed cognition is useful for thinking about situations involving 'humans working with instruments' and 'humans working in groups'. This is a focus on a specific type of collective, which uses an analysis of mediated action as a means of examining the functioning of such collectives. However, drawing attention to the use of semiotic tools in relation to the shaping of individual action *within* the collective broadens the discussion in somewhat ambiguous ways.

In the first case, the 'cognition' is collective, even if such collective cognition partly arises within human brains. 'An individual thinking in seeming isolation' could thus refer to the individual as a site of collective cognitive activity. However, 'an individual thinking in seeming isolation' might at the same time be 'thinking' in directions that are produced by their own history, conditions and current circumstances (Davis and Sumara 2006).[4] This second aspect is often eclipsed by the prominence of discussions of the collective aspect of cognition. In addition, individuals are *biological* beings, and both individuals and collectives are physically located in material *space* as well as *time*. An individual is not only not 'in isolation', it is also not only 'thinking'; at any moment in time a person is also responding to emotional pressures and disturbances, and manifesting behaviours and actions of which they may have little or even no awareness. Furthermore, the linguistic and semiotic tools which shape individual performance are not limited to the collectivity which is the focus of the analysis, but arise out of much bigger types of collectivity in which the community of practice or activity set is embedded.

The way that all of these things are interacting from moment to moment in relation to individual human beings far exceeds a person's 'perspectives' or interpretations, not least because the interactions of the many different, embedded systems involved constantly produce emergent effects which arise spontaneously (beyond the control of the individual), rather than being individually 'constructed'. These various issues can all usefully be investigated further with the help of complexity theory.

Complexity theory

The theoretical interest in the local and the concrete which is now evident in many areas of the social sciences draws attention to difficult issues not only of difference, but also of process, multifactoriality and dynamic flow through time. Though these issues are implied, and sometimes integral to, many social constructivist, sociocultural and postmodern/post-structuralist approaches, each of these groups of perspectives offers a unit of analysis or framing which focuses on only some of these aspects, from their particular position. Davis and Sumara (2006: 30) suggest that 'complexity thinking takes the discussion to realms that these discourses often ignore or evade', arguing that such thinking moves beyond the oppositional extremes of individual concerns and society's needs, introducing 'the biological across all phenomena'[5] (Davis and Sumara 2006: 30), and providing a way of articulating multiple levels of scale simultaneously. For Davis and Sumara, 'the vital question ... is neither, 'how are these discourses different?', nor 'how are they alike?' but 'at what level of complex organization is this theory a description?' (Davis and Sumara 2006: 120).

Ecologies of the social: the implicit connectedness of 'nested systems'

Complexity theory is not a unified theory, and though some writers suggest that it is 'relatively new in science' (Byrne 1998), others would argue that the perspective it represents is not new (Gare 2000). Though the emergence of complexity theory into public awareness is often seen to be connected to the establishment of the Santa Fe Institute in 1984, Gare lists von Bertalanffy's general systems theory, Whitehead's philosophy of organism, MucCulloch and Pitts on neural networks, von Neumann on cellular autonomata, Wiener on cybernetics and Prigogine on dissipative structures, as being precursors to the work of the Santa Fe Institute. He also discusses Waddington's work on epigenisis, Jansch's work on self-organization, Maturana and Varela's work on autopoeisis and Pattee's work on hierarchy theory. In his view, complexity has long been of interest to those philosophers and scientists who are part of what he calls 'a counter tradition within science', which has attempted to challenge 'a mechanistic, reductionist view of the world' with 'an organic view of the world' (Gare 2000: 335).

Complexity offers a view of the world as composed of multiple, nested, and open dynamic systems (Byrne 2005a). In contrast to 'the disorganized situations with which statisticians can cope' (Weaver, in Johnson 2001: 47), dynamic systems 'show the essential feature of organization' (ibid.); they have a coherence, an identity. Such systems, however, are neither static nor closed, and continually 'self-organize' in response to their environments. They can be very small (e.g. cells, amoebas), or very large (e.g. ecological or weather systems); they can be biological and physical, social and cultural, linguistic and political. One of the most important aspects of this perspective is that complex systems are embedded within each other, and therefore *cannot be considered in isolation from each other*.

Not all systems, however, are complex. Closed systems in which all the parts can be specified, which can be taken apart and then put back together again, and the workings of which can be clearly described on the basis of precise rules (Davis and Sumara 2006; Cilliers 1998), are not complex. By contrast, complex systems are open, characterized by dynamic interactions between multiple elements, and the rules which govern them 'can vary dramatically from one system to the next' (Davis and Sumara 2006: 11). This is a very important point in relation to systems that appear to be similar. Complex adaptive systems:

- are *open,* materially and energetically, and exist in a state which is *'far from equilibrium'*. There is a constant flow of energy and matter between the system and other systems in which it is embedded.
- have a *large number of components*, which are multiply connected, in *non-linear* ways. Information can feed back on itself, and systems affect themselves as well as other systems which they are connected to and embedded within.
- are characterized by interactions which take place at the *local level* only, as the system responds and adapts to changes in its inner and outer environments.
- *evolve through time* from specific *initial conditions*. Such systems thus have specific and unique trajectories through time.
- manifest *'sensitivity to initial conditions'*. Small changes in initial conditions can become amplified through time to result in very different results, even if the initial conditions of two systems appear to be the same. At the same time, two systems which appear to be very similar may be the product of very different initial conditions and histories of interaction.
- continually adapt, change and survive through processes of *emergence*. Emergent features and conditions arise as a result of the multiple interactions between elements, but transcend such elements. Emergence is difficult to explain and to understand, and is conceptualized differently by different researchers. 'Radical' versions of emergence state that there is no trackable pathway back to antecedents, even retrospectively (Goldstein 2005). Emergence arises out of a *diversity* of interacting elements (it is this

diversity, which includes elements which are apparently redundant, which make it possible for the system to continually change and adapt), and the interaction of such diverse elements *through time.*

- have structures, but these structures are not 'directed' or caused by any central organizing mechanism. Self-organization is *dynamic, responsive* and *distributed* (there are rules, but no 'underlying' or centralized generative forces).

- emerge not only 'initially' in relation to specific initial conditions, but also *continually*, in relation to a specific constellation of 'multiple presents' at any one moment in time.

- emerge within the *constraints* provided by other, larger and smaller systems which they embed, and are embedded within.

- exhibit *dynamic coherence.* A dynamic system has an identity, despite not having a centre or even, in many senses, a surround.[6]

- *evolve* and *learn.* 'A complex system learns that is it is constantly altering its own structure in response to emergent experiences ... its response to a virtually identical stimulus may change dramatically in a very brief span of time' (Davis and Sumara 2006: 100).

- are *mutually implicated.* Whatever complex system(s) may be the focus of analysis, it is always 'embedded in larger ecologies of relationships' (Davis *et al.* 2000). This means that researchers have to define the nature of the complex system in which they are interested (Byrne 2005a; Haggis 2006)[7] and also that they are always implicated in their subject of study (Haggis 2006; Davis and Sumara 2006).

- embody *unpredictability:* 'systems that are virtually identical will respond differently to the same perturbation. Hence, one cannot generalize the results from one system to another' (Davis and Sumara 2006: 100).

Any dynamic system which is a unit of analysis is both itself, and at the same time, because of its openness, simultaneously part of the interactions of a number of other dynamic systems. Dynamic systems of a similar type (e.g. schools, departments), therefore, will share in the interactions of the larger systems in which they are embedded (e.g. physical, ecological, cultural and social systems). The shapes and patterns of these larger system interactions, in combination with each system's own historically created patternings,[8] provide the *constraints which are necessary for emergence to occur* (at the level of the smaller system). Though the patterns of the larger systems may be shared, however, the patterning of the smaller systems, whilst remaining open to perturbations caused by other dynamics, is also always specific to that system's history and conditions. The result of this is that what emerges from the combined inter-actions (at the level of the specific system) will be specific *to* that system. It would make no sense for it to be otherwise, as the stimulus to emergence is the continuing survival of each particular system. Each system thus evolves in its own particular way, within shared sets of larger system constraints.

A system is particular in three senses. First, it has its own set of initial conditions. Second, these conditions have given rise to a specific history of emergent effects and ongoing conditions, in relation to that system's evolution through time. Third, the system is connected to and partly constituted by, a particular configuration of other, different systems, some of which exist at the same 'level' as itself (in the sense that they are all contained within the larger system interactions as listed above) and some of which exist beyond this. This combination of initial conditions, history through time and particular configuration of present systems make up the 'context' of each dynamic system, though it is questionable as to whether context is a meaningful notion in this situation. If it is, it would be tempting to say that context is both 'internal' to the system (in terms of initial conditions, and specific interaction history), and 'external' in the sense of connection to other multiple systems. This is only partly helpful, however, because the interactions of other, changing systems have been part of the 'internal' structure of the system which is the unit of analysis from the moment it emerged; indeed, it is the interactions of other multiple systems which produced the system in the first place, and which enabled it to become established and viable.

Emergence is the feature which might be said to most distinguish this perspective from others; or which perhaps develops vaguer notions of context and society most specifically. The individual system is not 'constituted by' the larger systems in which it is embedded. It continually emerges from within the constraints of these systems, transcending them at the same time as being constantly adjusted and constrained by the multiple, non-linear nature of the various interactions involved.

Conditions and time: 'Structure determinism'

One of the most important implications of the idea of 'sensitive dependence on initial conditions' is that any complex adaptive system is 'structure-determined' (Davis and Sumara 2006). Davis and Sumara (2006: 99, emphasis added) define structure-determinism as follows:

> It is one thing to try to make sense of where a complex unity begins and ends. But even if that issue could somehow be unambiguously settled, another at-least-as-difficult issue is the fact that *it is the system – and not the system's context* – that determines how it will respond to emergent conditions

In other words, not only are systems always specific and particular, but it is the specificity of a system's own dynamic structure which will determine its responses. From this point of view, comparing systems with each other may be of limited usefulness, in terms of understanding the kinds of dynamic systems which are of interest to educators. As discussed above, even two apparently similar systems will be emerging out of quite different initial conditions, past histories, and presently-connected other systems; likewise, apparently similar sets of initial conditions, histories and present constellations may give rise to two very different systems. This is why, as discussed above, the rules which govern such systems 'can vary dramatically from one system to the next' (Davis and Sumara 2006: 11).

The idea of 'structure determinism' provides an explanation of the genesis and evolution of difference; a difference which, from a complexity perspective at least, cannot meaningfully be aggregated into larger, 'overarching' categories or types. The assumption that general principles can be identified, which will meaningfully pertain to groups of diverse phenomena, is replaced by the idea that phenomena are fractal (i.e. they do not get any simpler at greater degrees of magnification [Davis and Sumara, 2006]) and therefore that they cannot be meaningfully simplified.[9] From this perspective, people, groups, institutions, cultures, societies, whilst continually emerging as a result of openness, connection and interaction, are nonetheless also specific to themselves. Many important aspects of such systems can therefore only be understood in relation to the particular histories and conditions (past and present) of each system. This is not an argument for an isolating, individualistic approach, however, as 'present conditions' refers to the need to study systems-in-themselves in relation to at least some aspects of the many other systems in which they are currently embedded. It also, crucially, implies a need to attend to relationship and patterns/characteristics of interaction, as the system is itself constantly emerging out of multiple dynamic processes.

In relation to learning and research into learning, 'structure determinism' provides one possible rationale for the investigation of specific systems through time (whether these systems are people, groups, vocational areas, institutional cultures or discourse systems). This approach implies a shift from seeking to identify general principles of correlation, cause and effect, to an analysis of *conditions* and *effects* in specific situations (Goldstein 2005; Byrne 2005b).

Learning and complexity

In relation to the discussion in the first part of this chapter, complexity theory provides a 'non-deterministic, non-reductionist' (Daniels 2001) way of acknowledging and exploring aspects of concrete particularity which is not based upon the centring, essentializing tendencies of previous cognitive approaches. It offers a way of both understanding and exploring why individuals within collectives might experience participatory practices differentially, or why apparently similar collectives may respond very differently to aspects of context which are assumed to be the same. Using this approach, it would be possible to investigate any kind of 'learning', including the questions discussed above about the differential engagement of people involved in intentional forms of collective learning activity (e.g. assessed learning in institutions), and the differential results (i.e. assessment outcomes) which emerge from the interactions of person-as-system and discipline-/tutorial group-/or institution-as-system.

Complexity theory is not a totalizing description which attempts to accommodate or explain all things. Instead, thinking of things in complexity terms arguably develops and opens out the potential for new kinds of creative thought, rather than closing such thought down. Describing things in terms of interaction and emergence, for example, does not attempt to describe *what* will emerge in any given situation; the framing of dynamic systems, the choosing of units of analysis, and decisions about what types of emergent feature may be meaningful all rest with the researcher.[10]

Complex adaptive systems, as discussed above, *evolve* and *learn*.

> A complex system learns, that is it is constantly altering its own structure in response to emergent experiences … its response to a virtually identical stimulus may change dramatically in a very brief span of time
>
> (Davis and Sumara 2006: 100)

As well as implying a different ontological basis for epistemology and methodology in more general terms, complexity theory also incorporates a very specific definition of learning, which may at first seem tangential in the context of education. The overall argument of this chapter, however, is that complexity offers radical challenges not only to many aspects of educational theorizing and research practice, but also to the often taken-for-granted nature of 'learning' itself.

Classes, teams, institutions, departments, students and/or disciplines can all be defined as interpenetrative complex adaptive systems. As complex adaptive systems, each of these units of analysis has to be considered not only as dynamic and continually emergent, but also in relation to the wider ecologies and sets of relationships in which they are embedded (thus allowing for progression beyond the conceptual fuzziness of 'mutual constitution'). Considered in this way, it can then be asked what the effect would be of defining 'learning' as the process by which a class, institution, or student might be 'constantly altering its own structure in response to emergent experiences …' (ibid.)

> Overwhelmingly, the word learner is used to refer to the assumed-to-be-isolated and insulated individual. By contrast, in complexity terms, learners can include social and classroom groupings, schools, communities, bodies of knowledge, languages, cultures, species … also organs and bodily sub-systems, cells, neurons. … It is not at all inappropriate to say that a discipline 'argues' or a cell 'knows' or a culture 'thinks'.
>
> (Davis and Sumara 2006: 14)

From this perspective, the changing dynamics and emergent effects which are produced by multiple and embedded complex systems are not merely implicated in a person's learning (whatever the focus of that learning may be), they *are* learning itself; if a learner is understood to be 'a complex unity that is capable of adapting itself to the sorts of new and diverse circumstances that an active agent is likely to encounter in a dynamic world' (Davis and Sumara 2006: 14). If a person is conceptualized as an embedded dynamic system, then the question is no longer how people create understanding/meaning (cognitive constructivism) or how social reality creates people (radical constructivism, critical theory). Rather, the question is how understanding and meaning may arise in particular ways from specific kinds of dynamic constraint. A complexity framing forces engagement with particularity, but not in an individualistic way, as the particularity cannot be separated out from the interactions of the many different dynamic systems within which it emerges. A complexity framing is also not simply 'social', in the sense that interpenetrating systems are both entities and environments (for other dynamic entities) as the same time.

Because of sensitive dependence on initial conditions, people, groups and institutions continually emerge uniquely, though within the constraints of the interaction characteristics of larger social, linguistic and cultural systems. As constraints which contribute to emergence, the patterns of 'the social' do not, as some social framings might suggest, mould and form people in predictable ways (though obviously there are limits to unpredictability; a person cannot emerge as a butterfly). Though it is possible to make general statements about the interaction characteristics of larger systems such as culture or society (e.g. gender, class), thinking of people as dynamic systems creates a way of understanding how larger system interaction characteristics *become transformed* when they become part of the specific dynamic system which is the person. The dynamics of larger social systems create constraints, but within those constraints, each person emerges slightly differently.

Learning and context

The idea of nested, dynamic, open systems, all implicated in each other, and yet all with their own identities and impetus to survive, changes many contemporary questions about learning. From a complexity perspective, learning is perceived not as 'being embedded in social and cultural contexts' (Boreham and Morgan 2004: 308), but *as a characteristic of embedded, dynamic systems*. It is also not 'best understood as a form of participation in those contexts' (ibid.) but as *a survival mechanism for such systems*. Complexity suggests radical (though embedded and dynamic) specificity, a response to which is that, as dynamic systems, people, groups/collectives, institutions, societies, cultures, all arguably have to be studied on their own terms, looking at conditions and effects in relation to initial and present conditions (i.e. the multiple systems in which they are embedded), and histories through time.

This understanding of learning develops the idea of a 'more fluid and relational set of practices' (Edwards and Miller 2007: 265) in very specific ways. It provides a unit of analysis, the dynamic system, which is itself profoundly fluid and relational, but which also has a form. Such a system is embedded in multiple other systems of interactions, and continually emerging. A complexity approach also goes beyond the current preoccupation with activity and practice. It suggests a need to understand how physical location, biology, activity, discourse, awareness, and intentionality work together to produce emergent effects across a range of embedded and mutually implicated systems; but with effects in each case being specific to *the survival of a particular system*. From this perspective, learning is far more situated than theories of situated learning imply.

Thinking of domains as complex adaptive systems raises questions about the idea of 'mobilizing learning' across them. Domains are specific, and also implicated in each other, producing emergent effects in relation to the changing diversity of elements which compose them, and the changing conditions within which they seek to survive through time. A domain such as 'family' seeks to survive *as* a family; a domain such as 'school' seeks to survive in the same way. A person carrying out an activity in either of these domains is, first and foremost, also seeking to survive; physically, emotionally, psychologically, communally and in relation to their own 'sense of themselves'. When they are part of the interactions that produce the family domain, a person will emerge in ways that attempt to further their survival as a part of that particular system; when they are part of the interactions that characterize and produce 'school', they will emerge differently. From this perspective, when a person moves from domain to another, it does not really make sense to talk of learning that they can 'take with them'. In each situation, different types of interaction come together, producing different types of effects. As conditions and agents are continually changing, even something that appears to be organizationally stable, such as 'class 3a, taught by Maria', is nonetheless subtly different every time it comes together (e.g. John is off sick today, Maria is stressed because she had a fight, this is a particularly hard chapter, the radiators are not working properly).

Arguably nothing that has been discussed here is news to teachers, or, for that matter, to doctors or ethnographers. Complexity is useful, however, because it outlines an ontology (and thus also epistemologies and related methodologies) of the 'irremediably contextual' (Greenhalgh and Hurwitz 1998). This provides both a theoretical and a practical starting point from which to begin multi-system analyses of conditions and effects in relation to specific learners, classes, schools, cultures and societies; not in order to replace forms of research which aim to identify correlation and generalization, but to make exploration of aspects of learning and education which these forms of research cannot accommodate become possible. Complexity opens the way for an exploration of 'difference' in its most radical sense.

Notes

1 Suggested by categories, types, classes, and 'key' features.
2 The notion of 'underlying structure' here is not necessarily literal, in a realist, explanatory sense. It can be simply instrumental, in terms of providing an interpretive framing.
3 The 'emancipatory' and social justice imperative which permeates a great deal of contemporary theorizing has, however, also arguably coalesced with other reasons to focus on collectives, resulting in the creation of strong, value-driven biases which are often taken for granted and not examined.
4 A further way in which cognition may be said to be distributed is 'across levels and areas' in the brain, which is different from the distribution of cognition seen in networks of humans working on a shared activity, or within a shared disciplinary area.
5 Though Davis and Sumara stress the biological, my argument is for ways of conceptualising *interconnection* between aspects of phenomena that are usually considered separately. Complexity insists that the physical and the biological be brought into discussions of 'the social', which otherwise often tend to ignore the urges and emotions of bodies, physical elements in space.
6 'The structures that define complex social systems … maintain a delicate balance between sufficient coherence to orient agent's actions and sufficient randomness to allow for flexible and varied response' (Davis and Sumara 2006: 148).
7 'What is a system of interest at any point in time is defined by observation and action. Boundaries depend on what we are looking for and at. This is not to say that boundaries are arbitrary relative or unreal …' (Byrne 2005a: 105).
8 A system is 'a pattern of causal organization' (Rosen 2000: 23).
9 Cross-sectional patterns, from this perspective, might be seem as representing aspects of the interaction patterns of the *larger* systems in which the systems which are being analyzed are embedded, rather than indicating 'underlying' structures-in-common in relation to these smaller systems (see Haggis 2006, 2007, 2008).
10 This is not to suggest that dynamic systems are simply the conceptual projections of the researcher. However, even if a realist position is adopted in relation to a 'real world' conceived of as being composed of dynamic systems, the researcher still has to make decisions about which of these multiply embedded systems to focus on and which aspects of the interacting features within such systems are of interest.

References

Bloomer, M. and Hodkinson, P. (2000) 'Learning careers: continuity and change in young people's dispositions to learning', *British Educational Research Journal*, 26: 583–98.

Boreham, N. and Morgan, C. (2004) 'A sociocultural analysis of organizational learning', *Oxford Review of Education*, 30: 307–25.

Briggs, A.R.J. (2007) 'The use of modelling for theory building in qualitative analysis', *British Educational Research Journal*, 33: 589–603.

Byrne, D (1998) *Complexity Theory and the Social Sciences*. London: Routledge.

Byrne, D. (2005a) 'Complexity, configurations and cases', *Theory, Culture and Society*, 22: 95–111.

Byrne, D. (2005b) 'Focusing on the case in quantitative and qualitative research', *ESRC Research Methods Programme, Workshop 4, The Case Study*. January 12–13, 2005 (oral communication).

Cilliers, P. (1998) *Complexity and Postmodernism*. London: Routledge.

Daniels, H. (2001) *Vygotsky and Pedagogy*. London: Routledge.

Davis, B. and Sumara, D. (2006) *Complexity and Education*. Mahwah, NJ: Lawrence Erlbaum Associates.

Davis, B, Sumara, D. and Luce-Kapler, R. (2000) *Engaging Minds*. Mahwah, NJ: Lawrence Erlbaum Associates.

Edwards, A. (2001) 'Researching pedagogy: a sociocultural agenda', *Pedagogy, Culture and Society*, 9: 161–86.

Edwards, R. and Miller, K. (2007) 'Putting the context into learning', *Pedagogy, Culture and Society*, 15: 263–74.

Engeström, Y. (1987) *Learning by Expanding: An Activity-theoretical Approach to Developmental Research*. Helskinki: Orienta-Konsultit.

Gare, A. (2000) 'Systems theory and complexity', *Democracy & Nature*, 6: 327–39.

Gee, J.P. (2000) 'The new literacy studies: from "socially situated" to the work of the social', in D. Barton, M. Hamilton and R. Ivanic (eds) *Situated Literacies*. London: Routledge.

Goldstein, J. (2005) 'Impetus without teleology: The self-transcending construction of emergence', paper presented at the Complexity, Science and Society Conference, Liverpool, September.

Greenhalgh, T. and Hurwitz, B. (1998) *Narrative Based Medicine*. London: BMJ Books.

Griffiths, F., Anto, N., Chow, E., Manazar, U., Van Royen, P. and Bastiaens, H. (2007) 'Understanding the diversity and dynamics of living with diabetes; A feasibility study focusing on the case', *Chronic Illness*, 3: 29–45.

Haggis, T. (2006) 'Problems and paradoxes in "fine-grained qualitative research": an exploration of "context" from the perspective of complexity and dynamic systems theory', paper presented at Higher Education Close UP Conference, Lancaster, July.

Haggis, T. (2007) 'Conceptualizing the case in adult and higher education research: A dynamic systems view', in J. Bogg and R. Geyer (eds) *Complexity, Science and Society*. Oxford: Radcliff.

Haggis, T. (2008) ' "Knowledge must be contextual": Exploring some possible implications of complexity and dynamic systems theories for educational research', *Educational Philosophy and Theory*, 40: 159–76.

Johnson, S. (2001) *Emergence*. London: Penguin.

Lave, J. and Wenger, E. (1991) *Situated Learning*. Cambridge: Cambridge University Press.

Law, J. (2004) *After Method*. London: Routledge.

Marsden, E. (2007) 'Can educational experiments both test a theory and inform practice?' *British Educational Research Journal*, 33: 565–88.

Nespor, J. (1994) *Knowledge in Motion: Space, Time and Curriculum in Undergraduate Physics and Management*. London: Falmer.

Rosen, R. (2000) *Essays on Life Itself*. New York: Columbia University Press.

Thomas, G. (2002) 'Theory's spell – on qualitative inquiry and educational research', *British Educational Research Journal*, 28: 419–35.

Valsiner, J. (1998) *The Guided Mind: A Sociogenetic approach to personality*. Cambridge, MA: Harvard University Press.

Chapter 5

Pragmatism's contribution to understanding learning-in-context

Gert Biesta

Introduction

One of the remarkable things about the recent interest in theorizing learning is the almost complete absence of references to pragmatism and more specifically to the work of John Dewey and George Herbert Mead. Whereas Mead's ideas influenced social learning theory and Dewey was a main source of inspiration for Kolb's work on experiential learning, their ideas do not seem to play a role in the recent wave of socio-cultural, situated and participatory theories of learning. This is even more remarkable given that many of the newer theories of learning explicitly try to overcome individualism, try to see learning as more than only a cognitive process, and try to understand learning as embedded in human action and interaction – ideas which are also central to the work of Dewey and Mead (see Hodkinson *et al.* 2007, 2008).

The easy explanation for this would be that Dewey and Mead have nothing to contribute to our understanding of learning – or at least nothing that is new and different from existing theories. This would suggest, however, that pragmatism was rejected after a thorough exploration of its potential contribution. A more likely explanation is that those working on pragmatism and those working on the newer theories of learning hardly ever interact because they belong to different academic communities and traditions. One reason for this is that the newer theories of learning were mainly developed in the field of the psychology of learning, particularly in relation to the work of Vygotskij and other Soviet theorists, whereas most of the work on pragmatism has been done in the context of discussions about the means and ends of (democratic) education (see Valsiner and Van der Veer 1988).

The purpose if this chapter is to explore the significance of pragmatism for the main theme of this book, the question of learning-in-context. For reasons of space, I will confine myself to a discussion of the work of John Dewey (1859–1952) (for Mead, see Biesta 1998, 1999, 2005). Dewey offers a theory of experiential and experimental learning in which learning is closely related to problem-solving. But Dewey has more to offer than just a description of how we can solve problems in a systematic and reflective manner. Dewey's views on learning are informed by (1) a *philosophy of action* which itself is based upon a *transactional* view of the relationship between human beings and their environments; (2) a *practical epistemology* in which knowing is understood as something we do; and (3) a *philosophy of communication* in which communication is understood in terms of *participation* in a common activity. The combination of these three elements results in a distinct contribution to the theory of learning, in which context is not seen as something that is outside of and disconnected from the learner, but rather as something that is always an inherent part of an ever-evolving transactional field.

Dewey's philosophy of action

In many philosophical discussions about knowledge it is assumed that the central problem to be solved is how the human mind can acquire knowledge about a world outside of itself. This question, which has been central to modern epistemology at least since Descartes, is based on a dualistic world-view in which it is assumed that reality consists of two different 'substances', mind and matter, and that the question of knowledge has to begin with the mind in order then to ask how the (immaterial) mind can get 'in touch' with the (material) world. The dualism between mind and matter has had a major impact on modern epistemology and, through this, also on modern theories of learning. Whereas many philosophers have tried to answer the question how it is possible for the mind to know the world, Dewey's work is not an attempt to generate a new answer to an old question, but rather an attempt to rethink knowing, learning and human action if we do *not* start from the 'impossible question' how 'a knower who is purely individual or "subjective," and whose being is wholly psychical and immaterial (...) and a world to be known which is purely universal or "objective", and whose being is wholly mechanical and physical' can ever reach each other (Dewey 1911: 441).[1] Dewey put forward a framework which begins with *interactions* – or as he later preferred to call it: *transactions* – taking place in nature, and in which nature itself is understood as 'a moving whole of interacting parts' (Dewey 1929: 232).

While *transaction* refers to interactions taking place in nature more generally, including interactions between inanimate objects, *experience* refers to the transactions of *living* organisms and their environments. What is distinctive about these transactions is that they constitute a *double* relationship. Dewey explains:

> The organism acts in accordance with its own structure, simple or complex, upon its surroundings. As a consequence the changes produced in the environment react upon the organism and its activities. The living creature undergoes, suffers, the consequences of its own behaviour. This close

connection between doing and suffering or undergoing forms what we call experience.

(Dewey 1920: 29)

In this quotation, Dewey presents experience as the very way in which living organisms are connected with and are part of reality. Contrary to what is suggested in the dualistic worldview, experience is therefore not 'a veil that shuts man off from nature', but rather 'a means of penetrating continually further into the heart of nature' (Dewey 1925: 15). It is this view of experience that is central to Dewey's philosophy of action.

Dewey developed his philosophy of action in the context of a critique of dualistic thought in psychology (see Dewey 1896). Interestingly enough, he did not focus his critique on old psychological theories but rather addressed something that was relatively new in his time, namely the use in psychological theory of the biological structure of the 'reflex arc', the system of afferent nerves, central nervous system and efferent nerves. By the end of the nineteenth century, psychologists were starting to use the idea of the reflect arc to explain human behaviour in terms of sensory stimulus, central processing and motor response – a development which would eventually lead to the psychology of behaviourism.

Dewey's main point of critique against this view was *not* that biology is used to understand human action, but that the principles of explanation and classification which the reflex arc idea wanted to replace were not sufficiently replaced. One of the main problems Dewey saw with the stimulus-response theory is that it assumes that it is the stimulus that sets the organism in motion. Against this, Dewey argued that the organism, as long as it is alive, is *always already* in motion, is always already engaged in dynamic transaction with its environment. Dewey did not want to do away with the notions of 'stimulus' and 'response' but wanted to understand them in functional terms and not as 'distinctions of existence' (Dewey 1896: 104).

In redefining stimulus and response, Dewey focused on situations in which the organism-environment transaction is disrupted, that is situations in which there is no pattern of action which presents itself as appropriate for establishing or maintaining a coordinated transaction of organism and environment. We could say that in such cases an appropriate response is lacking; yet we could also say that it is not clear what the stimulus is. 'The real problem may equally well be stated as either to discover the right stimulus, to constitute the stimulus, or to discover, to constitute, the response' (Dewey 1896: 106). The organism thus has to search 'for the state of things which decides how a beginning coordination should be completed' (Dewey 1896: 107). It is 'the motor response or attention which constitutes that, which finally becomes the stimulus to another act' (Dewey 1896: 101–2).

Dewey referred to this active search for the stimulus as 'perception'. Perception is not something which *precedes* action but has to be conceived as a 'factor in organic action' (Dewey 1912: 8). After all, the organism cannot stop its activities to find out what the stimulus actually is. The only way in which the organism can find the conditions of further action is by tentatively try-ing out different lines of action. While this process can be characterized as that of finding or constituting the stimulus, it is important to keep in mind that the stimulus is only found at the very moment in which an appropri-ate response has been found. It is only when the organism has 'hit' upon an adequate response that the stimulus has been 'found' as well.

The *act* of perception, if successful, brings about coordinated transaction. More generally we can say that an earlier open phase in which there is a ten-sion of various elements of organic energy, resolves into a later closed phase of integrated organism–environment transaction. Dewey stressed that in the case of higher organisms the outcome of this process on the side of the organism is not identical with the state out of which disequilibration and tension emerged. There rather is 'a change in the organic structures that con-ditions further behaviour' (Dewey 1938: 38). The behaviour of the organism becomes more specific or more focused. This modification is what Dewey called a *habit*. Habits are 'the basis of organic learning' (Dewey 1938: 38). Habits also embody meaning. Dewey emphasized that meaning is not some-thing mental but first and foremost 'a property of behaviour' (Dewey 1925: 141). It is literally embodied in the way in which the organism responds to the environment.

One way to summarize Dewey's theory of action is to say that it amounts to *a theory of experimental learning*. Dewey characterizes living organisms – including human organisms – as capable of establishing and maintaining a dynamic, coordinated transaction with their environments. Through this process the predispositions of the organism become more focused and specific, which is another way of saying that through the tentative, experimental way of establishing coordinated transaction, the organism has *learned*. This learning is, however, not the acquisition of information about how the world 'out there' really is. It is learning in the sense of the formation of a complex set of predispositions to act. In this process the world becomes more differentiated. It becomes, in other words, 'infused' with meaning.

Dewey's theory of experimental learning thus suggests that we learn through trial and error. In one sense this is the only way in which we can learn: we need to do something and need to undergo the consequences of our actions; but there is an important difference between blind trial and error and what Dewey refers to as intelligent action. The difference between the two has to do with the intervention of *thinking* – the intervention of symbolic operations. Coordinated transaction can result from the experimental, tentative exploration of possible lines of action. The problem with such experiments is, of course, that they are irreversible and therefore can ultimately be lethal for the organism. This can be overcome if we experiment with different lines of action *in imagination* instead of through overt action. This is precisely what thinking does. It is the 'dramatic rehearsal (in imagination) of various competing possible lines of action' (Dewey 1922: 132). The choice for a specific line of action should be understood as 'hitting in imagination upon an object which furnishes an adequate stimulus to the recovery of overt action' (Dewey 1922: 134). Whether this choice will actually lead to coordinated transaction will, of course, only become clear when the organism actually acts. Deliberation can in no way guarantee that the response will be successful, but what it can do is make the process of choosing more intelligent than would be the case with 'blind' trial-and-error. The ability to think relies on the use of symbols. 'By means of symbols ... we act without acting. That is, we perform experiments by means of symbols which have results which are themselves only symbolized, and which do not therefore commit us to actual or existential consequences' (Dewey 1929: 121).

Dewey's transactional theory of knowing

Dewey's philosophy of action has important implications for our understanding of knowledge and knowing. This is not only important in order to see how Dewey's views differ from mainstream modern philosophy. The question how we understand knowledge is also important in the context of theorizing learning, not in the least because from a dualistic point of view one way to define successful learning is to see it as the acquisition of true knowledge about a mind-independent world. Since Dewey does not start from the dualism between mind and world, the question he needs to answer is what it means to know and have knowledge if we think of the relationship between human beings and their environments in a transactional way. The concept of 'experience' plays a central role in Dewey's answer.

One implication of Dewey's transactional definition of experience is that it puts an end to the idea that we can only obtain a 'hold' on reality through knowledge. For Dewey, all modes of experience are equally real, since they are all modes of the transaction of living organisms and their environments. He argued that 'things – anything, everything, in the ordinary or non-technical use of the term "thing" – are what they are experienced as' (Dewey 1905: 158). For Dewey, this first of all means that everyone's experience is real. The horse-trader, the jockey, the zoologist and the palaeontologist will all have their own experience of a horse. If their accounts turn out to be different, there is, however, no reason for assuming that the content of only one of them can be real, and that the experiences of the others must necessarily be any less accurate or real. It simply reflects the fact that a horse-trader will have a different experience of the horse than a zoologist, because the trader 'enters' the transaction from a different standpoint, from a different background, from a different history and with different purposes and intentions. We do not have a contrast, therefore, between reality and various approximations to it; what we have are 'different reals of experience' (Dewey 1905: 159).

Dewey's postulate further implies that what is experienced is itself real. If someone is flustered by a noise, then that noise *is* fearsome. Dewey (1905: 160) stressed that 'it *really* is, not merely phenomenally or subjectively so'. This claim must be understood transactionally. If someone is frightened by a sound, then the fear is the immediate response of the organism. The sound *is* frightening because the organism reacts to the sound as being-a-frightening-sound. This implies, however, that *being*-frightened is not the same as knowing-that-one-*is*-frightened. Knowing what *caused* the fearsome noise (for example a burglar or a blow of wind) is a different experience. While this experience might be more *true* than the original experience of 'being afraid,' it is not more *real* than that experience. 'The question of truth is not as to whether Being or Non-Being, Reality or mere Appearance is experienced, but as to the *worth* of a certain concretely experienced thing' (Dewey 1905: 163).

The difference between experience and knowledge is therefore to be found in the *occurrence* of experience and the office of knowledge is precisely 'to discover the conditions and consequences' of its happening (Dewey 1929: 84). It is a search 'for those relations upon which the *occurrence* of real qualities and values depends' (Dewey 1929: 83). This is why knowledge is intimately and necessarily connected with action, because the discovery of the conditions and consequences of experience 'can take place only by modifying the given qualities in such ways that relations become manifest' (Dewey 1929: 84). For Dewey, therefore, knowledge is not concerned with reality 'as such' but with the relations between (our) actions and (their) consequences. This also means that knowing is not something which takes place somewhere deep down inside the human mind. Knowing is itself an activity, it is 'literally something which we do' (Dewey 1916a: 367).

The experimental transformation of organism-environment transaction results both in more specific habits and in a more differentiated 'world'. In this process, the 'world' gradually becomes 'a figured framework of objects' (Dewey 1922: 28), which is why Dewey refers to objects as 'events with meaning' (Dewey 1925: 240). The acquiring of meaning by sounds in virtue of which they become words is perhaps 'the most striking illustration that can be found of the way in which mere sensory stimuli acquire definiteness and constancy of meaning and are thereby themselves defined and interconnected for purposes of recognition' (Dewey 1933: 231).

In the case of language it is relatively easy to see that words, or 'sound-events', do not have a meaning of their own, but that they have *become* meaningful over time. It is more difficult to draw the same conclusion with respect to physical objects, such as chairs, tables, trees, stones, hills and flowers, 'where it seems as if the union of intellectual meaning with physical fact were aboriginal' (Dewey 1933: 231). Yet chairs and tables are as much events-with-meaning as words are. It is not, therefore, that through a process of inquiry we can find out what the possible meanings of, for example, a chair are. Rather, a chair specifies a particular way in which the transaction with the environment has become meaningful.

What does this mean for the truth of knowledge? For Dewey, there is no sense in asking about the truth of our immediate experience. Immediate experience simply is what it is. Truth and falsity only enter the scene when we raise questions about the *meaning* of experience, and are therefore not concerned with things as such, but with the *relationship* between our experience of a thing on the one hand and our possible actions or responses on the other. We approach a piece of paper as if we can write on it; the piece of paper *means* 'being able to write on it'; but it is only when we act that we can know whether this inferred meaning can become actual. This not only means that 'truth' is always contextual and related to action. It also means that truth is itself *temporal*. Truth does not refer to an alleged correspondence between a proposition and reality. It has to do with the correspondence between *suggested* meaning and *realized* meaning, that is, meaning 'put into practice'.

This does not mean that truth becomes disconnected from reality. The contrary is the case, not only because of the transactional framework that informs Dewey's theory of knowing, but also because of the *indispensable* role of action in the process that results in knowledge. Knowledge is therefore not a passive registration of reality 'out there'. Our intervention, our action, is a crucial, necessary and constitutive part of knowledge. In this sense, we can say that knowledge is always a human construction just as the objects of knowledge are, but it does *not* mean that anything is possible. We always intervene in an existing course of events and although our intervention introduces change, it will always be change of an existing course of events. We cannot create out of nothing; the only possible construction is a *re*construction.

One of the most important implications of Dewey's transactional approach is that knowledge does *not* provide us with an account or description or picture of reality as it is on its own and in itself. Knowledge always concerns the relationship between (our) actions and (their) consequences. This, in essence, is what a transactional conception of knowledge implies. It means that knowledge is a construction; or, to be more precise, that the objects of knowledge are constructions. However, contrary to how constructivism is often understood in the dualistic worldview (namely, as purely mental and hence subjective), Dewey's constructivism is a *transactional* constructivism, a constructivism that holds that knowledge is at the very same time constructed *and* real. This is why we can call Dewey's position a form of realism, albeit *transactional realism* (for this term see Sleeper 1986; Biesta and Burbules 2003).

Given that knowledge concerns the relationship between (our) actions and (their) consequences, knowledge will only ever offer us possibilities but not certainty. Sometimes we find that what was possible in one situation is also possible in other situations, but since the transactional 'determinants' of each situation are, in a sense, unique, there is no way in which we can assume that what was possible in one situation will automatically be applicable in another situation. This is why Dewey prefers to refer to the outcomes of our investigations with the notion of 'warranted assertions' rather than 'truths.' After all, the assertions we make about the consequences of our actions are only warranted in relation to the particular situation in which they were 'produced' and we should not make the mistake to think that they will be warranted for all time and all similar situations (see also Biesta 2007). This does not mean, of course, that conclusions from one situation cannot be useful for other situations; but the way in which knowledge from one situation transfers to another situation is in that it can guide our observation and perception and can suggest possible ways for resolving problems, for finding ways forward. Whether these possibilities will address the specific problems in the specific, new transactional situation can only be discovered when we act.

It is along these lines that we can understand the process of knowing as a process of learning; but the crucial difference between Dewey's transactional view and the dualistic view is that in the transactional view learning has no natural end point where we arrive at 'The Truth'. It is an ongoing creative exploration of possibilities in a process where learning feeds into action and action feeds back into learning.

Dewey's philosophy of communication

So far the focus has been mainly on individual 'human organisms' and the ways in which they learn as a result of experimental transactions with their environment. This is, of course, an important aspect of learning since, in a fundamental sense, learning is something that only individuals can do and that others cannot do for them. However, there is an important distinction to be made between our transactions with the natural world and our transactions with other human beings; and there is an important distinction to be made between learning about the relationships between our own actions and their consequences and learning from what others have learned. These questions bring us to Dewey's philosophy of communication, a philosophy which also plays a central role in Dewey's ideas about education (see also Biesta 2006).

Communication is not simply one of the 'themes' in Dewey's philosophy. In a sense, it is the most fundamental and most central concept of his whole philosophical system. This is because Dewey holds that mind, consciousness, thinking, subjectivity, meaning, intelligence, language, rationality, logic, inference and truth – all those things that philosophers over the centuries have considered to be part of the natural 'make-up' of human beings – only come into existence through and as a result of communication. Whereas older philosophies have taken social interaction to be a product 'of a ready-made *specific* physical or mental endowment of a self-sufficient individual' (Dewey 1925: 134, emphasis in original), Dewey argued that 'the world of inner experience is dependent upon an extension of language which is a social product and operation' (Dewey 1925: 137). Failure to see this led to the 'subjectivistic, solipsistic and egotistic strain in modern thought' (Dewey 1925: 137). Yet for Dewey 'soliloquy is the product and reflect of converse with others; social communication not an effect of soliloquy' (Dewey 1925: 135). This ultimately means that 'communication is a condition of consciousness' (Dewey 1925: 147). As Dewey explained: 'If we had not talked with others and they with us, we should never talk to and with ourselves' (Dewey 1925: 135). Along similar lines Dewey argued that 'the import of logical and rational essences is the consequence of social interactions' (Dewey 1925: 135), just as intelligence and meaning should be seen as 'natural consequences of the peculiar form which interaction sometimes assumes in the case of human beings' (Dewey 1925: 142).

Dewey was well aware that putting communication first meant that he had to think differently about the process of communication itself as well. He could no longer rely upon the idea – still common in our days – that communication 'acts as a mechanical go-between to convey observations and ideas that have prior and independent existence' (Dewey 1925: 134). In *Experience and Nature* (1925), he therefore unfolded an understanding of communication in thoroughly *practical* terms (see Biesta 1994, 1995), where communication was seen 'as the establishment of cooperation in an activity in which there are partners, and in which the activity of each is modified and regulated by partnership' (Dewey 1925: 141). Against this background, he defined communication as a process in which '(s)omething is literally made in common in at least two different centres of behaviour' (Dewey 1925: 141).

The starting point for Dewey's ideas about communication is the recognition that, in a sense, we all have our own, idiosyncratic 'view' of the world, we all have our own, idiosyncratic set of habits which structure and colour our transactions. For each of us, the world in which we live and act has a unique, individual meaning. As long as we do not interact with others, this is not really a problem, but when we engage in a *common* activity in order to achieve something *together*, it becomes important for the successful coordination of our activities that we adjust our individual patterns of being and doing. The point of Dewey's view of communication is that we do not first need to agree about our interpretation of the world and only then can start acting together. He argues that the change of our individual perspectives is the *result* of our attempts to coordinate our actions and activities and this is how we make something in common. It is not, therefore, that meaning is transmitted from one person to another. It is because people share in a common activity, that their ideas and emotions are transformed as a result of and in function of the activity in which they participate. This is how things are literally made in common. 'Understanding one another means that objects, including sounds, have the same value for both with respect to carrying on a common pursuit' (Dewey 1916b: 19).

For Dewey, communication is therefore about *participation* in a common activity. Participation is not simply about being in each other's proximity, nor about those situations in which people work together to achieve a common end. Communication, the process of 'sharing experience till it becomes a common possession' only occurs when all who participate 'are cognizant of the common end and all [are] interest in it' (Dewey 1916b: 12). It is only then that there is real participation and it is only this kind of participation, so Dewey holds, 'which modifies the disposition of both parties who undertake it' (Dewey 1916b: 12). Communication, in other words, only follows from situations in which one's activities 'are associated with others' (Dewey 1916b: 15).

Dewey's views about communication-as-participation are central to his answer to the question how we can learn from the learning of others, that is, how we can acquire the meanings available in a particular (sub-)culture. If we ask, for example, how a child can learn the meaning of a traffic light it is obvious that whereas a child can learn a lot about a traffic light through experimental interaction with it, the only thing it cannot discover in that way is what the colours of the traffic light actually mean. The reason for this is that the meaning of the traffic light is not to be found in the object itself, but is located in the ways in which people *use* the traffic light. It is located, in other ways, in the social practices that are regulated by the traffic light. The only way to get access to the meaning of the traffic light is therefore through participation in the practice that is regulated by the traffic light. It is only by becoming part of this practice and by trying to coordinate one's actions with the others in the practice, that the meaning of the traffic light can be learned. This indicates the inadequacy of 'learning by doing' as a summary of Dewey's views and suggests that it is more appropriate to summarize his ideas as 'learning through participation' or 'learning by doing things with others'.

Conclusions: Learning-in-context

They key concept in Dewey's theory of learning – and, for that matter, in his philosophy more generally – is the notion of 'transaction'. The idea of transaction, which is Dewey's alternative for the dualistic worldview of modern philosophy, suggests that human organisms should always be understood as actively connected with their environments. In his philosophy of action, Dewey characterizes this active engagement in terms of problem-solving and it is through this that the human organism learns about the relationships between its actions and their consequences. In this regard, we can say that for Dewey learning is always learning-in-context, but context is not the external situation in which learning occurs, but rather the engagement with the environment through which learning happens (see also Hodkinson *et al*. 2007). Dewey introduces the notion of intelligent action to characterize transactions mediated by symbols. Such mediation does not result in certainty, but only in more intelligent problem-solving, in a more intelligent approach to the selection of alternative lines of action. Although the use of symbols creates distance between the organism and its environment, this does not mean that the organism becomes disconnected from its environment; only that the character and 'quality' of the transaction change.

The transactional view of knowing shows that we do not learn about a static world disconnected from our actions; all our learning is about the relationships between our actions and their consequences. We construct a world of objects out of such learning processes; they do not precede them. This means that we do *not* learn about the contexts in which we act in order to adjust our actions better to the context. We only learn about the relationships between our actions and their consequences. If we wish to isolate contexts for analytical purposes, we can only do it on the basis of what we know about the relationships between our actions and their consequences. It is also important to see that the world that we are part of is not a static world; transaction is about real change, which means that as a result of ongoing transactions both we and 'the world' change. The transactional 'field' is therefore an ever-evolving one, not a field that is fixed. Knowledge therefore only ever expresses possibilities, never certainties. This is not to suggest that there is no continuity in our transactions, but it is to highlight that the field of transaction is not necessarily stable.

Dewey's views about communication and participation are, in a sense, nothing more than an application of his ideas about transaction to the social domain. One important implication from Dewey's ideas about communication as participation is that social contexts only exist *as* social practices and that the only way in which one can engage with such contexts is through engagement and participation. This again shows that, for Dewey, contexts are not outside of or external to individuals; they are part of the field of 'natural' and 'social' transaction. From an educational point of view, this means that a key task for educators lies in the organization of contexts. This, again, should not be understood as the organization or creation of environments in which students learn. In the transactional framework of Dewey's approach, organizing a context of learning means creating opportunities for participation in particular practices. The extent to which there are opportunities for all to participate and to engage with a plurality of different points of view is what Dewey had in mind when he connected the notion of 'democracy' to questions about the quality of educational process and practices (see Dewey 1916b).

Through the combination of a philosophy of (trans)action, a theory of knowing and a conception of communication as participation, Dewey provides us with a theory of learning which allows us to understand both the individual and social dimensions of learning, and does so in a way that is fundamentally different from the dualistic point of view which still permeates much of modern philosophy, psychology and educational theory. In this regard there is still a lot that can be gained from pragmatism's understanding of learning-in-context.

Note

1 All references are to the Collected Works of John Dewey, published by Southern Illinois University Press. I have referred to the original year of publication of Dewey's texts.

References

Biesta, G.J.J. (1994) 'Education as practical intersubjectivity: Towards a critical-pragmatic understanding of education', *Educational Theory*, 44: 299–317.

Biesta, G.J.J. (1995) 'Pragmatism as a pedagogy of communicative action', in J. Garrison (ed.) *The New Scholarship on John Dewey*. Dordrecht/Boston/London: Kluwer Academic Publishers.

Biesta, G.J.J. (1998) 'Mead, intersubjectivity, and education: The early writings', *Studies in Philosophy and Education*, 17: 73–99.

Biesta, G.J.J. (1999) 'Redefining the subject, redefining the social, reconsidering education: George Herbert Mead's course on Philosophy of Education at the University of Chicago', *Educational Theory*, 49: 475–92.

Biesta, G.J.J. (2005) 'George Herbert Mead and the theory of schooling', in D. Tröhler and J. Oelkers (eds) *Pragmatism and Education*. Rotterdam: Sense Publishers.

Biesta, G.J.J. (2006) ' "Of all affairs, communication is the most wonderful." Education as communicative praxis', in D.T. Hansen (ed.) *John Dewey and Our Educational Prospect: A Critical Engagement with Dewey's Democracy and Education*. Albany, NY: SUNY Press.

Biesta, G.J.J. (2007) 'Why "what works" won't work: Evidence-based practice and the democratic deficit of educational research', *Educational Theory*, 57: 1–22.

Biesta, G.J.J. and Burbules, N. (2003) *Pragmatism and Educational Research*. Lanham, MD: Rowman and Littlefield.

Dewey, J. (1896) 'The reflex arc concept in psychology', in Jo Ann Boydston (ed.) *John Dewey: The Early Works (1882–1898), Volume 5*. Carbondale and Edwardsville, IL: Southern Illinois University Press.

Dewey, J. (1905) 'The postulate of immediate empricism', in Jo Ann Boydston (ed.) *John Dewey: The Middle Works (1899–1924), Volume 3*. Carbondale and Edwardsville, IL: Southern Illinois University Press.

Dewey, J. (1911) 'Epistemology', in Jo Ann Boydston (ed.) *John Dewey: The Middle Works (1899–1924), Volume 6*. Carbondale and Edwardsville, IL: Southern Illinois University Press.

Dewey, J. (1912) 'Perception and organic action', in Jo Ann Boydston (ed.) *John Dewey: The Middle Works (1899–1924), Volume 7*. Carbondale and Edwardsville, IL: Southern Illinois University Press.

Dewey, J. (1916a) 'Introduction to essays in experimental logic', in Jo Ann Boydston (ed.) *John Dewey: The Middle Works (1899–1924), Volume 10*. Carbondale and Edwardsville, IL: Southern Illinois University Press.

Dewey, J. (1916b) 'Democracy and education', in Jo Ann Boydston (ed.) *John Dewey: The Middle Works (1899–1924), Volume 9*. Carbondale and Edwardsville, IL: Southern Illinois University Press.

Dewey, J. (1920) 'Reconstruction in philosophy', in Jo Ann Boydston (ed.) *John Dewey: The Middle Works (1899–1924), Volume 12*. Carbondale and Edwardsville, IL: Southern Illinois University Press.

Dewey, J. (1922) 'Human nature and conduct', in Jo Ann Boydston (ed.) *John Dewey, The Middle Works (1899–1924), Volume 14*. Carbondale and Edwardsville, IL: Southern Illinois University Press.

Dewey, J. (1925) 'Experience and nature', in Jo Ann Boydston (ed.) *John Dewey: The Later Works (1925–1953), Volume 1*. Carbondale and Edwardsville, IL: Southern Illinois University Press.

Dewey, J. (1929) 'The quest for certainty', in Jo Ann Boydston (ed.) *John Dewey: The Later Works (1925–1953), Volume 4*. Carbondale and Edwardsville, IL: Southern Illinois University Press.

Dewey, J. (1933) 'How we think. a restatement of the relation of reflective thinking to the educative process', in Jo Ann Boydston (ed.) *John Dewey: The Later Works (1925–1953), Volume 8*. Carbondale and Edwardsville, IL: Southern Illinois University Press.

Dewey, J. (1938) 'Logic: the theory of inquiry', in Jo Ann Boydston (ed.) *John Dewey: The Later Works (1925–1953), Volume 12*. Carbondale and Edwardsville, IL: Southern Illinois University Press.

Hodkinson, P., Biesta, G. and James, D. (2007) 'Understanding learning cultures,' *Educational Review*, 59: 415–27.

Hodkinson, P., Biesta, G.J.J. and James, D. (2008) 'Understanding learning culturally: Overcoming the dualism between social and individual views of learning', *Vocations and Learning*, 1: 27–47.

Sleeper, R.W. (1986) *The Necessity of Pragmatism: John Dewey's Conception of Philosophy*. New Haven, CT: Yale University Press.

Valsiner, J. and Van der Veer, R. (1988) 'On the social nature of human cognition: An analysis of the shared intellectual roots of George Herbert Mead and Lev Vygotsky', *Journal for the Theory of Social Behaviour*, 18: 117–36.

Part II

Cases of learning and context

Chapter 6

The textual mediation of learning in college contexts

Candice Satchwell and Roz Ivanič

A significant aspect of learning contexts is the way in which semiotic artefacts mediate learning within them. The *Literacies for Learning in Further Education* (LfLFE) project has researched the role of texts and associated communicative practices in constructing and mediating teaching and learning, in shaping communities, in constructing and sustaining relationships, and in helping students to achieve their goals. A particular aim of the project was to identify ways in which people can bring literacy practices from one context into another to act as resources for learning in the new context. Here we are specifically referring to literacy practices from Further Education college students' everyday lives in the UK being brought to bear in a formal educational context. In this chapter, we explain what we mean by 'literacy practices', demonstrate the textuality of learning contexts through examples from contrasting curriculum areas, and show how learning can be enhanced by mobilizing literacy practices from one context to another.

The concept of 'literacy practices'

The LfLFE project took its orienting theory from the New Literacy Studies (NLS) (Street 1984; Barton 2006; Baynham 1995; Barton and Hamilton 1998; Barton *et al.* 2000). NLS takes a social view of literacy, which entails several central tenets. First, it is revealing to think of literacy as the (social) use of written language to get something done in a specific context, rather than as the (cognitive) ability to read and write, independent of context. Literacy is not an autonomous set of skills for decoding and encoding linguistic structures, which can simply be learnt, measured by tests, and then transferred from one context to another. Rather, there are many 'literacies', each of which is situated in its social context, serving different purposes in different contexts, and varying from one context to another. Hence, it is more productive to speak of 'literacies' in the plural than a single literacy. Ethnographic observation of social life reveals that we live in a textually mediated world (Smith 1990): it is not long before a literacy researcher finds that almost any aspect of social life involves reading and/or writing of some sort.

Literacy researchers make their unit of analysis a 'literacy event': an activity in which reading and/or writing plays a part. They observe and gain participant perspectives on literacy events, seeking to understand their culturally specific characteristics. They pay attention to who does what, with whom, when, where, with what tools, technologies and resources, how, in what combinations, under what conditions, and for what purposes. They try to uncover participants' values, attitudes and beliefs about literacy, and what literacy means to them. They pay attention to issues of power and status in literacy events, and the consequences for identity of participation in them. From such data, they derive insights about 'literacy practices' – culturally recognizable ways of doing things with literacy in which people can be seen to be engaging. This account presents the learning of literacy practices as informal, situated, achieved through participation in socially significant action.

Most of the research in NLS has been undertaken in non-pedagogic settings – studies of the reading and writing people do to accomplish their lives at home, in the community, in the workplace. They have included studies of literacy practices in a variety of languages, of multilingual literacy practices, of the literacy practices of adults and of children (see, for example, Barton and Hamilton 1998; Barton *et al*. 1994, 2000; Martin-Jones and Jones 2000; Gregory and Williams 2000). These studies have emphasized the complexity, diversity and richness of literacies in which people engage as part of their lives as workers, citizens, family members and participants in widely varying communities of practice. These 'vernacular literacy practices' are very different from 'doing literacy' as a curriculum subject, and they are learnt through participation in the activities of which they are a part, not through instruction, drills and tests.

The situated view of literacy makes it essential to study written language not just as a set of linguistic structures that can be turned into electronic form, as do many linguists, but in their exact visual and material form. Even the simplest written texts are always multimodal, consisting of linguistic, visual and material modes. The visual and material characteristics of texts are shaped by social purposes and practices. To take this into account, the analyst needs to pay attention to the size of the writing and the surface on which it appears; whether handwritten or typed; the colour of ink, pencil, digital image, the paper, the screen background; the relationship between writing and space; the way parts of the writing are related to each other and/or to graphics; underlining, use of space, framing, overlaying of text, and other aspects of layout (see Cope and Kalantzis 2000; Ivanič 2004; Kress and van Leeuwen 1996, 2001; Moss 2001; Ormerod and Ivanič 2002). A social view of literacy recognizes that, in the same way that linguistic components of texts cannot be disentangled from other forms of visual semiosis, the textuality of learning contexts is not just linguistic, but multimodal.

Attention to the multimodality of texts leads to an interest also in the media, technologies, materials and tools for inscription, whereby texts-as-artefacts are made and received (Ormerod and Ivanič 2000). New technologies add enormously to the significance and diversity of literacy media and artefacts, leading them to interact with the linguistic aspects of literacy practices in complex ways. This factor proved to be highly significant in the LfLFE project, with students varying across the whole range from high-tech to low-tech in the media they employed and preferred for reading and writing.

The textuality of learning contexts

While the NLS view of literacy is not fundamentally an educational theory, it is central to any study of context, since almost all contexts are in some way textually mediated, and it is highly relevant to the nuanced understanding of, we suggest, nearly all learning contexts. As argued in chapter 2 in this book by Russell, texts are more than containers or conduits for meaning, in the same way that contexts are more complex than containers for communication. As he explains, within Activity Theory, texts and text-types (or 'genres') are among the most significant 'mediating means' (or 'socio-culturally shaped tools and artefacts') for achieving social goals, including the goals of teaching and learning. Literacy theory provides an elaboration of the means and mechanisms whereby these 'mediating means' operate. In this section, we identify the connections between a social view of literacy, as outlined above, and learning and teaching.

A central tenet of the LfLFE project is that literacy practices mediate learning in all subjects across the curriculum. However, it is crucial not to conflate 'literacy' with 'learning', since each can exist without the other. On the one hand, literacy can be used for purposes other than learning. People read and write to communicate, to organize their domestic life, to pass the time of day, to fulfil mechanical tasks at work, to keep records. These are functions of literacy which are not dependent on educational settings and are in fact much more likely to be part of people's work and home lives. Their main objective is not 'learning', although of course any social activity provides opportunities for learning through participation. On the other hand, learning is not necessarily textually mediated: learning how to knead dough is probably better done by watching and doing than by reading or writing. However, we have not had to look far to find written language somewhere in any learning context, even in the most practical curriculum areas. In most formal or informal learning contexts there is an astounding diversity and complexity of multimodal texts, and of the practices surrounding their use, and of ways in which literacy practices mediate learning.

A wide range of written texts are in use as mediating tools in learning contexts: texts such as booklets, websites, letters, handouts, overhead presentations, textbooks, logbooks, files containing notes on A4 paper, labels, maps, diagrams, writing on blackboards, white boards, measurements, lists. Each of these suggests not only a particular type of physical object, but also a particular type of multimodal communication of which that object is a part. The texts themselves invite questions about purposes, processes and the cultural situatedness of reading and/or writing in pedagogic contexts: who reads and writes what, how, why, when, where, and in what relation to other aspects of learning: cognitive, linguistic, material, social, and ideological.

Texts within literacy practices are, we claim, an extremely valuable locus for educational research, as they are tangible cultural artefacts of the teaching/learning event, which may or may not be enhancing learning. By eliciting participants' perceptions of their role in the learning process, we hope to increase our understanding of what makes texts useful to learning, of ways of using texts which are productive for learning, and of possible ways in which learning might be enhanced by texts and literacy practices which have not previously been used in educational contexts.

The *Literacies for Learning in Further Education* project

The LfLFE project took the New Literacy Studies approach to the study of literacy in two new directions. First, it extended it to a new group of people: we were studying the situated, multimodal literacy practices in the everyday lives of people who were attending a range of Further Education college courses. Second, we were bringing this theoretical approach to literacy into a pedagogic context: that of learning a range of curriculum subjects in colleges. To distinguish our approach to literacy from research that focuses on the teaching of literacy skills and on students' scores in literacy tests, we specifically did not research Key Skills Communications classes, where the teaching of 'literacy' is normally seen to be located in colleges. Rather, we based our research in 32 units of study from eleven different curriculum areas across four colleges of Further Education. We studied these learning contexts as textually mediated social spaces, in the same way as homes, community settings and workplaces are textually mediated social spaces. However, such learning contexts in themselves provide literacy-learning opportunities, especially when viewed from the perspective of learning-through-participation, so we cannot unproblematically separate literacy as a resource for learning from literacy development as a curriculum aim. Nor can we unproblematically identify certain texts and certain practices with educational contexts, and others with non-educational contexts, as is illustrated in our case study of AS Media Studies below.

The 16 teachers of these units acted as college-based researchers in collaboration with university-based researchers. First, we researched the literacy practices in which the students on those courses participated in their everyday lives: in connection with their families, domestic responsibilities, communities, leisure pursuits, travel, health, employment, and encounters with bureaucracy (see Edwards and Smith 2004; Smith 2005; Stanistreet 2004). We did this through iterative interviews, supported by clock-faces that students drew to show what they did in a 24-hour period of their lives, and for some students by photographs they took of the literacies in their lives. This is data about what people use reading and writing for, and was not necessarily focused on learning.

Second, we collected evidence of the literacy practices surrounding all the texts read and written by the students for the purpose of learning on each of these curriculum units, for the purpose of demonstrating learning, and for participating more broadly in college life (see, for example, Edwards and Smith 2005; Ivanič 2006). We did this through observations, interviews, in-depth study of the use of specific texts, and comprehensive collection of and reflection on the use of texts within each unit.

Noticing and collecting texts was a starting-point for our research into the literacy practices whereby these texts mediate, potentially mediate, or fail to mediate learning in the curriculum areas in our sample. We supplemented the collection of texts with data on the purposes and processes of reading and/or writing these texts – according to the teachers, according to the learners, on who does what with them, and how. In the next section we discuss the textuality of two contrasting learning contexts in colleges, showing how texts are to a greater or lesser extent constitutive of curriculum areas, and that texts play an important role even in relatively practical curriculum areas.

Texts and literacy practices in two college learning contexts

A textually saturated curriculum area: Media studies

Media Studies is a curriculum area in which students are expected to engage with a wide variety of different texts. In terms of the LfLFE project, this is an unusual area as it is not seen as a vocational subject. However, students on the course are often focused on a career in the Media. Texts do not just mediate but actually constitute this curriculum area. Reading and writing a wide variety of multimodal texts in a wide range of media is the main activity on the course, making it very different from, say, Painting and Decorating, or Catering and Hospitality – the area of our second case study. The particular unit looked at for the project was a three-month introductory unit of the AS course, which is the first year of the two-year A level. In this section we start with an analysis of the first text the students receive, both as an example of how a text mediates enculturation into a new course, and for the way in which it represents the literacy practices that constitute the course. We then expand

AS MEDIA STUDIES

COURSE OUTLINE

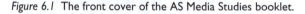

Figure 6.1 The front cover of the AS Media Studies booklet.

out, first to examine the other texts that the students encounter in their very first lesson, and then to consider the textuality of learning on the course as a whole.

The first text handed out on the course was a stapled introductory booklet consisting of 11 double-sided pages in black and white. It encapsulates semiotically the relationship between 'Media' and 'Studies' on which the course is based, illustrating the range of texts and literacy practices associated with the course, and suggesting links between them.

The front page is representative of the whole booklet in the way it intersperses the discourse of education with media discourses (see Figure 6.1). The title of the booklet is 'AS MEDIA STUDIES' and sub-title 'COURSE OUTLINE' – phrases which belong to the discourse of education; but sandwiched between these phrases is a picture of the poster for the film 'Gladiator' with two other photograph images on either side of it. The word 'GLADIATOR' is on the poster and also the words 'A HERO WILL RISE', but these words are almost illegible due to the quality of the printing. Directly beneath the words 'COURSE OUTLINE' are the advertising slogans: 'just do it.' (in lower case but with a full stop after it) and 'You bet it's delicious' along with the *Coca Cola* logo. So, while the title is in the discourse of education, the rest of the semiotic content of the front page is layered with images and words from a range of popular culture artefacts.

The rest of the booklet continues to intersperse the discourse of education with media discourses: written descriptions of the modules and their assessment methods and weighting are juxtaposed with a variety of images from films of various genres, advertising, newspapers and magazines. Side by side with these images are photographs of students in front of computers, and a close-up of someone handwriting an examination paper.

The juxtaposition of the images from media alongside student literacy practices in a range of different domains highlights the nature of the course – that the students will study elements of the media world all around them, using media to do so. In this respect the document suggests that the course itself is a borderland between literacy practices associated with media consumption and literacy practices associated with education. Although not many students made this connection when they were interviewed at the beginning of the course, the majority tending to see the course as unconnected with their everyday lives, this perception began to change as their involvement with the course – and with the research – progressed. An instruction towards the end of the introductory booklet is 'In short increase your media intake!' The content of the booklet itself indicates that this refers to accessing websites; watching films at home or in the cinema; reading books, newspapers and magazines; watching TV; listening to the radio. These are all activities in which students engage on a daily basis, but they alone do not ensure success on the course. This is acknowledged by the inclusion of images of the college resource centre and of people writing essays and sitting exams. The juxtaposition of these visual and verbal signifiers implies, we suggest, that it is only the combination of 'real world' media literacy practices and educational literacy practices which will enable students to succeed. Indeed, the *raison d'être* of Media Studies can be seen as the reification of that combination.

In subsequent sessions students were shown moving images from documentaries, advertising, news programmes, films, pop videos. After watching a clip, they were required to write notes and subsequently to develop their notes into an academic style essay, all the while being expected to translate their interpretation of the visual images into a standardized form of language, espoused by the education system but frequently flouted by the very texts under scrutiny. While the media texts they were analyzing are part of the everyday world, the way in which they are analyzing them is securely grounded in academic terminology and the literacy practices associated with that domain.

The LfLFE project attempted to uncover details about students' everyday literacy practices while also revealing the range and detail of the literacy practices required by their college courses. Media Studies as an academic subject throws into relief the complexity of the relationship between the two areas of our research, and highlights the difficulty of bringing the two together; while in each specific context texts mediate social action in a situated, context-specific way, the very same texts can be the focus of crucially different literacy practices in different contexts. While a student may 'idly' watch pop videos or read magazines in their spare time, the same video clip or magazine article can become the focus of a literacy practice that carries the values and identities of the educational system. For us as researchers to understand what sorts of texts can most usefully be employed in education – and how – we need first to understand the perceptions of the participants in the literacy practices which involve those texts.

A curriculum area with minimal textuality – or is it? Catering and Hospitality

Although Catering and Hospitality might seem a far cry from Media Studies, as the literacy practices associated with Media Studies are explicitly (in the title) and obviously many and diverse, we have found that Catering, both as a job and as a subject area, also requires engagement with a variety of literacy practices. When the Catering and Hospitality department was first approached as a subject area for inclusion in the project, the response was that there was not much literacy in Catering. However, observation of the college restaurant and kitchens – not to mention the theory classes – indicates that this is not necessarily the case.

Students on courses of level 2 and 3, including the NVQ Food and Drink Service (level 2) course researched, are given a logbook that has to be filled in as they complete different elements for assessment. The logbook is used to demonstrate knowledge and competence for the purposes of accreditation. The completion of the logbook is a formal literacy practice firmly grounded in an educational context, although the term 'logbook' itself may be an attempt to de-formalize the concept of a 'Record of Achievement'. This is a practice which students regard with varying degrees of enthusiasm, but is generally seen as a necessary and relatively manageable activity. Because completion of the logbook is crucial to students completing the course, they are in evidence throughout all activities in the restaurant and kitchens.

At the same time, as part of their college course students are 'working' in the restaurant, taking orders ('writing checks'), reading and explaining menus to customers, reading booking entries in the diary, working the bar and the till, reading the whiteboard in the kitchen with details of the dishes and who is cooking what, accessing the computer for information about customers' special requirements, and filling in electronic templates for customers' bills and cash summary sheets.

At other times they are designing and writing menus, posters and leaflets for direct use in the restaurant. In addition students are asked to complete assignments, such as, at level 1, researching how to find a job and complete a CV, culminating in a mock interview, and designing and costing a menu to fit given criteria. One student explained how he had learnt to describe the same dish in a variety of styles, ranging from a £7 meal to one for £40. This might appear to be the kind of activity required of an A level (level 3) Media student, rather than a level 2 Catering student.

The fact that a large part of the students' time in Catering even within college is spent in a simulated work environment means that once again the juxtaposition of different kinds of literacies is clearly in evidence. In this curriculum area, there is the requirement for formal academic literacy practice in the completion of the logbook, and the less formal but equally prescriptive workplace literacy practices involved in the effective and efficient running of a restaurant.

It may be significant that, although many students found no difficulty in completing their logbooks, some struggled with it. We observed two students requiring individual help with writing down what they had done in the restaurant, whilst apparently having had no difficulty in actually doing it. The same students had no problem with writing orders, checking the computerized restaurant bookings and so on, but they felt they needed help with spelling 'cafetière' and 'cutlery' and remembering where to put the full stops and commas. It is highly significant that it was the students asking these questions, not the tutors. It shows that the students were fully aware that the conventions of the formal literacy practice of completing a logbook were different from those of the workplace-based practice of writing a meal order check. Moving between practices involves recognizing their differences: these students demonstrated this recognition, and were able to identify the exact aspects of the new practice with which they needed support.

Textuality as a resource for learning across contexts

What we have described so far is our research into the semiotic artefacts and literacy practices which mediate learning on two contrasting courses. We have also studied the same students' literacy practices in domains of their lives other than their college courses: the role of multimodal texts in their domestic lives, their leisure, their travel, their communication with family and friends, their participation in community action, their religion and their part-time work. This revealed that most students are engaging in a wide array of practices and have a variety of expertise, and yet the students – and their tutors – often see these as separate from and irrelevant to their college lives. The LfLFE project worked with college tutors to identify ways in which the students' literacy practices and expertise outside college might be mobilized to increase their success on the courses on which they are enrolled (see, for example, Smith 2005; Ivanič and Satchwell, 2007; Satchwell, 2007).

Our hypothesis is that literacy practices, employed in the first instance for purposes of conducting aspects of everyday life, have the potential to be mobilized, or 'networked', as resources for learning in the FE domain. This 'curriculumization' of everyday literacy practices does not entail transferring practices wholesale and unaltered from one context to another, but is rather a transformation whereby some aspects of practices remain the same but others are changed. A new contextual configuration emerges from the new relationship among texts, practices, purposes, participants, time and place. So, for example, we were interested in how students on the *Media Studies* and *Food and Drink Service* courses described above could draw on their practices in other domains to serve the purpose of enhancing learning in these college contexts.

Some elements of a practice are more crucial than others for effectively engaging in that practice. For example, to play a computer game it is necessary to install the game following the on-screen instructions, to read directions as to which buttons to press and in what order, and to build up experience of playing such games over time. To play a computer game *successfully*, however, it is also a prerequisite to perceive a personal goal to be achieved. Such goals could be wide-ranging depending on the participants and the context, but could be, for example, a desire to reach the next level, to engage in extended play with a child, or to research for an article. If there is no such purpose identifiable by the participant, there is little motivation to engage in the practice, and certainly little hope of doing so effectively (for discussion of this, see Gee 2003). Similarly, to successfully create a poster advertising an event (an activity frequently required in an educational setting), there is a need to be convinced of a purpose, which again could be many and varied, but might be a belief in the validity of the event itself and the effectiveness of reaching the desired audience through this means, or might be a recognition that the process will provide benefit to the individual in terms of learning, earning respect from a tutor or, in a professional context, earning money. If tutors recognize the centrality of students seeing purpose(s) for the reading and writing they do, and identifying with those purposes as pertaining to who they are or who they want to become, tutors can adjust their teaching accordingly. This is not just a question of individual motivational differences, but of tutors' sensitivity to the possibilities of fine-tuning different aspects of their pedagogic literacy practices in order to make them relate more closely to students' own goals for themselves (for further discussion, see Satchwell and Ivanič, 2009; Ivanič *et al.* 2007).

Here we contrast two students on Catering and Hospitality courses, showing how one mobilized literacy practices across domains, and the other did not. We show how a lack of awareness of or engagement with certain elements of a literacy practice can differentiate between a student who succeeds on his course and one who does not. Complexity theory, as examined by Haggis in this book, contributes to an understanding of how learning contexts are experienced differently by different individuals as they bring the contexts of their wider lives and histories into play. Haggis introduces Complexity Theory concepts to explain that these differences should not be reduced to generalizations, but should be treated as 'dynamic systems' which each contribute to the 'emergence' of a learning context through ongoing interactions in time and space.

Separation of everyday literacy practices from the college course

Students on the level 1 Introduction to Hospitality course were required to design a leaflet related to catering in an environment of their choice. Two of the students in the project researched their chosen topic comprehensively, completed spider diagrams, and produced extremely effective leaflets which they handed in with their notes and evidence of research. However, another student involved in the project handed in a leaflet with no accompanying notes or evidence, entitled 'THE ARMED'. This student had chosen the armed forces as the environment on which to focus, as he related strongly to them in his everyday life. He had produced the leaflet at home on his computer, on which he frequently played games and surfed the net. However, he had clearly not engaged with the literacy practice required of him in producing the leaflet: he had not recognized the need for the text to be accessible to an audience and had apparently not noticed that the heading was incomplete. The literacy practice of creating a leaflet not only requires being able to use a computer and having an understanding of the conventions of the genre, but also requires a belief that there is a purpose in creating it and a potential audience for that leaflet. This student's lack of engagement with the task indicated his lack of conviction in this respect, culminating in him not taking ownership of the pedagogic practice.

When one of us interviewed this student, he clearly differentiated between his activities in and outside of college; in fact he was unable to recall most of his college activities, but was able to talk at length about his interest in playing computer games, teaching Army Cadets, and researching weaponry. In terms of topic and technology, therefore, one might have expected this college literacy practice to be resonant with his home practices. However, there were crucial differences between the two sets of practices, which militated against him being able to mobilize his resources effectively between domains: his sense of purpose and ownership in the pursuit of the literacy practices in his own time was clearly not replicated in his college literacy practices. In terms of Activity Theory, as explained by Russell in this book, we could explain this phenomenon as a contradiction between the different activity systems of the student's hobby and his course, in which the 'Objects', 'Subjects' and 'Community' of the different systems are too dissonant for his engagement in any of his out of college practices to carry over into college practices.

Facilitating the mobilization of the literacies in his life involves identifying and making explicit the contradictions between the activity systems of the two domains.

Everyday literacy practices as resources for learning on the college course

In contrast, a student on the Level 2 Food and Drink Service course made clear links between his college life and his life outside college. Logan, who had come into Catering and Hospitality with minimal GCSE qualifications, talked in an interview about producing an information sheet to accompany a menu in the restaurant at college. When asked whether this was something he was required to do for the course, he replied, 'It's, it is and it isn't!' indicating that, whether or not it was part of the course assessment process, it was worth doing for other reasons (see Ivanič 2006 for further analysis of this case).

Logan saw his work in the college restaurant as a reflection of himself – although not to the extent it would be if it were 'his own place'. Asked how he would feel about a spelling mistake on the menu, Logan replied:

> Well, it would matter and I'd feel, as soon as a customer pointed that out, whether it was me that wrote the menu or whether it was someone else, I would feel embarrassed because it's the place where I'm representing ... Yesterday the menus had a ... were done ... and Mr H [the college restaurant manager] had to add something quickly and it came up in a smaller font, and I was a bit, I don't like that, but not in the way that I would say 'oh we're going to have to print out eight new menus because of it', but I would feel like, if it was my own place I probably would, do you know what I mean?

The production of menus for the college restaurant can be seen as a literacy event which is situated in a time and place, following particular conventions of format and usage, but which was also – for Logan – imbued with values and attitudes to which he subscribed in a professional capacity, and which he envisaged as part of his imagined future. Logan, at the age of 20 and still part-way through his course, was already *maître d'hôtel* of a prestigious local golf club restaurant. We suggest that Logan was able to mobilize his everyday literacy practices as resources for learning and succeeding in a college context largely because crucial aspects of his college life were in harmony with his sense of who he was and who he wanted to become. The possibilities for self-hood held out by this educational context, and by the literacy practices it supported, were ones with which Logan could align himself, despite his disenchantment with education during compulsory schooling.

Conclusion

The LfLFE project shows the significance of the textuality of learning contexts in colleges, and the nature of the literacy practices associated with these multimodal texts. It shows how courses which are explicitly constituted by literacy practices, such as A Level Media Studies, recontextualize the everyday texts and practices of media consumption in pedagogic practices. This heterogeneity may go unrecognized by both students and staff, hindering rather than enhancing learning.

Further, the research shows how even curriculum areas which are thought of as mainly practical, and are chosen by students who do not think of themselves as good at reading and writing, such as Catering and Hospitality, are to a large extent textually mediated. First, the vocational areas for which such courses are preparing students are dependent on a wide range of largely hidden literacy practices. Second, there are pedagogic literacy practices surrounding learning and teaching and, more especially, the provision of evidence of learning on such courses. The textuality of such contexts is a major factor to be recognized and taken into account in the management of learning.

The project has also uncovered the literacy practices which mediate the activities and relationships in which students engage in other domains of their lives. These are characterized by the high degree of ownership and agency with which they participate in these practices: for many students there is a marked contrast between this ownership and agency and their lack of engagement in the literacy practices on their courses. The challenge is to identify factors which might provide the impetus for transforming the literacy practices demanded by the learning environment into practices with which students can identify. Success in their courses may depend on students being enabled to take ownership of these literacy practices in the same way as they engage with the literacy practices in the contexts of the rest of their lives.

References

Barton, D. (2006) *Literacy: An Introduction to the Ecology of Written Language* (2nd *Edition*). Oxford: Blackwell.

Barton, D. and Hamilton, M. (1998) *Local Literacies: Reading and Writing in One Community*. London: Routledge.

Barton, D., Hamilton, M. and Ivanič, R. (eds) (1994) *Worlds of Literacy*. Clevedon: Multilingual Matters.

Barton, D., Hamilton, M. and Ivanič, R. (eds) (2000) *Situated Literacies: Reading and Writing in Context*. London: Routledge.

Baynham, M. (1995) *Literacy Practices: Investigating Literacy in Social Contexts*. London: Longman.

Cope, B. and Kalantzis, M. (2000) *Multiliteracies: Literacy Learning and the Design of Social Futures*. London: Routledge.

Edwards, R. and Smith, J. (2004) 'Telling tales of literacy', SCUTREA Proceedings, *Whose Story now? (Re)generating Research in Adult Learning and Teaching*. University of Exeter.

Edwards, R. and Smith, J. (2005) 'Swamping and spoonfeeding: Literacies for learning in further education', *Journal of Vocational Education and Training*, 57, 1: 47–60.

Gee, J. (2003) *What Video Games Have to Teach Us About Learning and Literacy*. New York: Palgrave/Macmillan.

Gregory, E., and Williams, A. (2000) *City Literacies: Learning to Read Across Generations and Cultures*. London: Routledge.

Ivanič, R. (2004) 'Intertextual practices in the construction of multimodal texts in inquiry-based learning', in N. Shuart-Faris and D. Bloome (eds) *Uses of Intertextuality in Classroom and Educational Research*. Greenwich, CT: Information Age Publishing.

Ivanič, R. (2006) 'Language, learning and identification', in R. Kiely, P. Rea-Dickens, H. Woodfield and G. Clibbon (eds) *Language, Culture and Identity in Applied Linguistics*. London: British Association of Applied Linguistics with Equinox.

Ivanič, R. and Satchwell, C. (2007) 'Networking and transforming literacies in research processes and college courses', *Journal of Applied Linguistics*, 4, 1: 101–24.

Ivanič, R., Edwards, R., Satchwell, C., and Smith, J. (2007) 'Possibilities for pedagogy in further education: Harnessing the abundance of literacy', *British Educational Research Journal*, 33, 5: 703–21.

Kress, G. and van Leeuwen, T. (1996) *Reading Images: The Grammar of Visual Design* (2nd Edition). London: Routledge.

Kress, G. and van Leeuwen, T. (2001) *Multimodal Discourse: The Modes and Media of Contemporary Communication*. London: Arnold.

Martin-Jones, M. and Jones, K. (eds) (2000) *Multilingual Literacies: Reading and Writing Different Worlds*. Amsterdam: John Benjamins.

Moss, G. (2001) 'To work or play? Junior age non-fiction as objects of design', *Reading: Literacy and Language*, 24, 3: 106–10.

Ormerod, F. and Ivanič, R. (2000) 'Texts in practices: Interpreting the physical characteristics of children's project work', in D. Barton, M. Hamilton and R. Ivanič (eds) *Situated Literacies: Reading and Writing in Context*. London: Routledge.

Ormerod, F. and Ivanič, R. (2002) 'Materiality in children's meaning-making practices', *Journal of Visual Communication*, 1, 1: 65–91.

Satchwell, C. (2007) 'Creating third spaces: Helping further education students with course-related reading and writing', *The Teacher Trainer*, 21, 2: 11–14.

Satchwell, C. and Ivanič, R. (2009) 'Reading and writing the self as a college student: Fluidity and ambivalence across contexts', in K. Ecclestone, G. Biesta and M. Hughes (eds) *Transitions and Learning through the Lifecourse*. Oxon: Routledge.

Smith, D. (1990) *Texts, Facts, and Femininity: Exploring the Relations of Ruling*. New York: Routledge.

Smith, J. (2005) 'How students' everyday literacy passions (practices) are mobilized within the further education curricula', *Journal of Vocational Education and Training*, 57, 3: 319–34.

Stanistreet, P. (2004) 'We are losing students because we are not accessing the skills they have got', *Adults Learning*, 16, 1: 10–12.

Street, B. (1984) *Literacy in Theory and Practice*. Cambridge: Cambridge University Press.

Chapter 7

Mediating contexts in classroom practices

Carey Jewitt

Textuality is often thought of in linguistic terms; for instance, the talk and writing that circulate in the classroom. In this chapter, I take a multimodal perspective on textuality and context. I draw on illustrative examples from school Science and English in England to examine how image, colour, gesture, gaze, posture and movement, as well as writing and speech, are mobilized and orchestrated by teachers and students and how this shapes learning contexts. Throughout the chapter I discuss the issues a multimodal perspective raises for the conceptualization of text and learning context and how this approach can contribute to learning and pedagogy more generally. I suggest that attending to the full ensemble of communicative modes involved in learning contexts enables a richer view of the complex ways in which curriculum knowledge and policy is mediated and articulated through classroom practices.

A multimodal perspective

From a social semiotic perspective, communication can be understood as a product of people's active engagement with the semiotic resources available to them at a particular moment in a specific socio-cultural context (Halliday 1978; Kress 1997). This perspective has been elaborated to take account of modes and systems of making meaning other than speech and writing, including the resources of music/sound (van Leeuwen 1999), action (Martinec 2000; Kress *et al.* 2001), visual communication (Kress and van Leeuwen 1996) and their arrangement as multimodal ensembles (Kress and van Leeuwen 2001; van Leeuwen 2005). Each of these modes provides teachers and students with a range of meaning-making potentials or semiotic resources from which to choose. One way of examining pedagogic processes is to examine teacher and student selections and configurations of the semiotic resources available in the classroom.

A multimodal perspective offers a new way of conceptualizing texts and contexts. In the English classroom, for example, where common sense would have it that language is what really matters, teaching and learning is multimodal and so are the texts that circulate in the classroom (Kress *et al.* 2005).

The classroom is itself a multimodal place with visual displays and the arrangement of furniture in space that realizes particular discourses of the subject (Jewitt 2005). For example, talk and writing in school English is accompanied by image, gesture, movement, posture among other modes, all of which shape the production of curriculum knowledge and practices that lead to learning, such as analyzing texts. The selection from these available resources is made on the basis of the sign maker's interest, which can be individual or institutional interests. Textuality and the textual cycle – the selection of texts and the pedagogic processes and practices within which texts are embedded – can be seen as one kind of evidence of what it is that the maker of a sign 'wanted to say' at that particular moment.

Rethinking texts as multimodal

A multimodal perspective on texts attends to linguistic resources (speech and writing) as a part of a multimodal ensemble in which resources are organized, designed, orchestrated to realize curriculum knowledge and pedagogic relations. These orchestrated designs can be thought of as multimodal textual formations in which the concept of text is broadened out from texts as boundaried written/linguistic material objects to 'textual formations' in space and time. From this perspective, some textual formations have a persistence over time, a strong material physical presence; such as the written text books used across the curriculum, the physical environment of the classroom, models and objects, images on display and so on. Textual formations may also have a more ephemeral relationship to time and space, for instance the movement of teacher and students, their talk, look, gestures. Some textual formations 'hover' somewhere between these two positions, like the temporary written texts on the blackboard that shape interaction but only last for the lesson.

Here I turn to the illustrative example of three-dimensional models of a cell made by year seven students in a school Science lesson. My purpose is to show how thinking about text from a multimodal perspective is useful for 'getting at' learning, in particular the ways in which students mobilize a range of semiotic resources available to them to make meaning. This relates to Russell's discussion of activity theory and the conceptual framing of mediating artefacts in Chapter 2, in particular his assertion of the importance of texts and production in the activity of students and teachers and the need to broaden the notion of text. He calls for education to understand the classroom as a network produced through the complex interaction of students. Multimodality is compatible with activity theory and can usefully expand the notion of 'tool' through the analytical dimensions that it provides in ways that extend thinking about the mediating effect of tools within education.

In my example, the students used and appropriated the resources made available to them (school Science styles, conventions, analogy and metaphor, and materiality) for their own meaning-making purposes, in order to express their interests. The teacher offered a textbook image of cells as a key resource and this can be read as the authoritative sign 'cells', the knowledge at issue in its canonical form. In the representation, image was the foregrounded mode, in the form of a photograph and a diagram, with writing used for a variety of purposes, ranging from label to paragraph. The students' models are a transformation of the text book sign 'cell' on two levels: on the level of mode; and on the level of elements/content.

At the level of mode, the students' models transformed the sign 'a cell', as presented in the textbook, from a written and visual two-dimensional representation into predominantly visual, three-dimensional representations. The shift from the written-visual modes of the textbook to the more dominant use of the 3D visual mode in the models of students brought different representational potentials. The models then are an expression of *learning as a transformative process* that required the students to engage with thinking and learning in a way that would have not been the case in a purely linguistic task.

Analysis of the cell models demonstrates that tasks which involve material, visual, and three-dimensional thinking and decisions, promote learning through engaging students in questions and a range of decisions of a kind which a linguistic task does not. Linguistically it is enough to say: 'the cell has a cell membrane'. To draw a cell membrane involves considerations of thickness of line, depth, and medium. To construct a three-dimensional model of a cell membrane involves deciding what it looks like, what material can best represent it, where it is placed in relation to the cell wall, and so on. The construction of the models thus demanded different work from the students. Analysis of the textual 'evidence' of this work likewise makes available different resources for educational practitioners and researchers who want to understand learning processes in the multimodal environment of the classroom.

In the models, the students used texture and shape in ways that are not possible nor practical in a textbook; for example, using water to represent the liquid in the vacuole, and a piece of sponge to represent the nucleus. The expansion from the affordances of the page to those of a model, that is from two dimensions to three dimensions, made available different potentials for the representation of the cell elements as well as the relations between elements. The three-dimensional models afforded the potential for more complex spatial arrangements between the elements, e.g. layering and depth, than the textbook image.

In the textbook, the cell wall was represented linguistically as a 'rigid (firm) coating which helps the plant keep shape' and visually by a thick black line. In some of the student models a cardboard box was used to represent the cell wall (see Figure 7.1). The 'cell walls' were raised to enclose the elements of the cell, reflecting the common function of a wall, to keep things in and/or out. The students' different uses of shape and texture visually expressed notions

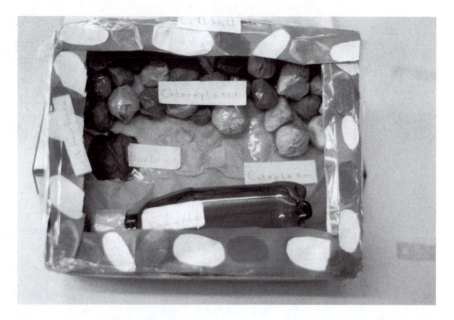

Figure 7.1 Student model of cell.

of 'containment' and transformed the 2D representation in the textbook into a 3D representation. Taking such signs as one kind of evidence of learning in this way moves well beyond the linguistic focus of assessment, and expands the concept of text.

In the textbook diagram, the bold line for the 'wall' contrasted with the lighter broken line representing the cell membrane. In contrast to the hard smoothness of the cell walls in the 3D models the cell membrane was represented as flimsy, shiny, crinkly, thin. The students' use of texture embodied the meaning of lived delicacy. One model used tissue paper (Figure 7.1), another used Clingfilm (Figure 7.2). Some used the thin edge of a plastic box. These materials realized students' understanding of what cell membranes are like – very thin, and delicate. The use of Clingfilm drew on the everyday function of these materials to express the function of the cell membrane to 'protect'. The students' choices of materials carried the meaning and function of delicacy in different ways and involved them in serious decisions around representation: how to imbue specific qualities and meaning to a model cell through the affordances of materiality.

The material realization of the chloroplasts in the models reflected the students' sense of what the characteristics and the functions of chloroplasts might be. The students' models transformed the shape of the chloroplasts in the diagram, from an oval irregular shape to square chunks and petals.

Figure 7.2 Student model of cell.

The chloroplasts were represented as something 'wrapped', whether in tissue paper, as in Figure 7.1, or as sweet wrappers in another model. The function of the chloroplasts is to store the chemicals required for photosynthesis, and the students' use of a wrapping appears to signify and imbue meanings of containment and storage; while the texture of the material used gave insight into what the students thought the 'skin' of the chloroplast might be and have as its function.

A multimodal perspective on text is significant for learning, as it serves to expand the texts that come into the analytical frame and that of assessment. A focus on multimodal texts raises questions that are important for learning, including how students move across and between modes in the course of learning and producing course work. The implications of multimodality for assessment are a part of this discussion, as teachers generally have a wide range of resources with which to make meaning, all of which students have to interpret and then 'translate' and 'transform' into primarily written (and occasionally spoken) textual forms for the purposes of assessment. My point here is not that all forms of meaning-making should be equal in formal education, but language, spoken and written, is the most socially valued form of communication in most contexts; language is embedded in an ensemble of modes and all modes play a central part in meaning-making. For the purposes of teaching therefore it may well be useful to know if a student is expressing scientific understandings across a range of modes and to consider how different resources challenge, extend or constrain thinking about the specific concepts to be learnt.

Multimodal textual cycles

Thinking of texts as the orchestration of an ensemble of modes in time and space opens up the idea of text beyond the examples of material 'fixed' texts. Here I turn to the idea of 'textual cycles', that is, the process by which meaning is given to texts, the selection of texts, and the pedagogic processes and practices within which texts are embedded and through which they are realized in the classroom. Multimodality offers a way of analyzing the interactions with and around texts. Drawing on two examples, one from the school English classroom and another from the school Science classroom, I explore how teachers and students mobilize a range of multimodal resources to construct the textuality of the classroom. This responds to text as a flexible, fluid and highly contextual entity, rather than a conception of text as a fixed bounded entity, in which the boundaries between conceptions of text and context are blurred. From this perspective text and context are intrinsically connected and 'woven through' each other.

The multimodal textuality of the English classroom: Macbeth

In this illustrative example I describe briefly how *Macbeth* was introduced and 'prepared for examination' at an inner London school over a series of 12 lessons. These lessons involved different phases of work and the text *Macbeth* features differently across each of these.

Macbeth takes some time to 'appear' in the classroom. The teacher does not inform the students they are studying *Macbeth*. Instead she attempts to connect *Macbeth* with the students' interest in witchcraft and superstition to offer them 'a way into' the text that relates to the demands of the National Curriculum (NC) course work requirement that a play be set in a socio-cultural context. The first lesson focused on 'witchcraft' and the students made a visual poster about witches. In lesson two, students explored, using the internet, the 'historical context' of life in 1603. Later they matched five pictures with five written characteristics that 'define' witches (e.g. 'They can fly through the air') and answered questions on a worksheet made by the teacher (e.g. 'What is a "Sabbath?" '). This use of worksheets produced English as a set of facts and studying Shakespeare as a kind of comprehension. This 'breaking down' of the process of study, and of the text *Macbeth* itself, into 'manageable chunks' reflects the department's response to the demands of the NC, classroom management issues and a perception of the students' ability. The teacher used worksheets to mediate *Macbeth* and the examination requirements: the scene from *Macbeth* 'became' a worksheet dislocated from the play. This fragmentation of the play was a material consequence of the examination requirements and the teacher's concern that *Macbeth* was too difficult for the students. Throughout the 12 lessons, students are given access to the first scene but not the whole play. They were given access to the minimum required to sit the examination. The textual cycle realizes the English department's focus on examinations and results.

The students analyzed the representation of the scene in a contemporary film of *Macbeth* in lessons four and five. They repeatedly watched the scene and the teacher focused attention and discussion on the setting, the witches' appearances, voices and effects. Through their performance of the scene, students' construction of a new text was the focus of lesson six. Students arranged their clothes, coats and scarves and hooded tops, to form cloaks and cover their faces to represent 'witchiness'. They used classroom space as a resource to create rhythm and played with the pitch, tone and pace of their voices to create the different characters of the witches. Later the students were given 14 images, with captions portraying key moments in the plot, to arrange in a sequence that reflects the plot of the play. In this way, the narrative was broken up and visualized and the plot took on a contextualizing function for the course work. All of this work on the text culminated in a written course work essay, titled 'Imagine you have been asked to direct *Macbeth*'. Explain how you would stage Act 1 scene 1 to engage a modern audience's attention and prepare them for the rest of the play'. The teacher 'retextualized' the students' retextualization of the play: (1) the written scene; (2) the multimodality of film, image, and performance; (3) a written commentary. The work of the previous lessons – studying Shakespeare – is transformed into a resource for 'preparing us for this essay'. The essay plan the teacher built 'with' the class matched the unfolding structure and sequence of lessons. The teacher broke up the task of writing for the students just as she broke up *Macbeth*: numbering paragraphs, ordering them, setting time limits to write into manageable 'chunks of time', that is, to write for examination.

A multimodal perspective to text and context enables a refocusing on the role of the text, by bringing into the analytical frame interaction that a linguistic account of text would not have attended to – the performance, the use of images, the role of the film. What appears to be the focus of interest – the written canonical text in the form of Act 1, scene 1 of *Macbeth*, is to a large extent 'absent' (or at least backgrounded) in the classroom. The written canonical text is actually made 'present', given presence, and made meaningful through its transformation by the teacher's and students' actions into non-linguistic modes. The mode of writing is then reintroduced for the purpose of assessment. To focus on language in the textuality of the learning environment alone would be to fail to recognize the multimodal resources the teacher and students use to weave this curriculum text – *Macbeth* – into the generalized communicative world of the students.

The multimodal textuality of the Science classroom: Blood circulation

The orchestration of modes in learning contexts is linked to curriculum subject matter and historical pedagogic practices. The kinds of images used, how they are used, how image is combined with other modes and so on is different in the school Science classroom than it is in the school English classroom. In short, texts and context connect with histories beyond the boundary of the classroom. This illustrative example focuses on a short (5-minute) excerpt of the textual cycle of a year nine school Science lesson on blood circulation in inner London. Over the course of the lesson the scientific entity 'blood circulation' was constructed. Having described the route of the blood, the teacher placed a model of the upper part of the human body on the bench in front of him (Figure 7.3).

The teacher handled the model heart while talking about the blood's movement through the heart and the contracting of the heart's muscles. Cyclicity was represented through the teacher's 'animation' of the model, and by his use of the verbs 'goes', 'comes'. The teacher used his finger to indicate the circulation of the blood on the image, providing a multimodal (visual, verbal, and gestural) summary of the lesson. Standing in front of the image on the white board he introduced the model of the insides of the human body, using his own body as a model for the outside. His body mediated the transition between the image on the board and the model on the bench, in a layering effect: his body overlaid the image; the model overlaid his body. Speech, gesture and model were fully integrated. Speech provided an explanation, gesture indicated the players, it acted out and dynamized the verbal account. The model provided an analytical representation of the

Figure 7.3 The teacher's manipulation of the model.

body as the physical location, and the relationship between the parts and the whole. The textbook image offered a detailed visual summary of all that had happened.

The semiotic resources mobilized by the teacher required the students to undertake specific kinds of imaginative work in order to make sense of different aspects of the circulatory system. The image required them to imagine the movement of blood around a circuit; to envisage the size and position of organs and the relationships between them in a highly abstract fashion; to think of the organs in a circuit, and of the cells as collected up into one place as an organ. The teacher's use of gesture and his body required the students to imagine what goes on 'beneath the skin'. The model required the students to think about elements of the cycle, for instance, the size and position of the organs, differently to that suggested by speech and image. The teacher's actions with the model realized movement and direction, which were named in his speech and required envisaging the agent of this action – the blood. Each mode repositioned the students in relation to the human body and demanded different cognitive work of them. The complex meaning of this part of the science curriculum was realized through this interweaving of modes. Throughout the lesson, the students were required to shift their view of the body between an internal and external entity. The direction of these moves can be interpreted as a pedagogic stance to the process of science as immersion and the role of observation in science.

I have attempted to show, through these two examples the links and connections across modes and texts in the classroom, the intertextuality of texts. I am arguing that the canonical text, whether it is *Macbeth* or the textbook image of the circulation of blood, is produced through the actions of teacher and students – the multimodal ensemble within which it is embedded. In both these examples, talk and writing are not the dominant forms of communication in the classroom and do not 'stand alone'. These examples also illustrate, in a limited way, how the texts and modal semiotic resources that circulate in the classroom connect to subject-specific practices, histories and knowledge. What is done to texts reflects, or refracts, aspects and qualities of the processes of knowledge production in a curriculum subject.

Now I turn to the question of context, and ask what a multimodal conception of text and textuality might mean for the idea of learning contexts, in particular classrooms.

Context: Classrooms as a multimodal textual formation

Texts and textuality are usually translated into the idea of 'texts *in* the classroom'. This produces the classroom as a kind of container. It is more productive to conceptualize context as a kind of network consisting of material, social, and historical strands woven together. Ideas of context as elaborated in Chapters 2 and 3 are pertinent here. In different ways, both chapters centre on the need to think of the classroom as a complex network. Fox outlines how an Actor Network Theory (ANT) approach views people and objects as fundamentally intermeshed through social networks. From this perspective, context is thoroughly materialistic and this means that the social does not, indeed cannot, exist outside of the material. Thus the character and potential of the materials that circulate in educational spaces, how these are mobilized through interaction, and how the learner is positioned within this complex web, is crucial for education. This also serves to foreground the need to understand the multimodal character and nature of the materials and interaction of the classroom. This positions the classroom as something clearly designed and *active*, as something that is dynamic and shaped by the agencies of those present in the context – the agencies of teacher and students, as well as by the agency of institutional and social and historical forces. The notion of context is, however, often made so stable that it becomes a 'solid given'. This serves to produce the classroom as a naturalized *physical space* as compared with an ideological space – although the design of the physical space is itself a part of the realization of ideology. From a multimodal perspective, the classroom itself can be understood as a complex sign. In other words, the classroom can be viewed as a textual formation in which the resources of space, furniture, visual display, and so on are discursively organized.

A multimodal approach to classrooms offers a way of looking at the design of learning contexts. Through the illustrative example below of two English classrooms in two schools to demonstrate how teachers' situated design of learning contexts can be examined from a multimodal perspective, I demonstrate how a multimodal analysis of the English classroom enables central questions to be addressed on the relationship between (and possibly the impact of) discourses of subject knowledge and learning contexts. For example, what do the texts, objects and furniture in a classroom represent as a part of English? Which representational and communicational modes are used to represent English? What is given importance through the resources of visual display and spatial arrangement?

English as competence in language communication

My first example is a classroom in an English department which is preoccupied, and not without reason, with getting students, mainly from ethnic minorities and working-class families, to perform well in GCSE exams at age 16. It assumes that it has to privilege a particular version of 'official knowledge'. This is materialized in the many official texts on the wall, which are mounted, framed and placed in prominent positions. The teacher selects and adapts the official policy (e.g. criteria and grades, key words in examination papers) and mediates these into sets of instructions for students that focus on examination. The layout of the classroom in neatly arranged group tables is another echo of departmental and national policies on group work and differentiation. In the process, it conveys to students that they are the kind of people who need a basic level of assistance to cope with assessment demands. In this sense it provides an example of a strategy for distributing what is seen as cultural capital in what are seen in both economic and cultural terms as impoverished places. Distribution, in this context, involves rationing.

The teacher's use of visual resources and her arrangement of these in the classroom displays combine to produce English as a coherent, 'bounded' and univocal space filled with language. The posters and displays are primarily written and word-processed and only a few include images. The content of the displays concerns writing genres, instructions on how to start a sentence, and so on. There is only one poster with several images on it: these are of Leonardo DiCaprio in the Baz Luhrmann film production of *Romeo & Juliet*. The images are derived from popular culture but are in a very literal sense cut down and tightly framed, so that the very thing that appears to have engaged many young people in the filmic reshaping of Shakespeare's play – the display of masculinity through the use of rap, dress and imagery of gang fighting – is the subject of the teacher's critique. It occupies a minor position in a classroom, which is a strongly 'boundaried' place, clear, sparse, and uncluttered, like the version of English that is produced there.

In this classroom 'What English is' is constituted as a completely explicit entity. The curriculum is displayed, the language of examination is literally written on the walls, the deadlines are clear. The politics of the English curriculum, as articulated in this classroom, is 'access to language': language is, literally, made available as a resource. An instance of this is the posters on the cupboard doors that contain dictionaries and thesauruses that list ways of starting a sentence. The visual display of the classroom fits into an instructional genre. Policy in the form of the National Curriculum is selected, condensed and strongly framed. Everything else has vanished. The curriculum is so pervasive that it is difficult to overlay it with anything. This genre of instruction positions the teacher and students in a particular relation to the production of English, beyond the obvious power relation that they are in. The teacher represents English as a series of competencies, that the students are to learn. The classroom display reminds them why they are there, why they must work. They are to aim for the teacher's idealized student text.

English and the life-worlds of students

The furniture and spatial arrangement of my second illustrative example classroom can be seen as an example of the organization of the 'progressive primary school' finding its way into the secondary school English and redefining the place to learn and the future of the school (Stuebing, 1995). The teacher has bought soft furnishings into her classroom: a carpet, several soft swivel chairs, a soft armchair and a sofa creating a home-like space in her classroom. She regularly reorganized the furniture and desks in the room and the arrangements were always non-symmetrical.

The teacher's design of her classroom can also be seen as a rejection of formal secondary school arrangements and an attempt to create a learning environment in which the curriculum is, as she commented, 'only a small part of what is actually going on within the whole learning experience'. The home furnishings of the classroom all attempt to distance the classroom from the school as an institution. They attempt to produce the classroom (and, by implication, 'school English') as a 'pseudo-liminal' space that is nei-ther school nor 'out of school', bordering on the style of a 'teenager's room'. This is echoed in the posters stuck quite literally all over the walls, over-lapping, angled, struggling for space in a jumble of film and music icons of youthful despair and early death (Kurt Cobain, James Dean, Tupac Shakur and more).

Alongside this cultural mix, the teacher has displayed students' texts, which are highly visual collages drawing on pop and film icons to represent the characters and relationships from, for example, *Macbeth*. These elements of the display reconstruct the relationship between writing and text within the domain of school English. In contrast to the use of popular culture as a visual annotation of aspects of the English curriculum in the first classroom, the teacher has here reframed English as popular culture (and in doing so she has reframed popular culture as English). In short, her visual display serves to position English and popular culture as interconnected forms of knowledge. The meanings of popular culture are foregrounded and the position of English in this is backgrounded (changed). The display reflects the teacher's comments on school English as being about 'different ways of reading the world and reading the text'.

The complex of signs realized via the visual display of the classroom is one of English as a space which collects the life-worlds of students. Here the world of popular culture is pervasive, and the curriculum is laid over it gently, offering the students a filter of 'school English' for viewing this everyday world in another way. The question 'what is English?' is raised and the role suggested to students is one of how to explore such a question in relation to the artefacts of their worlds.

These examples show how learning contexts are built up over time, but are nonetheless fluid, dynamic spaces created through the agentive work of the teacher as she or he is situated in the web of social, cul-tural and historical forces within which they operate. There is no container. This opens up the potential for the redesign of learning contexts, at the same time perhaps as it demonstrates the complex difficulty of change and redesign.

Concluding comments

In this chapter, I have shown how a multimodal perspective might be useful for rethinking texts, textuality and context. I have proposed that one way of viewing the classroom is as a transformative cycle of multimodal textual formations with different relations to time, some of which are ephemeral and others of which are more fixed through their sedimentation over time. From this perspective, the classroom is a dynamic textual formation. I have argued that moving beyond language to think of multimodal textual ensembles enables the semiotic work of students to be bought to the fore and offers ways of getting at what learning is, what senses students are making, and what connections and disconnections exist for them in relation to concepts to be learnt.

Pedagogy is shaped by a range of modes, as demonstrated in this chapter and elsewhere (Kress *et al.* 2001, 2005). This raises the question of what modes teachers are making available to students and how the textual environment of the classroom is established and worked with by students and teachers. It also raises the issue of what aspects of this textual environment are legitimated and which are not within the multimodal textual environment of school learning.

The orchestration of the textuality of learning environments is central to the realization of pedagogy in the classroom. How policy features in this orchestration is key to the production of pedagogy. Multimodality offers a way to think of the classroom as a complex social web of connections, woven into different patterns. Text and context are a part of the designed realization of these discourses.

References

Halliday, M. (1978) *Language as a Social Semiotic*. London: Edward Arnold.
Jewitt, C. (2005) 'Classrooms and the design of pedagogic discourse: A multimodal approach', *Culture and Psychology*, 11, 3: 309–20.
Kress, G. (1997) *Before Writing*. London: Routledge.
Kress, G. and Van Leeuwen, T. (1996) *Reading Images: The Grammar Of Visual Design*. London: Routledge.
Kress, G. and Van Leeuwen, T. (2001) *Multimodal Discourse*. London: Arnold and Macmillan.
Kress, G., Jewitt, C., Ogborn, J. and Tsatsarelis, C. (2001) *Multimodal Teaching and Learning: Rhetorics of the Science Classroom*. London: Continuum.
Kress, G., Jewitt, C., Bourne, J., Franks, A., Hardcastle, J., Jones, K. and Reid, E. (2005) *English in Urban Classrooms: A Multimodal Perspective on Teaching and Learning*. Oxon: Routledge.

Martinec, R. (2000) 'Construction of identity in Michael Jackson's *Jam*', *Social Semiotics*, 10, 3: 313–29.

Stuebing, S. (1995) *Redefining the Place to Learn*. Paris: OCED.

van Leeuwen, T. (1999) *Speech, Music, Sound*. London: Macmillan.

van Leeuwen, T. (2005) *Introducing Social Semiotics*. Oxon: Routledge.

Chapter 8

Worlds within worlds

The relational dance between context and learning in the workplace

Lorna Unwin, Alison Fuller, Alan Felstead and Nick Jewson

Introduction

Organizations, whether in the public or private sector, and regardless of their size and nature of activity, have different approaches to the way they create and manage themselves as learning environments. In developing an understanding of the nature of learning at work and the conceptualization of workplace pedagogy, it is necessary to build a picture of the contextual factors that conspire to facilitate or to hinder opportunities for learning. These factors would include an organization's identity, history and culture, the goods and services it provides, its organization of the labour process, its treatment and involvement of employees and the broader productive system in which it sits (see Braverman 1974; Darrah 1996; Koike 2002; Rainbird *et al.* 2004a; Fuller and Unwin 2004a; Evans *et al.* 2006). This chapter explores the ways in which these factors interact over time and space to create different types of learning environment. The term the 'relational dance' in the chapter's title was inspired by Cook and Brown's (2005) metaphor of the 'generative dance' between knowledge and 'knowing', which happens when individuals and teams make innovative leaps forward through problem-solving in the workplace.

It is important at the outset to acknowledge that the primary function of any workplace is not learning, but the production of goods and services and the achievement of organizational goals determined internally and/or shaped by others such as customers, head offices, parent companies, and government departments (see Rainbird *et al.* 2004a). Furthermore, organizations in both the public and private sector exist within the boundaries of a political economy and 'face a set of coordinating institutions whose character is not fully under their control'. (Hall and Soskice 2001: 15). This poses a considerable challenge for researchers interested in workplace learning, as it requires that attention be paid to a range of phenomena that stretch beyond the actual generation, acquisition and sharing of skills and knowledge. By arguing that contextual factors are central to the understanding of workplace learning, we are not suggesting that human agency has little or no role to play. Individuals can and do exert agency in terms of the way they engage with and create (personally and collectively) learning opportunities (see Billett 2002; Hodkinson and Hodkinson 2004). The extent of this engagement reflects individual biographies and dispositions to learning developed over time. We would argue, however, that examining individual agency in isolation from the way work is organized and the wider institutional and political features that constitute the workplace as a learning environment leads to a partial explanation of learning at work. As Rainbird *et al.* (2004b: 39) argue, learning at work has to be considered within 'the context of the power relations which characterize the employment relationship'.

This chapter draws on findings and analysis from an ESRC funded, multi-sector project,[1] which is employing a range of qualitative and quantitative methods in workplaces in the United Kingdom (UK). To illustrate our arguments, we provide evidence from two of our project sectors: hairdressing and automotive component manufacturing. The chapter is in three sections. The first section discusses the influence of context on learning (and vice versa) and then broadens the discussion to consider the influence of context on pedagogical practices. The second section provides illustrations from two of our case study sectors and the third section offers some concluding remarks.

Learning as part of work activity

There is still a strong tendency on the part of UK policymakers, employers and the agencies/providers that support workforce development, to conceptualize learning at, through and for work as a linear, fixed-time activity, and to use qualifications as a proxy for job competence and skills (see Felstead *et al.* 2005). This is understandable if the prime concern is the measurement of learning outcomes. Beckett and Hager (2002: 99) refer to this as the 'front-end model of occupational preparation', a model which relies on what Schon (1983) termed 'technical rationality', whereby it is assumed that people can and will apply this learning to everyday problems and situations in the workplace. Conceptualizing work-based or work-related learning in ways which mirror formal education helps policymakers to set standards for the design of vocational qualifications, allocate funding, measure outputs, and compile data on the volume of skills in the economy (see Felstead and Unwin 2001; Felstead *et al.* 2005). For their part, many employers prefer the acquisition of specific skills and knowledge to be organized in such a way as not to interfere too much with the business of producing goods and services. This acquisition model of learning is also important for individuals who need and want to attain qualifications in order to gain entry to the labour market, to gain promotion within their existing job, and to move from one organization or sector to another. Some learning in the workplace (involving structured instruction and assessment) can be accredited through formal qualifications, but much of it arises out of everyday workplace activity. It is situated, embedded and occurs through social interaction and, hence, it conforms much more to the participation and transformative models of learning that have been developed in response to the inadequacy of acquisition as a model for workplace learning (see Lave and Wenger 1991; Engeström 2001; Beckett and Hager 2002; Eraut 2004).

The embedded nature of workplace learning poses considerable challenges for researchers. In our project, we have used a variety of qualitative and ethnographic methods to excavate the nature of learning in our case study sites and this will be discussed in more detail later in the chapter. We also had the opportunity to employ quantitative methods through collaboration with the National Institute for Adult Continuing Education (NIACE). NIACE conduct an annual Adult Learning Survey in the UK and asked the project to design a new module of questions on workplace learning for a sub-set of the main survey sample. This sub-set comprised a random household survey of 1,943 employed people across the UK (Felstead et al. 2005). The questions sought respondents' views on the activities they felt best helped them to improve their skills and knowledge at work. The respondents reported that it was the nature of the work activity itself that generated learning. They cited activities such as doing the job, being shown different approaches, engaging in self-reflection and keeping one's eyes and ears open, as examples of how they improved their knowledge and skills and, hence, their work performance. Not all employees, however, were able to use their work practice in this way. For example, employees in jobs classed as 'elementary' and 'machine operatives' were less likely to be able to improve their work performance through day-to-day interactions with colleagues, clients and the job itself, because their tasks are tightly bounded and heavily prescribed. In that sense, learning does not float free, but is strongly anchored and manipulated by the nature of the context. Ashton (2004: 45), building on the work of researchers such as Darrah (1996), Koike (2002), Scarborough et al. (1999) and Lawler et al. (2001), has argued that an organization constrains or enables opportunities for learning through the following modes of behaviour: the extent to which it facilitates access to knowledge and information; the opportunity it provides to practice and develop new skills; the provision of effective support for learning and the extent to which it rewards learning.

Given our argument that organizations create different types of learning environment, we are, necessarily, interested in the role of pedagogical practices, the concept of a workplace curriculum and the role of artefacts and devices. In using the term pedagogy in relation to a workplace context, we are not just referring to what might be classified as 'formal', structured activity, such as planned instruction in new procedures or training sessions away from the work-site. There is a debate in the literature about the use of terms such as formal, informal, non-formal and incidental to describe learning at work (see Eraut 2004; Billett 2004; Colley *et al*. 2003). There is not the space in this chapter to review this debate, but we would argue that what matters is the extent to which organizations create the conditions which facilitate learning in general and then add value by extending opportunities to employees to deepen their learning. Previous research by project team members (see Fuller and Unwin 2004b) in the steel and metals sector revealed that employees, including apprentices, were engaged in forms of instruction in the workplace covering a range of matters from disciplinary knowledge (e.g. mathematical problem solving) through to adjustment of manual performance (e.g. more effective use of a machine). This involved pedagogical practices between peers, between apprentices and between apprentices and older workers. The extent of this varied from one workplace to another and depended upon four discernible and interrelated dimensions.

First, each of the companies in the study operated within parameters shaped by external contextual factors, including, for example, the nature of their product market and ownership, regulatory requirements set by government, the price and availability of raw materials and so on. Second, each company had created internal structures and processes, characteristics and mechanisms that Billett (2002), building on the work of Gibson (1969), has referred to as 'affordances' operating in the workplace. Third, these affordances and the extent to which each company encouraged the sharing of knowledge and skills and recognized the learning of all employees appeared to be stronger in companies which were able to take a longer-term view of their business goals and were more able to withstand external forces or winds of change. Fourth, the extent to which individual employees were able to and/or chose to take advantage of and even create learning opportunities partly reflected their own biographies and sense of worker identity.

In one company, which had created what Fuller and Unwin (2004a) refer to as an 'expansive learning environment', the continuation of apprenticeship training over a period of some 80 years meant that there was visible evidence of the company's strong commitment to the importance of substantive training for the long term. A significant number of experienced employees (including senior managers) had themselves been apprentices. Apprentices were, therefore, positioned at the centre of the company's workforce development strategy, with their knowledge and skills being valued by older workers. The richness of the pedagogical activity found in this company reflects the view of Edwards and Nicoll (2004) that 'pedagogic practices are embedded in the actor-networks of specific workplaces'.

Where pedagogical practices are visibly encouraged and valued in workplaces, they may be underpinned by the codification of relevant knowledge and skills into a workplace curriculum. Typically, this will take the form of workbooks for apprentices, training manuals and other artefacts. Previous research by the authors (see Fuller *et al*. 2003) showed that some organizations (for example, an accountancy practice) use specific artefacts such as legal documents as vehicles for bringing workers together to generate new working practices and, hence, employ the curriculum beyond the level of formation training. In contrast, some organizations use the curriculum as a device for controlling the level of autonomy deemed appropriate for their employees. For example, in one car dealership, the manager kept the procedures for calculating the part exchange value of cars in a file in his office so that his sales staff had to go to him each time they needed to carry out this function on behalf of a customer. In this workplace, sales staff were actively pushed to compete against each other, to the extent that one employee referred to the 'dog-eat-dog' nature of the work environment and described how sales staff would deliberately not share with colleagues their ideas for best practice in winning sales.

In the case of the car dealership, the sales staff were certainly learning all the time, despite the fact that their access to the knowledge they would need to exercise greater discretion in terms of completing sales with customers was denied. There has long been an assumed connection in the management and broader social science literature between increased levels of skill and the ability to exercise discretion. Yet Felstead *et al.* (2004) argue that this may be an illusion. They show that skills surveys in the UK between 1986 and 2001 reveal that, despite the fact that discretion is positively correlated with skill and despite many jobs becoming more complex, there had been a considerable decline in the number of employees reporting that they had a 'great deal of choice in the way they did their job' (ibid.: 163). In addition, between 1992 and 2001, there had been a 'marked decline in employees' perception of their influence over each of the specific aspects of the work task' (ibid.).

Felstead *et al*'s (2004) research is important to this discussion because it reminds us that workplaces are different from formal educational settings as employees are not, necessarily, afforded the identity of learners. In professional occupations, the notion of continuous learning is part of the historic fabric of community life, but in many other occupations, learning is regarded as an activity to be undertaken during the induction period, after which the focus must be on productive work. Even as these words are written, however, it must be acknowledged that the traditional rarefied notions of professionalism are being eroded in both the public and private sectors due to increased pressure to meet targets and deliver greater outputs. The point here is that pedagogical practices may be shared by educational settings and workplaces and may produce increased levels of skill and knowledge, but it does not necessarily follow that workplaces will combine increased learning with increased opportunities for employees to exercise judgement and take greater control over their work.

Sectoral illustrations

This section uses evidence from two of our case study sectors, hairdressing and automotive component manufacturing, to illustrate our arguments. The illustrations display the complexity of the interplay identified by Edwards (2006: 6) between the way in which learning is both dependent upon and the creator of the context in which it takes place: 'In other words, learning contexts are practically and discursively performed and performative. They co-emerge with the activities by which they are shaped and vice versa'.

Hairdressing

The hairdressing sector in the UK is characterized by small, single-owner establishments who operate in a market which stretches from the quick and cheap haircut supplied by the men's barber shop (average £5) to the lengthy and very costly (minimum £100) service supplied by salons in major cities, where the selling of products increases the client's bill way beyond the cost of the initial haircut. Our fieldwork has concentrated on two franchise organizations in England. These organizations comprise a head office, which supplies central services such as marketing, information technology and accounting to as many as 30 individual salons. They can be categorized as 'business format franchises', with highly standardized, controlled and regulated relationships (Felstead 1991: 52). Franchised chains have a reputation for high fashion and are well known for their innovations in both hairdressing techniques and styles (Drucker *et al*. 2002). They also have a reputation for investing heavily in training, many running their own 'in-house' training schools for apprentices, both inside and outside the organization (Mintel 1999).

In terms of the organization of work, franchise chains differ as to the amount of latitude they give to salon managers. Our case study franchisors exhibit a very 'top-down' culture and exert considerable control over the amount of inter-/intra-salon knowledge sharing and transfer. The use of the metaphor of the 'family' is common, with salons expected to conform to head office defined quality standards, extending to such factors as the design of the salon. The head offices not only dictate the physical environment of the salons, but also issue documents, in the form of booklets, which prescribe in detail the conduct and behaviour of salon staff in all aspects of social interactions with clients. Monitoring of these practices includes the use of mystery shoppers by franchisors and customer satisfaction questionnaires.

In terms of performance, one of our case study organizations employs a 'batting averages' approach for comparing the individual salons. This involves measuring stylists' performance in terms of the number of clients they retain (a stylist with a transient client base will be viewed with concern), the amount of products they sell over and above the cost of the hair procedure and the complexity of the hair procedure (colouring is a key way to earn higher returns). The daily pressures of meeting business targets and the maintenance of the standardization of the service across the salons has created a highly structured approach to learning and pedagogical practice, both on-the-job and in the off-the-job training sessions. There is a strong emphasis on continuous teaching and learning (for all grades of staff) in relation to codified knowledge (including the procedures set out in the booklets referred to above) as new products are constantly being introduced and new procedures invented as fashions evolve in a sector where the customer base is notoriously fickle. Learning to read customer behaviour, retain their loyalty and persuade them to spend beyond the basic hair procedure is also part of the considerable knowledge and skill-base of every stylist. The physical environment of the salons is key to the way in which learning and pedagogical practices are facilitated. Staff of all grades and functions are open to observation (and surveillance) by all co-workers and clients, enabling comments on, and corrections of, work practices to flow freely. One experienced stylist commented:

> Some of the youngsters are brilliant. I like learning new things. I mean often they'll go on courses and they'll come back and they'll say: 'Oh you should see what I did' ... you know, they show you. I think that's the nice thing about the job, especially working for a big salon.

A newly qualified stylist commented:

> ... my techniques are a lot newer than some that have done the training ten years ago. So if they have like a younger client in, that wants something a bit more trendy, it's, like, a more up to date technique that can be used. ... It's nice because everybody asks each other for advice. I can go to somewhere and asked them about a more classical haircut and they can come to me and say 'I've got somebody young and they want something a bit more ... how would you go about it?' ... And nobody's too busy to stop what they're doing to come and help you out.

Experienced stylists appear to take their teaching responsibilities very seriously and, as the following comment reveals, they are able to conceptualize teaching as a reflexive process:

> I've found that I've learnt an awful lot when I'm actually teaching somebody. Because it makes me stop and think again: 'How am I going to put this over to this person?' So it makes me remember the information I've been given in the past. And sometimes somebody will come out with something that makes me learn from a comment they've made or the way they've approached something. So sometimes you can actually almost re-educate an existing member of staff but by *them* being the one that's *teaching*.

The hairdressing salons we are studying employ a dynamic workplace curriculum that has evolved over time to ensure that standards can be maintained and business targets achieved. There are formal structures in place to deliver this curriculum, both on-the-job as part of everyday working practice and off-the-job through formal instruction. It is clear from our data that the commitment to learning throughout the salons is sustained by an organizational culture in which business (and hence employee) success is deemed to be the result of constant vigilance with regard to cross-salon standards. Employee agency is part of the recipe in that stylists aim to be as high up the batting list as possible and to do that they have to keep learning new techniques but, at the same time, they know that they will learn more effectively by sharing ideas with colleagues.

Automotive component engineering

The components sub-sector of the automotive industry employs some 200,000 people in around 2,000 businesses in the UK and supplies parts of vehicles (e.g. wheels, cylinder heads, panels, etc.) to the major manufacturers who assemble the vehicles (SMMT 2002). In recent years, vehicle manufacturers have been attempting to reduce their in-house costs by out-sourcing as many parts as possible to first-tier suppliers (see Doran 2003). The struggle to compete in the global market has brought many production and industrial relations' changes to the automotive sector and for Western owned companies the most challenging revolution has been the adoption of Japanese inspired 'lean' manufacturing and quality management approaches (see West 2000). In our project, we are investigating two first-tier suppliers, one in England, which makes parts for a German car manufacturer and one in Northern Ireland, which is owned by a French company and which makes parts for French and American car manufacturers. Both case study organizations suffer the same pressures common to all suppliers, namely meeting the ever more exacting demands of their customers in terms of achieving high levels of quality and efficiency for as little cost as possible.

The case study organization in Northern Ireland comprises a large factory divided into two main areas: one makes wheels and one makes cylinder heads. The workforce is divided along traditional manufacturing lines with a small senior management team responsible for four business units, which in turn employ production managers, technical engineers, maintenance staff, supervisors, and operatives. At the start of our research, the factory employed almost 1,000 people, but 18 months later the workforce has been reduced to around 600 in order to reduce operating costs. It is expected that the wheels division may only last another four years due to increasing competition from Eastern Europe. The manufacture of cylinder heads is far more complex than wheels and, therefore, it is expected that, for the time being, this part of the business will remain in the UK. This, then, is a learning environment in which the spectre of globalization stalks the factory floor on a daily basis.

Over the past ten years, the introduction of new production technologies has led to a reconfiguration of the jobs of operatives in the wheels division of the factory, requiring them to spot and solve problems as part of their daily activity and have a more holistic understanding of the production process. In order to improve operatives' skills, the company's training department identified 95 operatives to be trained as 'tutors' to the rest of the operative workforce. The tutors were given intensive off-the-job training, part of which involved them in the design of tutor packs containing basic, step-by-step, information describing the production of wheels. These packs were then placed on the various work stations round the factory floor so that operatives could consult them. The packs are much more than standard training manuals. They are designed to be 'live' artefacts. Operatives and their supervisors are encouraged to draw on their everyday experiences in order to adapt the packs by adding new information and better ways to describe the different stages of production. Thus employees engage in a collaborative process where learning crosses role boundaries and takes place on several levels. The packs are not limited to being mechanisms for training new recruits, but have evolved into vehicles for the consideration of how work is organized, how knowledge can be shared and, importantly, how new knowledge might be created.

The tutor pack approach meant the company could develop what one supervisor called a 'vocabulary for production staff', which enabled employees to talk about the different types of skills and knowledge used on the factory floor. As a result, they are enabled to become much more engaged in discussions about learning and training. As with the hairdressing booklets, the packs contain the factory's workplace curriculum, though in this case the document has been promoted as a much more interactive tool for learning.

Operatives, supervisors and managers all commented on the importance of the tutor packs and the approach to on-the-job learning that underpinned their use. However, whilst the initiative demonstrates a creative and inclusive approach to pedagogy, it is now struggling under the pressures of the stark business context. One of the tutors explained how he has less and less time to support the ongoing learning operatives in his team as, ironically, he was having to train operatives from other parts of the factory in order to make the workforce more flexible:

> I don't feel sometimes we're doing enough ... we're really under pressure, so I'm not actually getting to go through the tutor packs again with the guys that I should be going through it again. You know, there's quite a lot of cross-training, which means the guys on the platform doing casting, need to be trained up in our department as well. So it means not only have I the five or six people, the four or five people that I'm working with directly, but I also have all the casters as well to do. It's just at the moment with the pressures, I can't get those people freed up to do that and I can't be freed up either to do it.

The problem here is that a short-term approach to training is now push-ing out the time and space for the nurturing of newly acquired skills and knowledge. In addition, the business pressures have also had an impact on the opportunities for operatives within one section to rotate their jobs and, hence, experience a more varied working day.

Conclusion

This chapter has argued for a more holistic approach to the conceptualization and exploration of learning in the workplace. Such an approach positions learn-ing in context and requires researchers, practitioners and policymakers to pay much closer attention to the dynamic nature of the workplace environment. We do not seek to ignore the importance of individual agency, but rather we argue that individuals in the workplace are part of an organic enterprise, one that they both help to shape and are shaped by and one to which individuals bring pedagogical expertise formed as part of their learning biographies (see Felstead et al. 2006).

All learning and pedagogical practice in the workplace, as in formal edu-cation institutions, will be influenced by a range of factors and shaped by external as well as internal imperatives. The combination of those factors and imperatives will differ according to the nature of the goods and/or services being produced, the type of ownership and culture of the organization, its via-bility and status in its product market, and the extent to which outside forces (including government regulation) can interfere in its activities. At the same time, organizations will differ in terms of the range and capabilities of the staff it can utilize for specific pedagogic roles (e.g. trainers, mentors, coaches, workplace assessors, supervisors, line managers). However, the workplace has an advantage over formal educational institutions as pedagogic activity is likely to be spread across a much broader range of people. Those organizations, like the case study examples referred to above, that recognize the pedagogic potential of their employees are able to promote a stronger learning culture than those that conceptualize the transmission of skills and knowledge as a hierarchical, top-down process. This does not mean, however, that pedagog-ical good practice can overcome the power of context, although case study managers discussed here would argue that the maintenance of robust and appropriate learning activities helps an organization to withstand the winds of change.

A key challenge for our current research is to examine the extent to which the learning and pedagogical practices we are observing and attempting to capture across the diverse workplace and sectoral settings are only understand-able when analyzed within the confines of the contextual features discussed earlier in this chapter. Our arguments about the importance of context could be highly restrictive, in the sense that, ultimately, the context overpow-ers any sense of the transferable or transcendental potential of the learning.

Edwards (2005: 9) suggests that 'it may be the patterns of participatory process that are transferred rather than simply knowledge'. This would require researchers to move from 'a generalized notion of learning transfer to an understanding of the diverse specifics of a context that may be mobilized ... To focus on learning per se may not be helpful therefore' (ibid.). This causes us to think harder about the ways in which the hairdressers and the workers in the automotive plant are learning about how to (at the same time) adapt to and overcome the contextual features of their workplaces, as well as the everyday skills and knowledge that enable them to perform their job-specific tasks.

Regardless of their purpose, all workplaces are complex environments in which learning takes many forms and in which pedagogical practice can include the full range of activities normally associated with educational settings. The extent of pedagogical variety and the nature of the learning opportunities available to and created by employees exist within a set of contextual relationships that shift and change with time. In order to develop a better understanding of the pedagogical nature of workplaces, we need to build detailed maps of those relationships, ideally within a longitudinal research framework. This will require greater use of collaborative, multidisciplinary research studies in which the organizations being studied play a much more active role in the collection and analysis of data. In his classic ethnographic account of two American factories, Darrah (1996: 33) rightly cautioned against misguided notions that there can be a 'comprehensive, foundational description of the workplace', for, as he added, 'the diverse understandings of work are extraordinarily complex, reflecting assumptions about the self, its relations with other people, hierarchy, knowledge and causation'. We would argue, however, that light needs to be shone on as wide a variety of workplaces as possible (including educational workplaces, such as schools, colleges and universities) in order that we might learn more about the teaching and learning that occurs day in day out and which, for the most part, remains invisible.

Acknowledgment

The authors would like to acknowledge two former research associates of the ESRC project, Tracey Lee (University of Huddersfield) and Dan Bishop (University of Leicester), who collected data for the hairdressing and automotive case studies reported in this chapter.

Note

1 The project, *Learning as Work: Teaching and Learning Processes in the Contemporary Work Organisation* (RES 139250110), is funded under the ESRC's Teaching and Learning Programme. For more details, see http://learningaswork.cardiff.ac.uk/.

Worlds within worlds 117

References

Ashton, D. (2004) 'The impact of organisational structure and practices on learning in the workplace', *International Journal of Training and Development*, 8, 1: 43–53.

Beckett, D. and Hager, P. (2002) *Life, Work and Learning*. London: Routledge.

Billett, S. (2004) 'Learning through work: Workplace participatory practices', in H. Rainbird, A. Fuller and A. Munro (eds) *Workplace Learning in Context*. London: Routledge.

Billett, S. (2002) 'Workplace pedagogic practices: Co-participation and learning', *British Journal of Educational Studies*, 50, 4: 457–81.

Braverman, H. (1974) *Labour and Monopoly Capital*. New York: Monthly Review Press.

Colley, H., Hodkinson, P. and Malcolm, J. (2003) *Informality and Formality in Learning*. London: Learning and Skills Research Centre.

Cook, S.D.N. and Brown, J.S. (2005) 'Bridging epistemologies: The generative dance between organizational knowledge and organizational knowing', in S. Little and T. Ray (eds) *Managing Knowledge* (2nd edition). London: Sage.

Darrah, C.N. (1996) *Learning and Work: An Exploration in Industrial Ethnography*. London: Garland Publishing.

Doran, D. (2003) 'Supply chain implications of modularization', *International Journal of Operations and Production Management*, 23, 3: 316–26.

Drucker, J., Stanworth, C. and White, G. (2002) *Report to the Low Pay Commission on the Impact of the National Minimum Wage on the Hairdressing Sector*. London: University of Greenwich Business School.

Edwards, R. (2006) 'Learning in context – Within and across domains', paper presented to Seminar One of the ESRC Thematic Seminar Series, *Contexts, Communities, Networks: Mobilizing Learners' Resources and Relationships in Different Domains*, Glasgow Caledonian University, February.

Edwards, R. and Nicoll, K. (2004) 'Mobilizing workplaces: Actors, discipline and governmentality', *Studies in Continuing Education*, 26, 2: 159–73.

Engeström, Y. (2001) 'Expansive learning at work: Toward an activity theoretical reconceptualization, *Journal of Education and Work*, 14, 1: 133–55.

Eraut, M. (2004) 'Informal learning in the workplace', *Studies in Continuing Education*, 26, 2: 247–73.

Evans, K., Hodkinson, P., Rainbird, H. and Unwin, L. (2006) *Improving Workplace Learning*. Oxon: Routledge.

Felstead, A. (1991) 'The social organization of the franchise: A case of "controlled self-employment"', *Work, Employment and Society*, 5, 1: 37–57.

Felstead, A. and Unwin, L. (2001) 'Funding post-compulsory education and training: A retrospective analysis of the TEC and FEFC systems and their impact on skills', *Journal of Education and Work*, 14, 1: 91–111.

Felstead, A., Bishop, D., Fuller, A., Jewson, N., Unwin, L. and Kakavelakis, K. (2006) *Performing Identities at Work: Evidence from Contrasting Sectors, Learning as Work Research Paper No.9*. Cardiff: Cardiff School of Social Science, Cardiff University.

Felstead, A., Fuller, A., Unwin, L., Ashton, D., Butler, P. and Lee, T. (2005) 'Surveying the scene: Learning metaphors, survey design and the workplace context', *Journal of Education and Work*. 18, 4: 359–83.

Felstead, A., Gallie, D. and Green, F. (2004) 'Job complexity and task discretion: Tracking the direction of skills at work in Britain', in C. Warhurst, I. Grugulis and E. Keep (eds) *The Skills That Matter*. Basingstoke: Palgrave.

Fuller, A. and Unwin, L. (2004a) 'Expansive learning environments: Integrating personal and organizational development, in H. Rainbird, A. Fuller and A. Munro (eds) *Workplace Learning in Context*. London: Routledge.

Fuller, A. and Unwin, L. (2004b) 'Young people as teachers and learners in the workplace: Challenging the novice-expert dichotomy', *International Journal of Training and Development*, 8, 1: 32–42.

Fuller, A., Ashton, D., Felstead, A., Unwin, L., Walters, S. and Quinn, M. (2003) *The Impact of Informal Learning at Work on Business Productivity*. London: Department for Trade and Industry.

Gibson, E.J. (1969) *Principles of Perceptual Learning and Development*. New York: Prentice Hall.

Hall, P.A. and Soskice, D. (2001) 'An introduction to varieties of capitalism, in A. Hall and D. Soskice (eds) *Varieties of Capitalism*. Oxford: Oxford University Press.

Hodkinson, P. and Hodkinson, H. (2004) 'The significance of individuals' dispositions in workplace learning: A case study of two teachers', *Journal of Education and Work*, 17, 2: 167–82.

Koike, K. (2002) 'Intellectual skills and competitive strength: Is a radical change necessary?' *Journal of Education and Work*, 14, 4: 390–408.

Lave, J. and Wenger, E. (1991) *Situated Learning: Legitimate Peripheral Participation*. Cambridge: Cambridge University Press.

Lawler, E.E., Mohrman, S.A. and Benson, G. (2001) *Organizing for High Performance*. San Francisco: Jossey-Bass.

Mintel (1999) *Hairdressing Salons and Barber Shops – UK – June 1999*. London: Mintel International Group Limited.

Rainbird, H., Fuller, A. and Munro, A. (2004a) (eds) *Workplace Learning in Context*. London: Routledge.

Rainbird, H., Munro, A. and Holly, L. (2004b) 'The employment relationship and workplace learning', in H. Rainbird, A. Fuller and A. Munro (eds) *Workplace Learning in Context*. London: Routledge.

Scarborough, H., Swan, J. and Preston, J. (1999) *Knowledge Management and the Learning Organization*. London: CIPD.

Schon, D. (1983) *The Reflective Practitioner*. New York: Basic Books.

SMMT (2002) *Strengthening the Supply Chain: Improving the Competitiveness of the UK's Automotive Components Sector,* London: SMMT (The Society of Motor Manufacturers and Traders Ltd.).

West, P. (2000) *Organizational Learning in the Automotive Sector*. London: Routledge.

Chapter 9

Technology-mediated learning contexts

Mary Thorpe

Contexts that are mediated and virtual

Technology is often viewed as a carrier of an interaction that would otherwise happen face-to-face and unmediated. This assumes that the primary reality is the physically present interaction and that a virtual version of that reality can be delivered using digital technologies. This formulation tends to lead to analyzing technology-mediated learning contexts by reference to their ability to deliver the supposed key features of the face-to-face. In their analysis of the use of networked study bedrooms in a university context, for example, Crook and Light (2002) locate the challenge to technology-mediated learning in terms of how to replicate the combination of informal and formal discourse opportunities that characterize the face-to-face campus.

However, the use of the face-to-face experience as the route through which to approach the technologically mediated can suggest that there is a 'real' context that exists prior to the use of technology, and that this context is what we mediate in order for learning to be enabled in the virtual environment. This chapter challenges such a starting point. It analyzes the ways in which the practices that develop with the use of technology in particular settings do configure distinctive learning contexts rather than mediated versions of the face-to-face. These contexts may support as well as undermine learning, but it is through practices with technology, rather than the direct effect of the tools themselves, that we create learning contexts. These practices stimulate particular experiences of learning and configure learning contexts that may bear little resemblance to face-to-face learning contexts.

Technology is also portrayed as a tool that we choose to add into an existing context associated with a learning goal, in order to increase access, skill development, learning effectiveness and so on. However, deterministic approaches that assume technology can directly bring such effects have not been borne out by the research into how technology does impact on learning, or indeed on other social processes (Woolgar 2002). Technology can create virtual environments or 'places', and may thus implicitly foster a container view of context, perceived as being the technologically created 'space' within which learning happens. However, to perceive technology as an inert container or tool, separate from the practices of which it is a part, obscures the ways in which technology-mediated contexts are constructed and impact on learners. Technology self-evidently involves tools, understood as both the physical resources and practical skills required to make use of them, but to focus primarily on the tool or the virtual space would be to make a categorical error, mistaking a component part for the system as a whole (Jones and Esnault 2004).

We need to explore the ways in which technology-enabled practices construct learning contexts and distinctive modes of engagement in learning. As Satchwell and Ivanič argue in this book, 'new technologies add enormously to the significance and diversity of literacy media and artefacts'. As their account shows, learners may differ in the extent to which the expertise and resources they develop through technology-enabled practices are mobilized to expand their learning and achievement within institutional settings.

Issues of identity, textuality and trust

The use of technology for core aspects of higher education – discussion, communication and access to information – challenges learners' core assumptions and capabilities. Computer-mediated communication (CMC) for example, is a tool designed *for* communication that may be perceived, at least initially, as a *barrier* to communication. Feenberg (1989) relates this to loss of the cues and social embedding through which face-to-face communication happens. The task is to rebuild this context through textuality – using text to reconstruct forms of socializing, cue recognition and communicative process that generate the necessary conditions for learning.

Asynchronous conferencing, for example, makes communicative demands on contributors, in order to foster a positive climate that will nurture confidence to 'enter' a discursive space that novices typically experience as unfamiliar, even intimidating. Research on the impact of CMC has also identified a connection between textual practices and experience of identity online. The apparent neutrality of the online space has been shown to be just that, apparent rather than real, with text messages as carriers of many cues for the reader about the attitudes and intentions of the sender: 'in conditions of student diversity and unfamiliarity with online literacy practices, marginalization, isolation, and 'dissensus and conflict' (Blair and Monske 2003: 449) 'can undermine the goals of collaborative learning' (Goodfellow 2005: 483). Furthermore, there is evidence that students have particular issues about identity that directly affect what for them constitutes a positive learning context or otherwise.

In her research on masters students using computer-mediated communication (CMC), Bayne (2005) identified a marked awareness of the potential for identity management among students and a shared unease about where such 'untrue' presentations of who one is might lead. Students perceived this as a situation of risk – of losing contact with one's 'real' identity through coming to believe in an identity constructed online. This might result also from how others react and play into an identity that could take over and threaten the students' sense of control and balance: 'there is danger in the threat to the "real" self by the online, constructed self, as though the real self is something fragile, protected by a boundary which is too easily transgressed' (Bayne 2005: 32). These students demonstrated a need for transparency in how identities are played into learning contexts and for control of the process. Being able to reflect on and monitor what one believes and to retain a core sense of self directly affected their confidence and trust in the learning context.

Trust is also key in relation to judging the authenticity of knowledge sources. Access to the Internet is popularly seen as a connection to unlimited resources that empower the user. However, for students, the issue of warrantable evidence – who makes a claim and on what basis – is core to learning. There are possibilities for being misled and for getting lost amid a plethora of dubious material as much as for empowerment. Bayne (2006) develops this in terms of the authorship of digital texts, drawing on Foucault's concept of the 'author function' to pinpoint the way in which digital texts enable multiple authorship and weaken the notion of the author as a known identity with a stable relation to a text.

Digital texts are mutable and open to change by many 'writers', leading to a fluidity and instability that impacts on both authors and readers. The same hypertext can generate different readings through the multiple links and serendipitous connections its readers make. In the context of study, this reconfiguration of the roles of author and reader may constitute a challenge to, rather than a support for, learning. Bayne interviewed students in a study of the impact of learning technology on cultures of higher education. They expressed a distrust of digital texts unless these emanated from a recognizable authority, a known university or a well-known media site such as Guardian Unlimited. Such sites could be trusted because they are assumed to incorporate processes of checking and verification of authorship and text quality. As Bayne (2006: 22) notes, this reflects 'the tightness of the coupling of the stable, printed text and the individualized author and the position of this grouping at the heart of academic practice'.

Cyberspace therefore presents challenges for learners in higher education (Land and Bayne 2005), but it has also been positioned as enabling social constructivist approaches to learning through empowering students to collaborate, to find their own resources and connections and to construct complex personal understandings (Jonassen and Reeves 1996). A distributed cognition perspective sees networked learning as fostering interactions between learners in the network and between learners and a potentially unlimited range of resources (Jones and Esnault 2004).

However, the provision of technologically-mediated forms of interaction does not necessarily guarantee these positive effects. Students may not take up the opportunities offered, or may do so to little good effect. Asynchronous conferencing, for example, has fostered both utopic and dystopic views of its potential (Haythornthwaite 2006). However, the use of online conferencing and bulletin boards is a particularly important area given the centrality of written texts, dialogue and debate within higher education (Goodfellow 2005; Laurillard 2002). The case study which follows explores how the design of study practices using the Internet and CMC enabled participation and a positive learning experience for students at the Open University UK studying an undergraduate course in Environmental Studies.

Dialogue and collaboration in online networks

Computer-mediated communication (CMC) offers the possibility for students to develop the discursive practices and skills of debate relevant to their field of study. The Open University has a strong rationale for the use of this technology, as its students do not assemble in one location in order to engage in the variety of forms of interaction that a campus-based university offers. Most courses are delivered through a blend of multimedia resources plus online and some face-to-face interaction. Experience of online interaction has been mixed, however, and where a close link with learning outcomes and course assessment is lacking, there have been low levels of participation (Kirkwood and Price 2005).

Research funded by the Andrew Mellon Foundation set out to explore the impact of online interaction across a range of disciplines and courses (Thorpe and Godwin 2006). One course in particular was studied in depth, using a survey of a random sample of students, interviews with five tutors and ten students. The course, *The Environmental Web*, is a third-year course in the Environmental Studies programme, delivering at least half its study time through online activities, computer conferencing, and the use of software, enabling students to upload assignments as web pages and to use climate modelling tools.

Students are expected to spend at least half their time studying online, in searching, evaluating and using information from the Web. The course guide argues that Environmental Science is itself a Web-based practice and that the main aim of the course is 'to provide you with the skills needed to develop your own environmental literacy and to take part in informed environmental debate and action, rather than to expand your environmental knowledge as such' (Course Chair). Informed debate is thus foregrounded in an authoritative statement by the course chair and embedded in the learning outcomes for the course. Students know therefore that participation in online discussion and debate is a core course activity.

The tutor perspective

Five tutors (one quarter of all tutors on the course) were interviewed. A semi-structured schedule was used, interviews were recorded and transcribed, checking the text with the respondent. A grounded approach was used in the analysis (Strauss 1987), with detailed study of each transcript and building of rich connections between the perceptions communicated in each interview. The interview strategy was not to assume that CMC was the most important feature of the course, but to explore tutor perceptions first, to find out how they perceived the important issues. Progressive focusing enabled exploration of the significance of online communication and the form it took on this course.

Tutors were asked to identify whether particular aspects of the course teaching were key to its success. All tutors picked out aspects associated with online communication, with three tutors commenting on the conferencing, the high rate of participation and continuity of student contact with peers as well as the tutor. Tutors also highlighted the beginning of the course as key to its success. The first six weeks of the course focus on individual research of a small island state, feeding forwards into an online debate within each tutor group, which contributes a required part of the first assignment.

> ... Yes again going back to the beginning of the course, the way it starts, it's very intense at the beginning ... that particular aspect of getting everybody involved right at the very beginning really sets the scene for the rest of the course. It blends tutor groups, it gets students involved with other students on a national basis and it starts in a very interesting way where students can get very involved.

All students are allocated to a tutor in groups of approximately 20 students per tutor. All tutors were asked to reflect on what made the conferencing on this course work, when experience on other courses can be disappointing. Most cited the uncompromising approach of the course team and the integration with assessment. However, this compulsory aspect went along with high levels of interest and involvement that made the process enjoyable, not merely mandatory:

> ... with [*The Environmental Web*] there are marks in [assignments] for contributions and for writing up discussions, so in a way if they want marks ... they've got to contribute ... but it just seems to be that ... students have to to some degree and I think they then enjoy it – most of them enjoy it – and that as I say involvement of most of the tutor group actually stays after the initial really intensive small islands debate that we have.

This tutor and others emphasized the importance of the online activities in generating high levels of participation – again contrasting this with other less successful course approaches. These activities achieved genuine involvement – gave students a reason for being online, as this tutor expressed it:

> ... with [*The Environmental Web*] there are all these structured online tutor group conference activities ... We're given guidelines ... but with other courses we're not given that. It's very much up to individual tutors to get students to try and participate ... that's the difference with [The Environmental Web]. It's got these structured activities that hold students there and give them a reason for being there.

Tutor interviews therefore highlighted the success of the online activities and the interaction within online conference groups. This was taken forward into data collection with students, reported in the next section.

Student feedback on the design of a collaborative learning task

Tutors had identified the start of the course – the first six weeks approximately – as critical to its success. Students engage in two main phases of activity. These feed forward into the first assignment where 35 per cent of the marks are based on the student's reflections on their group collaboration and their own contribution to that. First, students prepare for their group collaboration by working individually on data collection and documentation. The tutor allocates each student in their group a different Small Island State to research, using the Web-related activities in their online course guide. They then upload their data and suggestions about the needs of Small Island States to their tutor group conference. They work together online to create a draft statement of demands, as if from the Association of Small Island States (AOSIS), to the United Nations. This statement is used within the first assignment they must each submit. All these activities are guided by online texts that are extremely clear, using a template for every task that identifies its focus, states the learning outcomes and the estimated study time, explains the rationale for the task and sets out clearly what the student has to do.

Ten students were contacted by e-mail about their experience of completing these activities, and three were interviewed by telephone, each interview lasting approximately one hour, using a semi-structured schedule. Interviews were transcribed and sent to students for checking. Most students logged on daily and all had been able to do the online tasks, though study times varied. Student feedback on the collaborative online group conference was very positive. Students were asked whether not having met their fellow students in advance made it difficult to participate. This student identified task clarity as key to being able to project herself socially (Rourke *et al*. 2001) and to make effective contributions from the beginning:

Interviewer: So did you find it difficult to contribute ... because you hadn't met these people first?

Student: No no not at all. Because in there we had an aim, we had a target so I didn't mind at all that I did not know the fellow students. We just exchanged views ...

All were asked whether it had been possible to express differences of view, since previous research suggests students tend to avoid argumentation online (McAlister *et al*. 2004). The mechanism of representing a small island state had had the positive effect of enabling students to express their views directly without fear of personal offence. They researched the vulnerabilities of their island before conferencing and used evidence to support their views, having genuinely engaged with the needs of their island.

Interviewer: did you find it possible to disagree?

Student: Oh very much so – people did disagree a lot and managed to put forward their points of view a lot, which I really liked, and backed it up with examples ... most people's decisions were informed and you could see that.

This group had taken the initiative to use a spreadsheet to plot their views – evidence of self-organization in a context where the group were clear about their task and not dependent on tutor facilitation. It was also possible to disagree with a majority view where that clashed with what was in the interests of the island that a student was representing, as this student made clear:

About halfway through we put everything on a spread sheet to see what kind of opinions were coming forward, and it was quite clear that three issues were coming forward from most people, so you ... thought ... if you weren't in that consensus you would be in a minority and probably you'd have more sway if you felt able to join the majority ... on most of the issues I could but there was one or two issues where I said no there's no way I'm going to compromise on that ... I was Haiti, so I was very poor ... there was a lot of wealthy islands, so some people didn't have the issues that Haiti did so there was some things that I just couldn't compromise on.

This comment reveals identification with the island being represented, so that the student feels that her arguments relate to something beyond herself or the preferences of other students. It enables her to disagree and to take an independent position from the group. The phased design of the activity motivated students to engage with the evidence about small islands before interacting with their peers and the role play freed them from unease in putting forward and justifying their positions – they argued for 'their' island, not for themselves.

This design in effect performs a mix of compulsion and engineered interaction that combines formality with informality (Crook and Light 2002) and which achieves a form of combined individual and group work that is quite different from anything found on the campus. Where the campus requires attendance at set times and places, in order to help students manage their resources of time and attention to best effect, here students have to engage online in order to be able to complete their first assignment. Virtually all students therefore do participate but not merely at a perfunctory level. Students confirm that they do feel free to differ with their peers and to make reasoned claims. The online activity may be mandatory, but students manage the process themselves – tutors do not actively moderate and do not need to, because the task is specific and clearly defined. Students are required to reflect in their assignment submission on their own role in the online process so are motivated to play a constructive role. The interaction between peers thus combines elements of informality with formality, some groups setting their own timetable for interaction over a defined brief period so that the interchange gets closer to being synchronous.

These practices deliver a positive learning experience as part of a successful course (see Thorpe 2008). They do not directly mediate the familiar formats of face-to-face seminars and discussion groups, but construct distinctive sequences of individual and collaborative activity. Carefully constructed online texts play a key role in enabling students to take control of their learning, working within the boundaries of their course and motivated by their study goals.

In the next section, the learning context is not one bounded by assessed study but by the interests and offline community involvements of teacher practitioners. Online texts here also play a key role, this time supporting exchange across boundaries of workplace and experience.

Texts and virtual talk in practice-based contexts

Taking an activity-theory perspective, learners can encounter through online interaction a diversity of texts and activity systems that create the potential for expansive learning (Tuomi-Grohn and Engeström, 2003). This is learning that crosses the boundaries of different activity systems, expanding involvement with others and developing both individual and collective learning (Cole and Engeström 1993). CMC offers possibilities for knowledge exchange and learning by practitioners participating from within their work context. In his chapter for this book, Russell describes the way in which texts can be seen as mediational tools through which the connections and differences between different contexts can be analyzed and negotiated. Texts generated by practitioners themselves can build networks online that bridge across constellations of communities of practice (Wenger 1998).

Online discussion forums provide an opportunity to share practice contexts and to develop one's own identity as a practitioner through learning at the boundaries between different practices. Knowledge creation by practitioners is one of the potential benefits of networked professional communities, particularly in education (Hargreaves 1999). Leach has used Wenger's concept of communities of practice to identify the significance of the social context of pre-service and in-service teachers in relation to their engagement in study. Such learners bring not just everyday practices of reading, listening, narrative and so on, but rich experience in the constellations of practice communities that are continually developed within and across schools (Banks *et al.* 1999). This experience can legitimately become itself the focus for study, if online discussion environments can be constructed that enable learners to mobilize that experience, to rework it and to use it in the construction of new understandings.

However, online interaction between practitioners may not demonstrate the shared tasks, repertoire and mutual engagement characteristic of a community of practice. It may be more appropriate to conceptualize it as a form of networking rather than a virtual community. Jones and Esnault (2004) have countered the positioning of community of practice as a dominant form of social organization, preferring to see communities and networks as different types of social organization. The community of practice is characterized by strong ties between its members whereas the network makes connection between weak links possible. A network is not best seen as a weak form of community but as an organizational form in its own right with benefits as valuable, potentially, as those of a community of practice. Weak ties through connections with those far outside close community contacts may prove the most useful where we need to change perspectives or learn radically new ways of practising. Online communication enables such connections to occur, but this raises the question of whether online networks create contexts that do support practices of professional learning and knowledge sharing.

Talk in virtual contexts

Opportunity to explore these issues arose in research undertaken with the National College for School Leadership (NCSL) in England, which has developed an online environment for over 30,000 teachers involved in its leadership programmes. NCSL uses its *talk2learn* online environment for a variety of conferencing forums, drawing on a range of school-based communities such as bursars, departmental and school heads and deputies. Data on contributions to most of the forums was analyzed to show levels of participation over time. A sample of forums was observed and tutors on assessed programmes were surveyed (Thorpe *et al.* 2007).

Although the metaphor of community-building is used within NCSL, research of the many forums set up, each lasting for several weeks or months, identified a model of readership by many, with occasional 'drop-in' contribution by a minority of the participants (Thorpe et al. 2007). Extended interactions were unusual and this raised questions about the appropriateness of conceptualizing these online interactions as communities of practice. We explored the form of interaction and its significance for participants through a detailed analysis of one forum that generated a relatively high level of contribution using a 'hotseat' format. This gave centre stage to an Australian practitioner-expert in 'students' voices', who responded to questions and comments from teachers about how best to bring pupil views genuinely into decision-making within a school.

The forum lasted 17 days with 110 contributions (44 from the hotseat guest) from 42 participants and a total of 346 readers at the maximum, falling to 15 for the last contribution. Most contributors made only one contribution and tended to address each other rather than the hotseat guest. Contributions were generated by the concerns of place-based practice and some contributors expressed strong emotional convictions, portraying teachers in favour of pupil voice, but blocked by the realities of the classroom:

> Usually teachers start by seeking pupils' perspectives as a starting point for new topics. I think we often use this to assess what pupils know and understand to then move on with our clearly planned learning outcomes. If pupils feel we aren't listening, maybe it's because teachers feel they are restricted in what they are 'supposed' to teach; and teachers then refocus pupils along the planned path.

Other contributors described school experiences that showed progressive practice or responded to requests for how to tackle particular issues. One took on the role of a kind of leading practitioner for a period, as she retold the inspiring practice of a head teacher:

> The previous head was a great visionary and strived hard to properly listen to the pupils' needs and desires. The school vision and aims were written in conjunction with the children, and are directed to the children in easily understood language. They are not written for the benefit of the governors, teachers or other stakeholders. As a result of this ethos and belief in including the pupils in the way in which their school is run, standards dramatically improved, and the school is now a fun and creative place to learn.

Evidently the online interaction did draw in resources from the place-based communities of schools, generating emotional identification and engagement online. In some cases contributors described taking back their new awareness to share with others in their own school community. It matters therefore that these participants are members of practice communities offline, but the casual drop-in nature of their online interaction did not build a virtual community of practice. It did constitute a network of weak links, that bridged between diverse practice contexts and developed a knowledge base around what might constitute strengths and weaknesses of different ways of incorporating pupil views into school management. Through their online talk and story telling, contributors analyzed the weaknesses of different methods of eliciting pupil views, the risk of parental influence, the links between effective representation and effective learning. They were also challenged to reflect on their own values by the hotseat guest, who responded directly to most contributors.

What was co-constructed by this process of online communication was a kind of hybrid form – a mix of community (drawn upon in the form of identifying contributors and their emotional commitments) and network (the connection to experience beyond the boundaries of immediate experience). This hybrid form of interaction, in which exchange and learning did occur, was enabled by the construction of a communicative genre, the 'hotseat'. This enabled the expert (in this case) to use the language of a practitioner with shared interests in order to challenge, without personal confrontation, some of the more emotionally self-justifying discourse that the topic generated. Her approach demonstrated critical questioning, rather than the dominance of an authority or academic assessor and encouraged practitioners to move beyond the boundaries of their familiar assumptions as well as of their school community contexts (Thorpe *et al.* 2007).

This genre of exchange of experience also created a space where bridges between different practice contexts were made, and local knowledge was taken up and developed intertextually (Russell 2001). Connections were made with formal academic texts introduced into the discussion and with the reflexive knowledge of an expert practitioner. The hotseat metaphor enabled strangers, with no other connection than their involvement with the NCSL, to read, contribute and learn in an area that mattered to them. They drew on the resources of their place-based communities and used the weak links between contributors, and an expert operating beyond their practice boundaries, to debate the contradictions between their many practice contexts and thus to learn not by transfer but by expanding (Tuomi-Grohn and Engeström 2003).

Virtual settings: Real learning in real contexts

This chapter has questioned the assumption that technology directly mediates in an unproblematic way forms of learning that already exist, creating a virtual learning context in place of the face-to-face context. The idea of context as a pre-existing format or container for learning that technology can replicate in virtual space, has not been helpful in formulating effective ways to develop learning through practices with technology. The provision of an online discussion space, for example, does not directly remediate a formal study context such as a seminar or tutorial. Knowledge sharing between practitioners in communities of practice cannot simply be transferred online. A context has to be reconstructed and participation invited through the use of activities, structured formats and textual genres operating at various levels. These are practices with technology that work synergistically with the actions of learners as they navigate through and contribute to online environments. Context is the product of these interactions and relational developments over time.

Barnett and Coate (2005) comment on the way in which academic identities are now constructed partly through digital networks in which students engage with the world 'in ever wider ways', changing their relationship to knowledge. Work-related learning has also demonstrably drawn on the potential of networks to support cross-boundary sharing, the development of new identities related to changed work practices and a supportive context through which new practices can be encountered and tried out (Allan *et al*. 2006, Hodgson and Watland 2004).

Early emphasis on communities of practice (Dirckinck-Holmfeld and Sorensen 2004) has given way to greater interest in networks and the potential of loosely linked relationships for learning at and across the boundaries between practices (Ryberg and Larsen 2006). Engeström (2007) has also emphasized the importance of learning across multiple activity systems where knowledge is being developed across many sites, from the formal academic context through practitioner-focused websites and fora to the workplace. Technologies, such as social networking, can be used to construct personal learning environments designed by the learner precisely in relation to their interests and goals across a range of practice boundaries (Anderson and Dron 2007; Leslie and Landon 2008). Learner-generated contexts are now an active area for research and development. These opportunities for new modes of learning and engagement require a conceptualization of technology as embedded in practices through which contexts for learning are constructed. Such contexts are diverse in terms of their use of technology, their meaning and significance for learners and their success in supporting learning. It is the practices with technology that drive activity and context, not the tool in isolation or the affordances of particular technologies.

References

Allan, B., Hunter, B. and Lewis, D. (2006) 'Four years on: A longitudinal study assessing the impact of membership of a virtual community of practice', in S. Banks, V. Hodgson, C. Jones, B. Kemp, D. McConnell and C. Smith (eds) *Proceedings, Networked Learning Conference 2006*, http://www.networkedlearningconference.org. uk/past/nlc2006 (accessed May 23, 2008).

Anderson, T. and Dron, J. (2007) 'Groups, networks and collectives in social software for e-learning', *Proceedings of the 6th European Conference on e-learning,* Copenhagen Business School (accessed May 23 2008).

Barnett, R. and Coate, K. (2005) *Engaging the Curriculum in Higher Education.* Maidenhead: Open University Press with the Society for Research in Higher Education.

Banks, F., Leach, J. and Moon, B. (1999) 'New understandings of teachers' pedagogic knowledge', in J. Leach B. and Moon (eds) *Learners and Pedagogy.* London: Paul Chapman.

Bayne, S. (2005) 'Deceit, desire and control: The identities of learners and teachers in cyberspace', in R. Land and S. Bayne (eds) *Education in Cyberspace.* Oxon: RoutledgeFalmer.

Bayne, S. (2006) 'Temptation, trash and rust: The authorship and authority of digital texts', *E-Learning,* 3, 1: 16–26.

Blair, K. and Monske, E. (2003) 'Cui bono? Revisiting the promises and perils of online learning', *Computers and Composition,* 20: 441–53.

Cole, M. and Engeström, Y. (1993) 'A Cultural-historical Approach to Distributed Cognition', in G. Salomon, *Distributed cognition – psychological and educational considerations,* 1–46, Cambridge: Cambridge University Press.

Crook, C. and Light, P. (2002) 'Virtual society and the cultural practice of study', in S. Woolgar (ed.) *Virtual Society? Technology, Cyberbole, Reality.* Oxford: Oxford University Press.

Dirckinck-Holmfeld, L. and Sorensen, E.K. (2004) 'A theoretical framework for designing online communities of practice', *Networked Learning Conference, 2004,* Lancaster and Sheffield Universities.

Engeström, Y. (2007) 'From communities of practice to mycorrhizae', in J. Hughes, N. Jewson and L. Unwin (eds) *Communities of Practice: Critical Perspectives.* Oxon: Routledge.

Feenberg, A. (1989) 'The written world', in R. Mason and A. Kaye (eds) *Mindweave: Communication, Computers and Distance Education.* Oxford: Pergamon Press.

Goodfellow, R. (2005) 'Academic literacies and e-learning: A critical approach to writing in the online university', *International Journal of Educational Research,* 43: 484–94.

Hargreaves, D. (1999) 'Teaching as a research based profession', in B. Moon, E. Bird and J. Butcher (eds) *Leading Professional Development.* London: Paul Chapman.

Haythornthwaite, C. (2006) 'Facilitating collaboration in online learning', *Journal of Asynchronous Learning Networks,* 10, 1: 7–23.

Hodgson, V. and Watland, P. (2004) 'Researching networked management learning', *Management Learning,* 35, 2: 99–116.

Jonassen, D. H. and Reeves, T. (1996) 'Learning with technology: Using computers as cognitive tools', in D. Jonassen (ed.) *Handbook of Research for Educational Communications and Technology.* New York: Simon and Schuster Macmillan.

Jones, C. and Esnault, L. (2004) 'The metaphor of networks in learning: Communities, collaboration and practice', *Networked Learning 2004 Conference Proceedings.*

Kirkwood, A. and Price, L. (2005) 'Learners and Learning in the 21st Century: What do we know about students' attitudes and experiences of ICT that will help us design courses?', *Studies in Higher Education,* 30, 3: 257–74.

Land, R. and Bayne, S. (2005) *Education in Cyberspace.* Oxon: RoutledgeFalmer.

Laurillard, D. (2002) *Rethinking University Teaching: A Conversational Framework for the Effective Use of Learning Technologies*. London: RoutledgeFalmer.

Leslie, S. and Landon, B. (2008) *Social Software for Learning: What Is It, Why Use It?* The observatory on borderless higher education, London. Online. Available http://www.obhe.ac.uk/products (accessed May 2008).

McAlister, S., Ravenscroft, A. and Scanlon, E. (2004) 'Combining interaction and context design to support collaborative argumentation using a tool for synchronous CMC', *Journal of Computer Assisted Learning*, 20: 194–204.

Rourke, L., Anderson, T. and Garrison, R. (2001) 'Assessing social presence in asynchronous text-based computer conferencing', *Journal of Distance Education*, 14, 2: 1–16.

Russell, D. R. (2001) 'Looking beyond the interface: Activity theory and distributed learning', in M. Lea and K. Nicoll (eds) *Understanding Distributed Learning*. London: Routledge.

Ryberg, T. and Larsen, M. (2006) 'Networked identities – understanding different types of social organization and movements between strong and weak ties in networked environments', *Proceedings, Networked Learning Conference 2006* (accessed 10 January 2008).

Strauss, A.L. (1987) *Qualitative Analysis for Social Scientists*. Cambridge: Cambridge University Press.

Thorpe, M. (2008) 'Effective online interaction: Mapping course design to bridge from research to practice', *Australasian Journal of Educational Technology*, 24, 1: 57–72. http://www.ascilite.org.au/ajet/ajet24/thorpe.html (accessed 23 May 2008).

Thorpe, M. and Godwin, S. (2006) 'Interaction and e-learning: The student experience', *Studies in Continuing Education*, 28, 3: 203–21.

Thorpe, M., McCormick, R., Kubiak, C. and Carmichael, P. (2007) 'Talk in virtual contexts: Reflecting on participation and online learning models', *Pedagogy, Culture & Society*, 15, 3: 349–66.

Tuomi-Grohn, T. and Engeström, Y. (2003) 'Conceptualizing transfer: From standard notions to developmental perspectives', in T. Tuomi-Grohn and Y. Engeström (eds) *Between School and Work: New Perspectives on Transfer and Boundary-crossing*. London: Pergamon.

Wenger, E. (1998) *Communities of Practice*. Cambridge: Cambridge University Press.

Woolgar, S. (ed.) (2002) *Virtual Society? Technology, Cyberbole, Reality*. Oxford: Oxford University Press.

Chapter 10

'The boundaries are different out here'

Learning relationships in community-based further education

Beth Crossan and Jim Gallacher

Introduction

Community-based further education in Scotland as a context for teaching and learning plays a considerable role in implementing the widening participation to learning opportunities strategies that have become increasingly important aspects of the policy agenda over a number of years (Gallacher *et al.* 2002). We have undertaken research designed to explore the distinctive aspects of these community learning contexts. In this chapter, we focus on the roles of staff, both teaching and core staff, in helping to create the distinctive learning cultures found within these centres. We argue that staff working in these centres have complex roles and face significant challenges in undertaking these and suggest, as do other contributors to this book, that they need to understand learners' lives outside the specific learning context under investigation. We focus on the importance of the *learning relationships* formed within and outwith the centres, and use the concepts of *emotion work, underground working,* and *habitus* to deepen our understanding of these relationships.

Following Edwards and Miller (2007), we allow for the idea of context to be extended into the dimension of relationships between individual learners and variously defined others, in particular centre staff, mediated through a range of social and organizational factors. We argue that for learners in community learning centres to mobilize their full resources for learning, that is, their funds of knowledge, literacy practices and experiential learning, understanding and enhancing the relationships formed between learners and between learners and all staff plays a key role.

The studies

We draw on data generated in three completed research projects based in the Centre for Research in Lifelong Learning. The first, entitled *Understanding and Enhancing Learning Cultures in Community-based Further Education*, was part of the Economic and Social Research Council (ESRC) funded Teaching and Learning Research Programme (TLRP),[1] and was undertaken in partnership with two of Scotland's further education colleges. This study aimed to better understand the distinctive features of the learning cultures of community-based further education. The aims, methods and outcomes of this study are reported in Gallacher *et al.* (2007). The study was based in two community learning centres (CLCs), each of which was attached to a college in the west of Scotland. A total of 81 interviews were conducted over three phases of field-work, including both staff and learners. These comprised 29 staff interviews and 52 learner interviews, and included repeat interviews with some staff and learners over the duration of the project.

The two other studies upon which we draw were smaller in scale, but built directly on the TLRP project. The first of these focused specifically on transitional issues.[2] Here the experiences of students who had made 'successful' transitions to the main college campus from CLCs were investigated. This enabled an exploration of students' experiences of transition, exploring what and who acted as bridging resources. In the third project, we focused on the relative absence of men among the learners in the two centres and the reasons why they are more attractive to women. This was a small scale study involving 25 students in either one-to-one or focus group interviews and five members of staff.[3]

Theoretical frameworks of analysis

In this chapter, three perspectives underpin our analysis of the role of staff working within the centres studied. The first of these emphasizes the importance of learning relationships. This emerged out of the work of Mayes *et al.* (2001) on vicarious learning, which led to a direct focus on the nature of the relationships between learners, and then on the nature of the relationships between learners and people who shape their learning. There is a clear link between this work and the various strands of theorizing that have flowed from the work of Vygotsky (1978), and the more recent influence of Lave and Wenger's (1991) work on situated learning and communities of practice.

A learning relationship exists when we learn from or through others, or when a human relationship has an impact on a learner's fundamental disposition to learning (Mayes and Crossan 2007). These include relationships with others in the learning environment, or relationships with people not directly connected to the learning, but who have an influence on how the learner views learning and whether they view themselves as learners at all. In our work, we have recognized and explored the impact within community-based learning of relationships which learners have with family members, friends and non-teaching staff, as well as the more obvious ones with tutors and fellow students (Gallacher *et al.* 2007).

However, in understanding how these relationships are structured and shaped, the work of Bourdieu, and the ways in which his approach has been utilized in the *Transforming Learning Cultures* (TLC) project has been central to our own approach (Bourdieu and Passeron 1977; Bourdieu 1989; James and Diment 2003; Hodkinson *et al.* 2004, 2007). Bourdieu's concept of habitus has been helpful in developing an understanding of the ways in which the dispositions and practices of both learners and staff have been shaped and have, in turn, shaped the learning cultures and the learning contexts which have emerged within the community-based centres.

We are particularly interested in understanding how the habitus of staff has influenced their preparedness to take on the challenging roles which they have as community-based tutors and the impact this makes to mobilizing the full resources of learners. In understanding how the learning cultures and learning relationships within these contexts are shaped, it is also important to consider the relationships between the centres and the wider world of further education. In this respect, Bourdieu's concept of field is valuable as it enables us to see community-based further education as a sub-field that 'connect(s) with, and partly share(s) the principles of the superordinate ...' field of further education at a national and college level (Grenfell and James 1998: 20). We will consider below how these ideas from Bourdieu have influenced our analysis.

Learning relationships and the staff within community learning centres

Our analysis has led us to recognize the complexity of the roles of all staff who work within these centres. We use the concept of learning relationships to explore this complexity.

Learning relationships and the teaching staff

A key feature of the learning cultures found within the learning contexts of CLCs is that relationships between staff and students, and within the student groups, are relaxed and informal, and this is highly valued by learners. Relationships with tutors, which were of relative equality, rather than the more formal relationships found in other learning contexts such as school, were important aspects of the CLCs. Indeed, students had very clear views about how they expected staff working in CLCs to behave, and these were most often accepted by staff. A number of cases were reported of staff who had too 'teachery' an approach, and staff of this kind did not survive in the CLC. In this sense there is a strong element of what Wenger has referred to as 'horizontality' of learning relationships (Wenger 2005). This is summed up by the comment made by one of the tutors:

> One big thing, the students have remarked to me ... it's very, very important, and that is that they don't feel they come into a classroom situation where you're the teacher and they're the student, we are as one.
>
> (S12A)

All of the tutors interviewed referred to this as a key feature of their role. Among those who also worked on the college campus (some were part-time tutors who only worked in the centres), this was recognized as an important way in which relationships differed between the CLC and the campus. These differences are expressed by one member of teaching staff who suggests that 'the boundaries are different out here ...' (S11A); staff protect themselves more in the college and are less open with students. Another tutor from the same centre referred to the way in which she sits among the students in the CLC, but tends to stand at the front of the class when on the main college campus.

Associated with this idea of horizontality was an emphasis on a role of providing support and encouragement for students, rather than a more traditional teaching role. This was expressed by a member of the staff in Centre B who describes herself as a 'facilitator'.

> I would say a facilitator ... as I've mentioned in the past, and quite a lot of the courses we do and it's quite a lot of encouragement that I do. I believe in what I've read and what I've learned in sort of helping people to help themselves and taking a back row and helping them facilitate their own learning as opposed to teaching them in perhaps a way they remember from years back ...
>
> (S04B)

However, while in these respects there was an emphasis on equality and horizontality in these relationships, there were also other dimensions to the role of tutor that made it more complex. First, the personal and social histories of students meant that many found processes of re-engaging with learning difficult. Many had negative experiences of schooling, demanding family lives, unsatisfactory labour market experiences and, in some cases, also had significant health problems, either for themselves or within their families. We have referred in our earlier work to the 'permeable boundaries' that enabled people to bring many of these issues with them into the centres (Gallacher *et al.* 2007). This refers to the way learners' personal and emotional lives are explicitly part of the learning contexts of CLCs. This can make the role of the tutor a very demanding one, where they have to work with the students to enable them to overcome their problems and develop the self-confidence that they need to be successful students. Thus, the tutor referred to above, as well as being a facilitator, also referred to the defensiveness and even aggression that she initially encountered within a class:

> I think my students definitely influence how I take the class because you have to adjust to who is there and initially there was a lot of aggression at first in that class because it was very difficult ...
>
> (S04B)

This tutor suggested that the aggression was partly associated with the fact that the students were initially unhappy with the treatment they received, because the material they needed for their course was not available, and they had found the first tutor they had unsatisfactory because she was too 'teachery'. However, she also suggested that the students were 'defensive' when they came in because they had not been in this type of environment for many years. As a result, they needed support and 'confidence boosting', which she described as a key aspect of the role. This then transformed the students' perceptions of themselves, and their relationship with the tutor:

> ... once they settle into the environment and they realize that it's not going to be something that's going to point out what they can't do, it's going to be something that's more concentrated on what they can do or what they've learned or what they've said they couldn't do and now can do and that sort of brings them on ...
>
> (S04)

As a result, by the time of the interview, the tutor was able to report that 'you could almost say that they looked after me in a way now, for getting them through'.

A further important aspect of the role of the tutor is the more formal one of the teacher. While staff and students emphasized the relaxed and informal nature of the learning cultures which distinguish CLCs, both groups also emphasized the importance of the formal learning that takes place, and the important role which tutors have in supporting this learning. Thus, when asked to define the characteristics of a good lecturer from the students' point of view, S04B commented:

> Well first and foremost someone who can provide what they need material wise and answer wise ... I think somebody who just adjusts, that can teach them what they need to know in a manner suited to their age, something that works as a balance across the class.

Similar views were expressed by other tutors who emphasized the need to work with the students to help them acquire the knowledge and understanding they needed. They also commented on the high academic standards of some of the work within the centres, which equalled that achieved on the campus. Students also emphasized the importance for them, not just of the social dimensions of their experiences within the centres, but also the 'teaching' role of the tutors and the importance of obtaining recognized qualifications (Gallacher *et al.* 2007). Thus, being a strong subject specialist and being able to engage students effectively cannot be underestimated as a central role of tutors within the CLCs.

Staff outlined a further aspect of the complexity of their role, which is balancing the relative informality of the relationships found within the CLC with the more formal structures associated with the colleges, the Scottish Qualifications Authority (SQA) and other bodies responsible for qualifications, such as the European Computer Driving Licence (ECDL). We have suggested in earlier work (Gallacher *et al.* 2007) that Bourdieu's concept of field can be of value in helping to understand this aspect of the culures and learning relationships found in CLCs. If community-based further education can be understood as a sub-field of further education more broadly, then the force-field of further education has an important impact on the CLC. Bourdieu also recognizes that fields can be characterized by conflicts and tensions and we can observe this within the sub-field of community-based further education. The learning cultures and learning relationships which exist within the CLCs are developed partly through a negotiation with rules, norms and expectations associated with the wider further education learning culture, and the negotiation of formality and informality was a key aspect of the tutor role. For example, an important task for the tutors is to enable the students to take assessments without undermining their confidence and detracting from the learning experience. In order to achieve this, tutors referred to differing approaches to introducing assessment, depending on the needs of the student group involved. Sometimes, especially early on in the process, this could involve referring to 'tasks' rather than 'assessments'. In other cases, it could involve giving students as much control as possible over the timing of assessments, and the circumstances in which they were taken, for example ensuring that ECDL assessments were taken together as a group. In this way, the teaching staff in the centres mediated the impact of the requirements of the more formal academic world. In this regard the suggestion by Colley *et al.* (2003), that attributes of formality and informality can be found in all learning situations, is helpful in understanding the learning cultures of CLCs, and the role of staff in shaping these cultures.

However, it must also be noted that many staff who work in these contexts feel that their work is relatively marginal and of lower priority than campus-based work. This can, on the one hand, create more scope for flexibility, as has been noted above and was noted by Hodkinson *et al.* (2004) in their discussion of courses seen as marginal to mainstream college activity. However, it can also mean that the control which they are able to exercise over their activity can be more limited. Despite this issue of control, there is considerable evidence that the teaching staff had relatively high levels of success in negotiating this relationship with the more formal academic world on behalf of the students within the centres.

As well as the complexity of roles undertaken by teaching staff, our work found that other staff working in these learning contexts form key relationships with learners. We will now consider the roles and relationships of these staff, before considering some common characteristics of the roles of all staff in the centres.

Learning relationships and the core centre staff

While the core centre staff within the two centres we studied are officially employed as managers/administrators, secretaries and janitors, it became increasingly clear in the course of our research that they had a key role in maintaining and developing learning relationships which were important in contributing to the informal and supportive learning environment found in the centres. One learner made this comment with respect to these roles:

> Really, really positive, if you've got a problem or you need something done, but that's not really their jobs but they would help with anything at all. You know they're even ready to listen to you, you know if you've got a wee problem in the house and you come up here and maybe you're a wee bit upset or something like that and they'll say 'listen do you need a wee word? Do you need a wee minute?' They're just great with everything, there's nothing I can say about them and [receptionist] she's there to keep track of everybody as well, try and keep the attendance right, trying to keep time keeping and that to a standard.
>
> (Learner 26, Centre A)

Staff in both centres recognized this as a central part of their role, even though it was not part of their official job description. Thus the centre manager in Centre A commented:

> We try and keep it more relaxed so the students are more comfortable and not feeling under pressure ... We want them to have a good learning experience here, so then hopefully they will take it into college and go further with their learning.
>
> (S69A)

These become key learning relationships in which students feel they are able to discuss a wide range of issues in their personal and family lives which, in turn, can impact on their role and experiences as students. An important reason why these staff are so significant in this respect is that they are present in the centres on a permanent basis, whereas the teaching staff come and go and are often only in the centres for short periods of time while they take their classes. They are also often the first point of contact for students, both when they come to the centres in the first place and when they come in and out for their classes. This enables them to build up close personal relations with the students and a high level of trust. The centre manager in Centre A summed up these relationships in the following way:

> Yeah I think the relationships with the centre staff are really good, [receptionist] is great with the students, she's the first person they see when they come in and because they're in every day and they bring the children in, you get to know them quite well, so you can tell if they're upset about something. A lot of them will come in and tell [receptionist] things and what's happening, so if we can help them with any other agencies we can then get them in touch with other people that could help them, or even just somebody for them to talk to and sharing their problems because we're here to listen to them and help them in any way we can. So a lot about it is about relationships and them feeling comfortable enough when they come in that they can tell you things …
>
> (S69A)

A second important set of learning relationships were the ones between the core centre and teaching staff. The CLCs lack the resources and infrastructure found on the main campuses, although both centres in our study were in some respects well equipped. The manager in centre B suggested that the core centre staff provided the 'main support' for many tutors who are part-time, and can in other ways feel quite isolated from the college campus and peer group, although this 'doesn't come under my remit' (S16A). The secretary in this centre suggested that they 'nurture' the tutors through the support which they provide for them.

In addition to these supportive relationships with the tutors, centre manager A referred to a rather different relationship between the core centre staff and tutors, which she describes as being a 'go-between'.

> I see them as a kind of go-between, between the tutor and the students. We've been really lucky in the tutors that we've got from [college], they've been really great, but maybe if a student's struggling with something and they feel they don't want to say to the tutor, we can sometimes pick up on things like that and let the tutor know …

This relationship refers again to the extent to which these staff perceive a 'caring' dimension as a key aspect of their role, and a responsibility to support learners who have difficult lives. It also reflects the point that they are the staff who are there on a full-time basis and have the opportunities to get to know the students very well.

The third set of relationships which affect core centre staff are those between themselves and the college campuses. Core centre staff in the centres see themselves as having an important role in interacting with campus-based staff, and particularly more senior staff, to convey what is needed to ensure that appropriate and good quality provision is available, and that managers understand the needs of the centres and the challenges associated with attracting and retaining students. Differences are evident between the two centres in this respect, as centre A is attached to a college with a very strong tradition of community-based work, and has a structure that links the college to the community-based centres. By contrast, in centre B the relationships were much weaker, and the centre manager expressed concern about her relative lack of control over key issues such as course provision and staffing.

Emotion work and underground workers

It has been increasingly recognized in recent years that in many occupations emotional engagement by employees with the people with whom they work is expected and indeed required. In some occupations, this has been referred to as 'emotional labour'. However, the broader concept of 'emotion work' has been developed to cover a wider range of different activities of this kind (Simpson and Smith, 2005). This emotion work can take a wide variety of forms, and it is recognized that it can place a new range of demands on workers. As we have indicated above, staff in the CLCs would appear to see this as a key aspect of their role. They refer to the 'caring' aspects of the role, the importance of 'listening', to undertake 'confidence building' and to engaging with students' personal and emotional lives.

Many staff reported readily accepting and even enjoying this aspect of their role, and for those with experience of both campus-based courses and work in the CLC, this is often seen as one of the key defining differences between the two settings. This was expressed in the following way by one of the tutors in centre B: '... I think that less focus on the academic and more on the developing confidence, so I think it's very much more a supportive role in that sense' (S15A). While this type of emotion work is recognized by many staff as a positive aspect of their role, it can also lead to additional challenges. Thus one of the tutors in centre B referred to the dangers that there were 'people who were looking for too much from you, and you felt this wouldn't be a good idea ...' (S28A). Other tutors referred to the need to maintain balance.

This preparedness to undertake work which goes well beyond the official expectations of the role has been discussed previously by James and Diment (2003), aspects of which they describe as 'underground working'. This describes activities beyond the official definition of the work associated with the role. Underground working of this kind can be observed in the work of many CLC staff. For example, the secretary in centre B outlined the additional elements in her role as follows:

> Yeah the caring side of it, obviously if you've got a student coming in with worries and financial worries and things we sit down and talk to

them and if somebody's not happy, any problems going on at home, they seem to bring them in and they'll sit and have a chat and its almost like being a counsellor I suppose, but that's not part of the job description, we just, well I do it anyway, just as a caring person.

(S08 Centre B)

Many of the tutors also provided interesting examples of this underground working. One commented:

... but you've got to get over all the other obstacles as well as teaching a class, so it's not the same thing as being in a class in a college. I enjoy it, but I can see that a lot of people maybe wouldn't.

(S10A)

The same tutor later outlined the work she undertook in order to find placements for her students. She felt a need to secure placements which she was convinced would provide them with the experience they would need to help them to progress to employment.

... I tramped through the streets to get work placements, round the employers because I didn't want to, I said I wouldn't put them out to do work placements in a place I wouldn't want to go and work myself, so I shot myself in the foot a wee bit, because it took me hours and hours and weeks and weeks and months to sort that out ...

(S10A)

Another rather different example of this underground working is provided by the tutor in centre A who had responsibility for the oversight of community-based provision. He recognized that tutors, particularly part-time tutors, in community centres can feel rather isolated. In response to this, he had taken on his own form of underground working by providing a level of support for these staff well beyond what would normally be expected.

Staff have got to be supported. Lonely – staff feel lonely when they're working out there [in the Centres]. I always give every member, every part-time member of staff, my home telephone number. I give them freely, and if there's any problems ... I obviously say don't phone after ten o'clock, or if football's on TV ... But you know to establish a relationship with them ...

(S68A)

All of the staff who worked in these centres referred to the need for various kinds of 'flexibility' in their approach to their work, which often led to a range of different kinds of underground working. It was also recognized that, while they enjoyed this work, not all of their colleagues would be prepared to take on the difficulties associated with this type of work. In the final section of this chapter, we will consider why these staff seemed prepared to take on these types of roles.

Habitus and the staff who work in community learning centres

We have argued that a general characteristic of the staff who work in these centres is a very positive commitment to their work, even though it often provided them with distinct and demanding challenges. These ranged across the emotion work and underground working we have discussed, through the difficulties of working in an off-campus location with limited support for the academic side of the work, to dealing with some of the campus-based staff who viewed community-based work as a relatively low level priority.

For many CLC staff there is a strong view that working in the community is a very positive choice. In this context, one tutor in centre A reported that she had turned down six offers of permanent contracts with the college which she felt would have led her away from community-based provision to more campus-based work. Another tutor in centre B referred to his positive choice to work in the centre, despite the practical difficulties and suggested that 'it's a breath of fresh air getting away from the college ...' (S11A).

We argue that Bourdieu's concept of habitus can be helpful in developing an understanding of the ways in which the dispositions and practices of staff have been shaped. Hodkinson *et al.* (2004) suggest that habitus can be seen as social structures operating within and through individuals, rather than being something outside of us. Utilizing this concept, we can see how structural issues, associated with class and gender, have shaped the life histories and dispositions of staff, and in these ways have influenced their preparedness to take on the challenging roles they have in the CLCs.

A common characteristic among many of the staff was their own complex histories as adult learners. This is well summed up by one of the computing tutors in centre A. She referred to having built up her own company, but then leaving this for personal reasons and deciding at this point that she would return to college. She recalled this experience in the following way:

> ... now I remember walking into College A, at my age, a mature student and thinking 'wow this is scary' and that's a thing I do tell my students because I know exactly how they feel and I think that's quite important that we should always remember or be able to recall how we felt in their situation because I do remember that quite vividly.
>
> (S12A)

She then went on to recount how she completed a Higher National Certificate and Higher National Diploma in the college, whilst 'juggling' a family and problems in her life. She described herself as a 'problem-solver' in this respect. She was then given the opportunity to go to a local university to complete a degree in one year, but had to be persuaded by her daughter, who was herself a university student at this time, that it was worthwhile to take the risk. Others described how coming to college themselves, for example many years before as apprentice in the shipyards, gave them a taste for learning, opening up new opportunities for them.

A number of other staff recounted similar life histories with respect to their learning careers. This seems to have led them to see work with adult returners as a particularly rewarding activity. In centre B there were younger tutors with more conventional educational histories, but they also showed strong dispositions towards this type of work. Thus, one of the young women referred to a history of volunteer tutoring and community work which went back to her school days and stretched through university. She and others referred to a very strong positive choice to work in a community setting rather than at the campus. Many staff who worked in these centres on a regular basis were people whose own life histories had led them to dispositions which were very positively oriented towards the opportunities to work with adult returners within community learning centres.

Conclusions

In this chapter we have utilized the concepts of learning relationships, emotion work, underground working and habitus to deepen our understanding of the demands, complexities and challenges for staff who work in community-based further education. With regards to relationships, we have illustrated that, while key characteristics of these are associated with informality, equality and horizontality, they are much more complex, involving a high level of emotion work and underground working. The staff role also involves the complex negotiation of aspects of informality and formality, which are demanded by the different learning contexts of community-based provision and the main campus college.

We have suggested that a useful way to understand both what staff do, and importantly why they do it, is to explore their own life histories and dispositions to learning, which are shaped by their habitus. Many staff in the centres see these roles as very positive, in which they are very happy to be involved. A key feature of this work in this learning context is the importance of understanding learners' lives outside the Centres. In this book, Satchwell and Ivanič highlight the variability in the ways in which students in main campus colleges integrate or keep separate their 'college' and 'everyday' lives. We argue that a key feature of the learning context of CLCs is the permeability of the boundaries between the CLCs and other aspects of students and staff lives.

We would also suggest, however, that the nature of their work and the complexity of roles that CLC staff undertake raises important issues regarding training and support needs. Many staff engage in aspects of emotion work and underground working and are taking on roles beyond any official job description, including the need to engage with the complex emotional lives of students. This, in turn, raises the need to recognize staff development and support issues for centre staff who are undertaking roles for which appropriate training and support is required. The manager in centre B referred to the need for better training for centre-based staff in relation to guidance and counselling. Teaching staff also referred to the relative isolation of work in these off-campus situations, and the difficulties of getting the academic and peer group support. We conclude that our work raises the need to ensure that a proper structure of support is provided at college level for centre-based staff which will improve the learning experience for students who attend the centres.

Acknowledgements

We would like to thank the staff and students who participated in the three studies, and who gave so generously of their time, experiences and expertise. We would also like to thank the funders of the three studies: The Economic and Social Research Council, The Nuffield Foundation and the West of Scotland Wider Access Forum. We would like to thank the other members of the TLRP research team for their work on the project: David Watson, Lorna Smith, Terry Mayes, Paula Cleary and Bryony Duncan.

Notes

1 The project has involved researchers at the Centre for Research in Lifelong Learning (CRLL), Glasgow Caledonian University, working in partnership with two FE colleges in Scotland. It is a 'Scottish Extension' project, linked to the Phase II TLRP project *Transforming Learning Cultures (TLC) in Further Education*, to whom we are grateful for their support.
2 The project was funded by the Nuffield Foundation. Full details of the aims, methods and outcomes are in Crossan and Cleary (2007).
3 The project was funded through the West of Scotland Wider Access Foundation. Full details are provided in Cleary *et al.* (2007).

References

Bourdieu, P. (1989) *Outline of a Theory of Practice*. Cambridge: Cambridge University Press.
Bourdieu, P. and Passeron, J. (1977) *Reproduction in Education, Society and Culture*. London: Sage.
Cleary, P., Brodie, J., MacFarlane, K., Brown, F., Galacher, J. and Boyd, V. (2007) *Motivation and Attainment in the Learner Experience (MALE)*. Final Report to the West of Scotland Wider Access Forum, Glasgow: CRLL.

Colley, H., Hodkinson, P. and Malcolm, J. (2003) *Formality and Informality in Learning: A Report for the Learning and Skills Research Centre*. London: Learning and Skills Research Centre.

Crossan, B. and Cleary, P. (2007) *What Supports Transitions from Community-based Further Education to Main Campus College?* Final Report to The Nuffield Foundation, Glasgow: CRLL.

Edwards, R. and Miller, K. (2007) 'Putting the context into learning', *Pedagogy Culture and Society*, 15, 3: 263–74.

Gallacher, J., Crossan, B., Mayes, T., Cleary, P., Smith, L. and Watson, D. (2007) 'Expanding our understanding of the learning cultures in community-based further education', *Educational Review*, 59, 4: 501–17.

Gallacher, J., Field, J., Merrill, B. and Crossan, B. (2002) 'Learning careers and the social space: Exploring fragile identities adult returners and the new further education', *International Journal of Lifelong Education*, 21, 6: 493–509.

Grenfell, J. and James, D. (1998) *Bourdieu and Education – Acts of Practical Theory*. London: Falmer.

Hodkinson, P., Biesta, G. and James, D, (2007) 'Learning cultures and a cultural theory of learning', *Educational Review*, 59, 4: 415–27.

Hodkinson, P., Anderson, G., Colley, H., Davies, J., Diment, K., Scaife, T., Tedder, M., Wahlberg, M. and Wheeler, E. (2004) *Learning Cultures in Further Education*, paper presented at the British Educational Research Association Conference.

James, D. and Diment, K. (2003) 'Going underground: Learning and assessment in an ambiguous space', *Journal of Vocational Education and Training*, 55, 4: 407–22.

Lave, J. and Wenger, E. (1991) *Situated Learning: Legitimate Peripheral Participation*. Cambridge: Cambridge University Press.

Mayes, J.T. and Crosson, B. (2007) 'Learning relationships in community-based further education', *Pedagogy, Culture and Society*, 25, 3: 291–301.

Mayes, J.T., Dineen, F., McKendree, J. and Lee, J. (2001) 'Learning from watching others learn', in C. Steeples and C. Jones (eds) *Networked Learning: Perspectives and Issues*. London: Springer.

Simpson, R. and Smith, S. (2005) 'Introduction', *International Journal of Work, Organisation and Emotion*, 1, 1: 1–3.

Vygotsky, L.S. (1978). *Mind in Society: The Development of Higher Psychological Processes*. Harvard: Harvard University Press.

Wenger, E. (2005) *Learning for a Small Planet: A Research Agenda*, available at www.ewenger.com/research (accessed 20 May 2008).

Part III

Inferences for learning and context

Chapter 11

The implications of learning contexts for pedagogical practice

Mary Thorpe and Terry Mayes

The chapters in this book range widely over a complex landscape of ideas which span not only educational concepts but also disciplinary perspectives. The main purpose of this chapter is to bring the reader back to pedagogy. We reconsider the pedagogical implications of learning in diverse contexts. We also reflect on the insights offered by some of the other chapters in this book, and the seminar series from which it was drawn, in helping us rethink pedagogical practice. We group our reflections into a number of broad themes that seem to us to impact directly on pedagogy.

Complexity, contingency and unpredictability

In her chapter which directly addresses the conceptual difficulty of aligning different theoretical viewpoints and discourses about learning, Haggis starts with a direct quotation from Davis and Sumara (2006) which nicely summarizes the issue we face here: 'The field of education is greatly dispersed. It must be simultaneously attentive to issues and phenomena across many levels of organization'. The question this raises for us is whether a complex account of learning necessarily implies an equivalently complex pedagogy. Haggis describes a fundamental tension that still characterizes contemporary theory: how to align accounts of individual cognition within a framing of the social: 'Theorizing, on the whole, seems only able to seesaw backwards and forwards across the individual/social binary. ... Discussing how individual affects social, how social affects individual, or which of the two is the most influential, is relevant to some questions but not to others'.

The basic point here is that the current focus on the social and on collective participation makes it difficult to deal with the differences that emerge amongst individual learners. Haggis turns to complexity theory to escape from the oppositional extremes of individual concerns and society's structures, to produce a way of describing multiple viewpoints about learning simultaneously. Complex systems are open, each system is simultaneously part of the interactions of a number of other systems. Haggis helps us by giving the examples of schools or departments as systems which share in the

interactions of the larger systems of which they are part. The emergent characteristics of the school or department, however, will always be specific to its
history and conditions. Haggis considers what the notion of 'context' means
here. Is it the combination of initial conditions and the history of interactions with other multiple systems? Yet, in a sense, it is the interactions of
other systems that produced it in the first place, so the idea of context loses
its meaning when multiple viewpoints are expressed simultaneously. More
useful, Haggis suggests, is the concept of emergence – particular systems
continually emerge from the constraints of larger systems in which they are
embedded.

Where does complexity theory leave us in our task of unpicking the practical implications for teaching? Haggis suggests that it should shift us away
from seeking to identify general principles of correlation, cause and effect,
to an analysis of conditions and effects in specific situations. The approach
encourages us to investigate learners, groups, vocational areas, institutional
cultures or discourse systems over time, though we must be mindful that these
systems cannot be studied in isolation from the many systems in which they
are embedded.

We take this argument essentially as making us wary of trying to describe
general principles of learning and teaching, rather to sensitize the teacher to
the fluid nature of the classroom or the learning group. As Haggis puts it
'even something that appears to be organizationally stable, such as "class 3a,
taught by Maria" is nonetheless subtly different every time it comes together'.
In a sense, this urges us to regard context as all important, though context is
a shifting, dynamic and essentially unknowable set of interactions. Wherever
we look – at society's attitude to gender, at the influence of physical space or
the virtual learning environment, at a particular learner's early childhood, at
the organizational policy or the influence of new technologies, at the pedagogical technique, we must not think we have spotted the key to successful
understanding of learning and teaching.

Complexity theory is an antidote to 'one best way' thinking. It is a plea for
humility. As Haggis herself says 'arguably nothing that has been discussed
here is news to teachers...'. Yet, the teacher might protest. To acknowledge
that an account of how and why one learner might be more successful than
another will have to range over factors ranging from individual dispositions
and individual histories right through to cultural and organizational issues,
must not imply a prescription against trying to find broad-based, effective ped-
agogical/methods. The need for the learner to be active in the performance of
tasks from which learning emerges, for example, is arguably one such method.
However there is a potentially unlimited number of ways of implementing
such an approach and its results will be unpredictable. It will not work for
all tasks and for all learners, nor even for the same tasks with the same learners on different occasions; but, as Haggis acknowledges, that won't surprise
most teachers. Good practice is contingent upon subject, goals and context.

It requires a trade-off between the available resources, including a teacher's ability to devote attention to individuals, and the need to acknowledge that every learner represents, in Haggis' terms, an emergent system. Good pedagogy should seek to link the immediate learning tasks with wider contexts that connect with the world-views of the teacher, the learners and the discipline. Even so, the complexity of the interactions across all levels of context render the outcomes unpredictable for individual learners.

In attempting to bring some clarity to the confusion around the concept of context, Cole (1996) distinguished between two general uses of the term: between 'that which surrounds us' and 'that which weaves us together'. These two meanings played out in the discussions of the seminar series from which this book originated and in the chapters of the book itself.

The container or environment metaphor is associated with a view of context as a boundary within which teaching and learning 'happens'. This is sometimes represented as a set of concentric circles representing the different levels of context. As we move from the inner circles – representing the micro-level interactions between learners, teachers and the more immediate environmental factors – to the outer circles, our view of context widens, from the personal and social factors influencing learner identity, to the cultural, global and historical. Unwin and her colleagues use the metaphor of a Russian doll in order to give a sense of the 'worlds within worlds' that characterizes workplace learning (Unwin et al. 2005). This paper interpreted workplace learning within what is described as the multi-layered landscape of pedagogical practices: 'we take those ideas further..., to try and make better sense of the Russian doll-like composition of workplaces. That is not to say we hope to end up with the tiny baby at the core, but rather seek to understand the role and function of the various layers, which, only when brought back together result in a meaningful whole'. They raise interesting questions about what can transfer between contexts, if the specificities of each context take on such great significance. It may be that pedagogy should broaden its purview to consider how best to transfer the specificities of particular contexts that support learning. The mobilization of learner resources across domains may need more than a focus on learning theories and pedagogical strategies. The second meaning of context offered by Cole has been expressed by Jewitt and Jones (2005) as a metaphor of the woven cloth, where threads connect every stitch to the larger pattern. In their paper on textuality, Jewitt and Jones drew attention to how the classroom can be viewed as a woven dynamic network, where the threads spin right out to government and policy initiatives which are inflected in micro mechanisms. Jewitt, in this book, draws attention to how micro analysis of semiotic resources such as space, movement and body posture, visual resources, speech and voice quality, writing, gaze and gesture can be utilized in the classroom by teachers to draw in pupils' experiences outside school to help them access the curriculum and pass assessments. The point illustrated by this paper is that some

teachers, while still curriculum- and examination-focused, have found strategies which give them space to connect their teaching to the wider social
experiences of their students. The teacher makes links to social and moral
issues by drawing on her own and her students' life experiences, to make cultural connections with the texts studied. Thus, even within the description of
the apparently constrained pedagogy of the school classroom, we see multiple
layers of context.

Looking at the interaction between classroom and home in an interestingly different way, Hughes (2005) contrasts the continued emphasis
within the school domain on learning as acquisition, in contrast to the
dominance in other domains of a participation model of learning. Through
research carried out for the 'Exchange in Knowledge between Home and
School to Enhance Children's Learning' project it was found that many
practices which have a strong school-like quality are present in out-of-
school contexts. Activities such as children working with tutors, playing
'educational' computer games or doing puzzles in children's magazines,
have been attributed to the development of the culture of assessment and
testing in schools. The colonization of home contexts by school practices with which parents collude was noted. Hughes raises the distinction
between domain and site in relation to these types of colonizing practices which appear to belong to the domain of school but are located in
the physical site of home. This raises questions what it is about an activity or event which determines why we should locate it within a particular
domain.

Some of the research on higher education has also focused on the influence
of wider contexts on the narrower constructs of pedagogy. This reveals conceptualizations of learning outcomes that are formulated around ways of thinking
and practising in a particular discipline. These are intended to describe 'the
richness, depth and breadth of what students might learn through engagement
with a given subject area in a specific context (McCune and Hounsell 2005).
Reacting against the narrowness and fragmentation of learning outcomes statements, lecturers were found to hold a broader and more fundamental set of
ideas about what their students should achieve, described in terms of changing
their view of the world. Here, contextual factors such as space for community building and activities such as placements, become central to whether or
not the intended shifts in thinking are achieved by students. Context plays
a pedagogical role, therefore, interweaving with the actions taken by a teacher.
Essentially, though, this work makes the same point about stretching the learning experience across all levels of context – out to the cultural 'world-view'
represented by a discipline. By recognizing that the particular subject being
studied can impact directly on learning outcomes, the pedagogy is shaped by
the cultural factors that distinguish one discipline from another.

Nevertheless, in this work, Entwistle (2005), for example, has come to
a similar conclusion to Haggis: that the complexity of the various elements of

physical, social and interpersonal structures, and their unpredictable inter-weaving, means that the learning outcomes of the actions of a human pedagogue are also unpredictable. Pedagogy is not value-free and choosing a particular context for analysis serves particular purposes. One of the implications for research of these approaches to context is the need for greater sensitivity around what is included or excluded by our decision to focus on a particular level or unit of analysis. We cannot avoid focusing selectively, of course. It is impossible to give equal attention at the same time to everything that is pertinent to learning. One of the contributions of research is to characterize the research problem and to justify the unit of analysis, using appropriate theoretical and analytical argument. In their chapter in this book, Crossan and Gallacher, for example, employ Bourdieu's use of 'field' to discuss the appropriate level at which to describe the learning that is observed in community-based further education. The consequent focus on learning relationships makes possible a characterization of learning that is functionally different from that found in mainstream colleges. This was a choice of context that is capable of describing learning at a level that can influence policy, and is therefore appropriate for that purpose.

The appropriateness of a defined level or unit of analysis, then, depends on the purpose to which the explanation is directed. In research terms, 'learning' is too broad to be useful, and the specification of its use as a construct is a way of adopting a particular perspective in order to make the term researchable. Pedagogy is also a term that is increasingly hard to pin down unless the context of its use (its purpose) is addressed. The meaning of the term has drifted in recent years, now being used more widely than the teaching practices underpinning child education. The term is used loosely to describe both a prescribed set of teaching practices highly bound by organizational context, as in 'the pedagogy of the classroom or the workplace', and also a theory-driven approach which can be applied across a whole range of contexts, as in 'constructivist pedagogy', which places the emphasis more on the role of the learner.

Unwin et al. (2005) argue that the purpose of choosing a particular field of view in describing workplace learning is itself a key issue. They discuss how policy is tending to urge organizations (and training providers) to concentrate on developing coaching and mentoring skills rather than providing formal learning opportunities. Research has shown 'coaching and mentoring to be necessary processes in the facilitation and maintenance of a learning culture in the workplace, and that the closer the synergy between what is needed to be learned and real work activity, the more likely it is that individuals will be motivated to respond'. Unwin et al. object to this on the grounds that 'it implies that learning (and teaching) at work is solely a matter of human interaction and agency, a phenomenon which floats free of context'. The analysis provided by the policymakers is flawed by a failure to take account of a sociological view of context.

Pedagogy and horizontal relationships

The workplace challenges conventional perceptions of pedagogy as workers fulfil a range of pedagogic activities; 'the workplace has an advantage over formal educational institutions in that pedagogic activity is likely to be spread across a much broader range of people' (Unwin *et al.* in this book). Crossan and Gallacher's study of the learning that occurs in community learning centres also challenges those conventional concepts of pedagogy which imply inequality in expertise and professional status. An important dimension of pedagogy in community learning is the formation of trust and mutual respect which is a prerequisite for learning. In these cultures the role of 'teacher' must be approached first through the tutor's 'legitimate peripheral participation' in the implicit community of practice that is represented by the cultural identity of the local community. In many community contexts it is equally valid to view the teacher as moving into the community represented by the learners as in the more common representation of the process working in the opposite direction. Using Wenger's (2005) term, describing the learning that is rapidly emerging through social software on the internet, such learning has the quality of 'horizontality'. It involves a negotiation of mutual engagement and the establishment of a shared repertoire of issues and responses. To be successful this process is complex and subtle and is enormously challenging for an institution to pin down as a set of skills to be trained (in fact such training is not attempted). Some tutors have described the checks and balances necessary for the process of horizontality to operate successfully. Full engagement with the personal issues presented by many students in community learning centres is neither possible nor desirable, but a balanced acknowledgement and understanding of the wider cultural context is key.

Crossan and Gallacher report the emergence of learning relationships as a key concept in a number of connected studies of the learning cultures of community colleges. Interviews with students explored their relationships in the family, work and community as well as with staff and the impact of these relationships on their learning. Particular relationships could be pivotal for many learners – sometimes turning them away from educational institutions, at other times encouraging them back in. However, the research stresses the significance of the *culture* of the community college in terms of the way in which staff handle issues of power and the boundary between college and personal life.

There is a dynamic between staff and college users that operates to maintain a sense of equality between them. Staff report not adopting a physical stance that would signal the conventional unequal power relationships of formal education. They call themselves 'tutors' in the community but 'lecturers' in the main college campus. Their approach to their role is also directly affected by the personal lives that students bring into the community college – they facilitate and encourage rather than teach. While facilitation is a familiar practice elsewhere, it is clear that the role requirement on staff here goes beyond what would conventionally be seen under this heading. Staff accept the indivisibility of personal histories with learning. They report that working with students' emotional needs is part of what they do in order to foster learning – that the quality of their relationship with students is key to that learning.

Learners build their confidence through the community college and then move to the main campus; but is this the only form of transfer that should be considered? Would the main campus benefit from recognizing the importance of learning relationships? If this became the ethos of the campus as a whole, would the burden of emotional labour fall less heavily onto the staff in one area and be more effectively dispersed across the institution as a while? The main campus of the college itself might better achieve its goal in bridging between community and formal education if it allowed the community to exert more influence on some aspects of its mainstream culture. In this regard, it would act as a counter to the idea of the college being out in the community, allowing the community culture to influence how being in the college is experienced by both students and staff.

Learning occurs through social relationships, but also through observation and vicarious participation in the learning of others. Vicarious learning focuses on learning through the act of watching others learn, and thus expresses another form of horizontality in learning. Cox (2005) argues that it is an under-researched aspect of pedagogy, hardly addressed in the educational literature, yet it is pervasive across all contexts in which some kind of learning community can be identified. He chose to take a highly applied domain in which to study vicarious learning, where the learning outcomes are specific to the task of case-based reasoning in clinical practice in medicine and health science. The approach is aimed at developing a technology-enhanced pedagogy, where trainee clinicians are given access to virtual patients. The project is exploiting the effectiveness of vicarious learning through capturing videos of either other clinical trainees discussing the case, or a tutor–student dialogue about it. The new trainee now has access not just to the virtual patient, but also to a range of examples of tutors and learners reasoning about the details of the case. If we assume that the effectiveness of vicarious learning depends on the extent to which the new learner can identify with the old, and with the task being undertaken, this approach gives in principle a way of operationalizing context. Thus only those aspects of context that the learner finds relevant will influence the effectiveness of learning vicariously.

Virtual learning contexts: A case of emergent practices

Thorpe's chapter takes technology-mediated learning as the special situation for study and analysis. She starts by challenging the notion that this situation should be described as a mediated version of the face-to-face experience, but rather it should be seen as a set of emergent practices that constitute distinctive and diverse learning contexts. She implicitly makes a point that resonates well with complexity theory – that to focus primarily on the technological tool, or the virtual space, would be to make a categorical error. To put it in complexity theory terms – it would ignore the interactions with larger systems within which it is embedded.

Nevertheless, the experience of virtual contexts is not disconnected from the embodied and the face-to-face. Computer-mediated communication needs to 'reconstruct forms of socialising, cue recognition and communicative processes that generate the necessary conditions for learning'. However, these constructions of a communicative context generate forms of interaction that do not directly replicate place-based versions of the seminar, the debate, the drop-in coffee bar, the noticeboard and so on. Thorpe takes a case study of online conferencing at the Open University, UK to develop her analysis. She first quotes Bayne's (2005) work investigating the sense of identity challenge felt by many learners using online environments, where identities may be projected that are at odds with those of 'the real' person – or at least the person they encounter face-to-face. Online environments can disturb the sense of a settled identity, just as they also may break the conventional relationship between an author and a text. A text on the web may be the product of multiple contributors, indeed current pedagogy advocates collaborative approaches to text construction. However, for many learners this raises the issue of both authorship and trust – where do texts originate and what trust should be placed in them? Thorpe addresses these issues of how a virtual context can become supportive of learning, taking examples that focus on two pedagogies that are associated with the features and functionalities of virtual environments – peer interaction and community building for knowledge development. In Thorpe's first case study, the tutors on an online university course emphasized the importance of interpersonal interaction for student engagement and learning effectiveness. Sequences of carefully designed online texts and activities were identified as key to the pedagogy here. The peer interaction achieves a successful combination of formality and informality without directly reproducing the face-to-face campus-based forms. Tasks prescribe activity while at the same time enabling students to take control over their own learning and interact with each other with a degree of self-organization. Here, implicitly, are methods that work at the level of the online course but that will be subject still to the impact of 'emergent context' on each student, creating differences of experience and success with the same pedagogic strategy. The purpose of such a study is not to build overarching theoretical principles, like community of practice, or legitimate peripheral participation, but rather to build our empirical understanding of how virtual learning contexts are experienced and how they might be designed for. Thorpe concludes, for example, that at the design level, metaphors for recognizable patterns of interaction and for the construction of textual genres need to be available to participants. At the level of the interaction itself, communicative prompts, templates to guide dialogue inputs and structured forms of 'speech' all emerge as features of good practice.

In a second case study Thorpe describes the use of an online environment which was developed for over 30,000 teachers involved in programmes with the National College of School Leadership. The online interaction did 'constitute a network of weak links, that bridged between diverse practice contexts and that developed a knowledge base'. The study of how such online communities develop, or fail to develop, over time is important for our building of understanding of the potential role for CMC environments of this kind. Particularly emphasized was the construction of a 'hotseat', in this case being used in a 'horizontal' manner, demonstrating critical questioning rather than the dominance of an authority or assessor. Effective practice is emergent in these examples, and Thorpe emphasizes that technology as tool should not be the focus for analysis, but rather its embedding into the practices of both teachers and learners.

These two cases also point towards the transformations of contextual boundaries and and the emergence of polycontextuality as a feature of the use of technology increasingly in all aspects of our lives. Mobile phones enable the learner to make important connections with other learners in the midst of their social lives and their daily tasks, no less than within the walls of a campus. Learning can become an activity running alongside other aspects of our lives, as when we listen to an iPod while we walk round a gallery or museum, travel to work, browse the web or do the shopping. Learners can personalize their own learning environments, using RSS feeds to draw in the information they want, to update the searches they have set up, to scan the blogs they have selected. They can select their own learning relationships using social bookmarking tools, which offer them tagged bookmarking and links with others using the same tags, or selecting items of shared interest. Virtuality, in other words, can break through the boundaries of different sites, can merge different forms of activity, can enable new domains such as user-generated content, and can foster new forms of relationship between learners and between learners and the construction of knowledge. The implications for pedagogy are profound, and unpredictable – continually emerging as we react to, come to terms with, sometimes reject, and sometimes adopt into our own ways of learning, the continual wave of virtual tools and practices that are now part of our daily experience as learners and teachers.

Life is the context for literacy and learning

Since its emergence as a separate discipline in the late nineteenth century, psychology has placed learning at the centre of its domain. The discipline has adopted many contexts for this study, ranging across animal learning in the wild, highly artificial learning in laboratories, naturalistic human learning, learning by babies, social learning in groups, and so on. Learning in formal educational settings has always been regarded as just one of many learning contexts, with its own particular characteristics but, for psychology, the classroom has never been afforded a significance that sets it apart from other contexts in which learning occurs. With such a perspective, it is natural that the question of how learning transfers across contexts has been a central issue in learning theory, and transfer from outside-school to the learning that happens inside is a natural focus for research. For educationalists, in contrast, a pedagogy that capitalizes on the informal learning that students bring with them from the home or the peer group is still a challenging idea, since it seems to reverse the logic by which learners are equipped for life outside by their educational experiences in formal settings. Many of the chapters in this book bring these disciplinary traditions closer together by exploring the idea that the 'outside' contexts must be mobilized in an effective pedagogy.

A good example of this is found in Jewitt's chapter. This takes as key elements in pedagogy the multimodal dimensions of image, colour, gaze, posture and movement, and gives these equal prominence with writing and speech in classroom activity. The key argument here is that the language the students bring into the classroom – a language derived from 'the generalized communicative world of the students...an everyday world of animated film, TV, cartoons and rap' – should be exploited in a pedagogy that scaffolds the students in deeper meaning-making.

Jewitt favours the idea of representing the classroom as a complex network, consisting of material, social and historical strands woven together. 'From a multimedia perspective the classroom itself can be understood as a complex sign'. Jewitt tries to unpack this notion with reference to two contrasting 'designs' of English classrooms. The first of these is an 'official' curriculum representation – involving predominantly written material. The second is a secondary extension of a 'progressive' primary school where the multimodal design positions English and popular culture as interconnected forms of knowledge. These examples make clear how a teacher can regard the classroom as a 'dynamic textual formation'. Jewitt seems to say to a teacher: think about your own role in creating context. You are part of the network, and you have an influence over the way the representational strands are woven together.

In their account of research into literacies for learning in Further Education, Satchwell and Ivanic adopt a social view of literacy as the use of written language to get something done in a specific context. They focus our attention not on the skills of reading and writing, but on 'the literacy event' – a holistic view of the cultural specificities of how texts mediate learning. Again, their research explored the characteristics of literacies used by learners in their lives beyond the classroom as well as within it. They discovered that both teachers and learners did not see the relevance of these 'vernacular literacies' to the literacies required in the college. The first implication of this research, therefore, is the value simply of knowing about such practices. If literacies are not best viewed as autonomous skills, it matters that teachers are aware of the experience learners have of actively constructing and using texts in contexts constituted by their social and work lives. Such awareness at minimum influences attitude – or has the potential so to do. A teacher who is aware of a student's literacy practices outside of assessed learning can bring this to bear in reflecting on their performance in the assessed tasks of the classroom and may be better able to support improvement of that performance.

Everyday literacy practices can only constitute a resource for learners if they are aware of them and convinced of their relevance to formal learning contexts. Satchwell and Ivanič provide examples of a student who was not able to mobilize his vernacular literacy abilities for his course tasks, because he lacked a sense of 'purpose and ownership' for his college course. Although his use of the computer and extensive learning to do with military topics did resonate with literacy practices required in college, he himself saw little or no connection and did not draw effectively upon his existing literacy abilities. Other students did see the connection between the college task and their espoused goals for themselves and were therefore able to draw on their existing literacy practices to support achievements working within the formal literacy requirements of their college course.

This raises the issue of identity in learning and Satchwell and Ivanič see this as part of the literacy practice. However, it is not subject to inquiry in the way that a teacher may be able to find out about the way in which their students use texts in their social and work lives. It does suggest that teachers need to take on the mantle of the ethnographer to some extent, researching the cultural backgrounds of their students and engaging with their view of themselves and their purposes. How might the student who could not mobilize the resources of her everyday literacy abilities be helped so to do? While the research is less explicit here, the implication is that teachers and learners need to engage – and probably on a continuing basis – in reflecting on the links between the literacies of their everyday practices and those of the college. This may lead teachers to change the texts they themselves construct in order to increase their resonance with practices that learners have mastery of outside the classroom and their ability to identify with the tasks they are asked to do inside the classroom. However, while it may be readily acknowledged that socially situated literacy practices generate a range of effective vernacular literacies, the relationship between these texts and those required in formal learning contexts is complex and raises questions about the relationship between teacher and learners. For students unable to identify with the goals of their course, it may require resources of empathy, insight and persuasion on the part of staff to develop a relationship through which students come to see things differently.

Back to Dewey

In looking back at the preceding chapters from the viewpoint of their practical implications for teaching and learning, we are reflecting in a sense Dewey's emphasis on action. The research and experiences on which they draw can, as Biesta puts it, 'guide our observation and perception and can suggest possible ways for resolving problems'. However, the test of these possible solutions can only be discovered when we act within a specific situation and experience the consequences of our actions. Dewey's philosophy also constructs a framework where there are many points of connection with the preceding chapters. One of these is an emphasis on the reality of experience and the validity of different kinds of experience. The horse-trader, the palaeontologist, the zoologist and the jockey may give different accounts of the horse, but one is not truer than another – they reflect the different experiences of how each interacts with the horse. This emphasis on experience as the only way through which we can construct knowledge of the world echoes the focus on practices in several of our chapters. Literacy has to be experienced as a specific practice, for example, and the specificities of that practice will differ between the classroom, the workplace and the learner's social life, both on- and off-line. We have also argued that learners' experience of learning outside the boundaries of formal education has value and that ways need to be found to enable learners to mobilize the resources from this learning. This valuation of the everyday, the workplace, the vernacular, gains significance in the light of Dewey's argument that all experience is valid and, at least potentially, a source of knowledge.

Dewey's perspective indeed is to argue that 'context' is not seen as something that is outside of and disconnected from the learner, but rather as something that is always an inherent part of an ever-evolving transactional field. Context is only separable for analytical purposes, since it is the product of our own interactions through engagement and participation with what is. Dewey's philosophy also underscores the unpredictability of pedagogy, in that all transactions are specific to situations that have unique determinants – 'there is no way in which we can assume that what was possible in one situation will automatically be applicable in another situation'. (Biesta, in this book). This is not a countenance of despair but an injunction to modesty in matters of pedagogy. We should aim for warrantable assertions rather than 'truths' and continually test out our knowledge through action and reflection on its effects.

In a consideration of pedagogy as brief as this, issues can only be raised selectively. However, one theme has dominated our analysis here. Within educational institutional contexts, pedagogy is challenged by socio-cultural approaches to learning that demonstrate the impact on learners of what happens beyond its immediate boundaries. This challenge comes in terms of both what there is to learn as well as how it might be learned, and by a range of different learners. The implication for pedagogy is to set both a new realism about what it can deliver, and at the same time, to create a new agenda for what pedagogy must address. Pedagogy as a result needs to build connections across different areas of experience, between the classroom, the workplace, the home and social life, where these connections can provide points of engagement for learners and ways of enabling them to draw on the resources of their own experience. These experiences now include, for many learners, the virtual as well as the face-to-face and symbolic, and these too must be within scope for pedagogy. If the scale of the challenge is sobering, we have at least identified both theoretical and practical tools that may help us in the task.

References

Bayne, S. (2005) 'Deceit, desire and control: the identities of learners and teachers in cyberspace', in Land, R. and Bayne, S. (eds) *Education in Cyberspace*, 26–41, Oxon: RoutledgeFalmer.

Cole, M. (1996) *Cultural Psychology: A Once and Future Discipline*. Cambridge, MA: Belknap.

Cox, R. (2005) 'Vicarious learning, case-based teaching and educational ICT', a paper produced for ESRC TLRP Thematic Seminar Series: *Contexts, Communities, Network: Mobilizing Learners' Resources and Relationships in Different Domains*, October, Open University.

Davis, B. and Sumara, D. (2006) *Complexity and Education*. Mahwah, NJ: Lawrence Erlbaum Associates.

Entwistle, N. (2005) 'Learning outcomes and ways of thinking across contrasting disciplines and settings in higher education', *The Curriculum Journal*, 16, 1: 67–82.

Hughes, M. (2005) 'Exchanging knowledge between home and school to enhance children's learning', paper produced for ESRC TLRP Thematic Seminar Series: *Contexts, Communities, Network: Mobilizing Learners' Resources and Relationships in Different Domains*, February, Glasgow Caledonian University.

Jewitt, C. and Jones, K. (2005) 'Managing time and space in the new English classroom', paper produced for ESRC TLRP Thematic Seminar Series: *Contexts, Communities, Network: Mobilizing Learners' Resources and Relationships in Different Domains*, June, Lancaster University.

McCune, V. and Hounsell, D. (2005) 'The development of students' ways of thinking and practising in three final-year biology courses', *Higher Education*, 49: 255–89.

Mayes, J.T. and Crossan, B. (2005) 'Learning relationships in community based further education', paper presented at the ESRC Teaching and Learning Research Programme (TLRP), Thematic Seminar Series: *Contexts, Communities, Networks: Mobilizing Learners' Resources and Relationships in Different Domains*, Glasgow Caledonian University, February.

Unwin, L., Ashton, D., Butler, P. Clarke, J. Felstead, A., Fuller, A. and Lee T. (2005) 'Worlds within worlds: The relationship between context and pedagogy in the workplace', paper produced for ESRC TLRP Thematic Seminar Series: *Contexts, Communities, Network: Mobilizing Learners' Resources and Relationships in Different Domains*, February, Glasgow Caledonian University.

Wenger, E. (2005) *Learning for A Small Planet: A Research Agenda*, available at http://www.ewenger.com/research/ (accessed 18 June 2008).

Chapter 12

Implications for researching learning contexts

Kate Miller

The chapters in the previous sections of this book all develop varying conceptions of learning contexts drawing on a range of different theoretical frameworks. What becomes clear is that there is a very rich array of theoretical thinking across these chapters upon which we can draw when developing new research endeavours. In this chapter, I will consider these conceptions of learning context and some of the implications for research in terms of the research methods, practices and ethics that may be drawn from the theoretical thinking that has been developed. I will also consider some models of research and their implications for researchers and research participants and the learning contexts of which they form a part. Finally, I will suggest some strategies for engaging research participants in research processes which may prove productive in terms of exploring the hard-to-reach aspects of learners' lives. The chapter is exploratory rather than definitive and a spur to more in-depth discussion of the work of research practices in producing learning contexts as much as reflecting on them.

Methods, practices and ethics

The theoretical framing of a research project has consequences for what is taken up as the unit of analysis and the units of data. The methodological approach and methods used to investigate the research questions reflect the theoretical orientation of the research. If one starts with an idea of context as container, then research practices are shaped by the relevant containers envisaged as the contexts under study. For example, cognitive approaches to learning focus analytically on the individual. Consequently the unit of analysis is individual cognition. Situated approaches to learning also tend to take the individual as the unit of analysis though socio-cultural factors are given weight. Distributed cognition takes the team or group as the focus for learning and knowledge. Actor-network theory (ANT) and activity theory move from the individual to the interaction between the individual and the collective. Thus, the network or activity system become the unit of analysis. The theoretical, methodological and ethical orientations of researchers are partly shaped through personal preferences and partly through pragmatic considerations and will play their part in the processes and practices of research, which in turn help in the selection and shaping of units of analysis.

These varying units of analysis and the focus that they provide obviously call for different methodological approaches and techniques. If the learning context is envisaged as a container, then looking at what happens within that context is framed by the boundaries of the container. If the unit of analysis is the relationships and networks between actors and actants and the context is shaped and constituted by the social practices engaged in by them, then it is difficult to know where the limits of the unit of analysis are. There are both methodological and ethical dimensions to making judgements about the limits to which one can or should go in exploring people's learning contexts.

This raises two questions to consider. First, how do we usefully define and limit our units of analysis when researching learning contexts? Second, how do we research ethically people's life contexts in order to understand their learning? The unit of analysis initially chosen will reflect the type of research questions that initiate the research, but may well need to be reconsidered in light of data that does not fit neatly within these units. Similarly, ethical considerations can be tricky to identify at the beginning of a research endeavour and may only materialize as the process unfolds. The units of analysis, i.e. containing the context to be explored, may initially seem to be easily defined, but may become more difficult and limit our understanding, depending on how the research process categorizes and draws boundaries between its selected units of analysis. To explore learning in the home as a specific bounded context seems straightforward, but the home is not simply a container, as people, objects, discourses, practices, etc. flow through that particular space and make it in particular ways. The research processes themselves may define or indeed blur container-like boundaries as they develop. In this sense, we need to be alert to the ways in which the theoretical and methodological approaches we take to investigate any research object will contribute to the constitution of the objects of research.

There are various metaphors of context that have emerged in this book that have implications for research. There is the container which neatly delimits what is inside and what is outside. There is the Russian doll with its different layers of practices from the macro to the micro. There is the woven cloth where the threads stretch from the micro practices of the classroom out to the other domains of learners' lives. There is the community of practice, the activity system, complexity and the network, all of which relate actors to other actors. It is probably worth noting that all of these metaphors use the concept of containment in some form or another, even as some try to move beyond the limitations set by bounded containers and take a leakier view of the world. At the very least, though, all use some form of categorization as a means of creating boundaries. Without them, it is impossible to even start to think about things. So it is prudent to remember that containers can be of many different sizes and of many different forms and have different ways of being permeable.

One of the implications for research of the more relational approaches to context is the need for greater sensitivity around what is included or excluded by our decisions to focus at a particular level or unit of analysis. We cannot avoid focusing selectively, of course. It is impossible to give equal attention at the same time to everything that is pertinent to a research question. Conceptualization of context as a container separates out the micro from the macro without necessarily taking account of the boundary work being done in establishing something as a learning context. There is simply a focusing in on what is inside the taken-for-granted context and a fading out of what is outside. This may result in an inability to relate the macro level factors to the micro level of social and cultural interactions. Consequently, there is a tendency to treat less than adequately certain highly abstract factors, such as power and social class, when we come to researching learning contexts.

However, if we accept that educational institutions do not exist as isolated containers of their own, but that what goes on in them is intimately related to other domains of people's lives, then we have to consider how far we should go in tracing the complicated strands of people's lives that go into shaping these learning contexts, if indeed they are practised as learning contexts by those involved; and if we do journey into these areas of people's lives, how do we establish and manage these research relationships which have their own implications in terms of power and social positioning?

If we take the more relational metaphors for context and consider people and their tools through their interactions as actively shaping these learning contexts, then we have a complex and in some ways fuzzy model of what constitutes a learning context. The problem is that it is hard to know on what to focus in our research. There is a need to relate local practices to wider macro structures. To understand these local events and the networks of practices that link them, ethnographic methods, sometimes loosely construed, are often employed in order to explore how participants in these networks both participate in and view their own practice in relation to others and the wider macro structures in which they operate; but here, of course, the research practices engaged in by researchers and participants in the research process have their own impact and play their own role in constituting the learning contexts which are the focus of their investigations. Certain approaches to research from an action or participative perspective are specifically designed to impact on the learning context and build in processes of evaluation. However, there are always the unintended consequences of research which need to be considered in their complexity which are often difficult to measure or capture due to their elusive or unexpected character.

The practicalities of research in terms of time and money, however, often limit an ethnographic approach to particular time slots in particular settings. It is not often possible to spend extended periods of time with people and become sufficiently integrated into the various domains of their lives to capture a rich insider perspective. One alternative is to utilize ethnographic-type methods that elicit information about a range of practices in which people engage across the varied domains of their often complex and intricate lives. The researcher may benefit from interacting with the people in a range of settings and find ways of playing down the possible perceived uneven relations of power that can limit the scope and flow of any interactions. Here, though, there is an increased danger of the researcher framing the research process according to their own imperatives without reaching an in-depth understanding of the cultural and social semiotic landscape of the research participants. The research techniques which are designed from a particular theoretical framework may actually limit the ability of the research participants to build different meanings and interpretations of practices and events. In other words, while opening up new contexts for research, the research practices themselves also set boundaries that may limit the capacity to understand learning across the different domains.

A relational approach to learning contexts, however framed, requires a certain amount of sensitive ethical decision-making around where to go and where not to go, what to uncover and what to leave covered up. Often these types of ethical decisions are made implicitly and spontaneously, making their impact on the research process less visible than other more explicit decisions about research design. In this sense, a fixed and standardized ethical code concerning research practices is not always very helpful and is inevitably too general to be of much utility to those engrossed in a particular research process. An interesting question is what informs these mostly hidden ethical decisions and on what basis are they made. Researchers often talk about difficult situations that arise in the research process and maybe a more careful look at these critical incidences could be illuminating in terms of how researchers' personal ethical decision-making impacts on the research process in establishing limits to what may or may not be considered a learning context.

Lankshear et al. (1996) draw our attention to how conceptualizing is a form of boundary-making. Bowker and Star (2000) make the point that to categorize is fundamental to being human. Categorization is about the setting of boundaries, including those of learning contexts. This indicates that the notion of a learning context is an effect of categorization, including that undertaken in research, and does not pre-exist such practices.

Edwards and Fowler (2007) explore this idea in locating research as an 'intellectual technology', drawing attention to the material, discursive and rhetorical practices of research. They describe the difficulty of opening up new discursive spaces for research when, in order to conceptually clarify and develop theoretical thinking and its position in relation to empirical work, we need to uptake and mobilize concepts already established within the domain of research. One way of exploring this process is to question the status of the objects of research, which are often treated as pre-existing in the social world and instead consider them as 'an effect of stable arrays or networks of relations' (Law 2002: 91). If we follow this line of thinking, then we can consider the part played by research practices and how they contribute to modes of ordering which produce certain forms of organization. In the view of Pels *et al.* (2002:11) 'objects need symbolic framings, storylines and human spokespersons in order to acquire social lives; social relationships and practices in turn need to be materially grounded in order to gain spatial and temporal endurance'. Edwards and Fowler (2007: 110) point out that research provides a range of intellectual technologies through which there is an attempt to represent and order phenomena and that 'research is as much embedded in these processes as it comments upon them', providing resources that attempt to represent and order social practices, while being subject to boundary-marking about what constitutes 'research'. In this sense, then, we should be aware of the performative nature of research processes and the limitations imposed on these practices.

An awareness of the spaces we create and the processes of enclosure that we perform through our research practices can be helpful when considering how learning contexts are performed in different ways through various networks of actors. It can also draw to our attention how the view varies from different perspectives and from different magnitudes of scale. The physical and material actors associated with particular locations, along with their associated modes of interaction, play an important role in shaping learning context and the research practices which investigate them. The resulting research practices can be either productive or restrictive depending on the particular combination of actors at work and the outcomes desired.

When researching in educational domains, the institution or organization that is organizing the learning may appear to act as a relatively clearly defined context if we are working with a container-type view. On this assumption, research can be carried out relatively easily within the bounds of that learning context. If research is being carried out on learning in a school, college or workplace then the institutional trappings will, to some extent, shape the type of research methods. They will tend to be formalized to at least some extent and the relations of power between researcher and participants can be relatively clearly defined so that each knows where they stand in relation to the other. There are ways in which these situations can be manipulated in order to attempt to trace the activities and practices of subjects' lives in other domains which are significant in the institutional learning context. However, the physical positioning of the research relationship in the institutional setting will impact on whatever techniques are used to bring the outside in or even the inside out. An awareness of the influence of the symbolic and material aspects of research locations can be useful as these are aspects which tell their own stories and can also be manipulated for research purposes.

If we take a more relational view, then it is the relationships between different domains that seem to be important. The issue of relationships across domains is certainly crucial in all of the research that has contributed to the chapters in this book. The points and practices of interaction vary across the chapters from texts to human relationships to boundary objects and human interactions. This raises the question of what is visible to whom, what is valued by whom and how that contributes to constituting learning contexts. The way in which research is set up in terms of funding, theoretical conceptualizations, methods and practices will impact on what is visible to whom and what is valued by whom. What is uncovered and what is left hidden and what is valued and what is not all play their part in the constituting of learning contexts through the research process. 'Concepts and boundaries co-emerge through the practices in which we engage in conducting research. It is not a question of escaping this process, which is illusory, but of bringing forth the basis for the particular wounds we inflict and living with the aporias that involves' (Edwards and Fowler 2007: 121). The chapters in this book point to the reflexive importance of considering our understandings of learning contexts in shaping the particular configurations of boundaries and relationships that we identify as such.

The swamplands of researching learning contexts

If we take a relational view of context and view it as something that is at least partly constituted through practice, then research practices will also be implicated in the forming of those contexts. The ethical questions arising from this understanding of context are more complicated than if we view research as something that is done impartially. Objectivist research traditions have taken the view that if the research impacts on the unit of analysis, then this is a problem in terms of validity of the research. This is referred to as 'the observers paradox' (Labov 1966) in sociolinguistic research or 'the Hawthorne effect' in sociological research (Draper 2003). The ideal in this type of research is to minimize the effects of the researcher on the research context. The researcher is supposed to be neutral and objective. In this case, the danger is that the focus on the objectivity of the research process can blind the researchers to the impact they may be having in all sorts of unpredicted ways.

However, if we accept that it is not possible to do research on something without having some impact on the object of research, then it is helpful to consider what type of impact we may wish to have. It is also important to consider that research is a learning context itself, which is intricately bound up with the learning contexts it takes as its objects of study. The research process will have an impact on the object of study right from the first conception of the research questions. Simply by categorizing something in such a way that it becomes the focus of research bestows a meaning to the object of the research.

From a Deweyan point of view, organizing a context for learning first and foremost concerns the creation of opportunities for participation in particular practices. An implication of this is that in order to research a learning context one would have to participate in those particular practices. Biesta (2006) argues that there are two central concepts in Dewey's understanding of contexts for learning: transaction and participation. 'Transaction' refers to the ongoing interactions between living organisms and their environments. At the more complex level of social interaction learning is also understood transactionally. Contexts for learning exist as social practices and transaction with such practices takes the form of participation. It is through participation that meaning can be communicated. Biesta argues that the most important transition in Dewey's theory of learning is the shift from action at the level of trial and error to intelligent action. Intelligent action is action mediated by symbols. According to Dewey the ability to use symbols – that is, to make a distinction between 'things' and their meaning – itself has a social origin. Symbols do not have an objective existence; they only exist in social practices, which means that access to symbolic resources can only be gained through participation in such practices (Biesta 2006).

If one was only observing or even observing and asking about the practices engaged in by research participants, then the understanding would be somewhat different to that gained from an active participation in those practices, which would enable a shared understanding of the symbolic resources available. This would suggest that, if the researcher wants to gain access to the meanings associated with symbolic practices, s/he will need to participate in the practices in a way which would enable engagement in the meaning-making process. In other words, they will have to become immersed in the contexts they are researching.

This view points to the tension inherent in any research endeavour that aims to investigate research questions through a method involving observation of practice, whether this is framed in terms of participant observation or non-participant observation (though I am not sure how you could actually do the latter without an invisibility cloak). There are various ways in which researchers can participate in the symbolic practices of their subjects. However, unless the researcher actually gives up the research endeavour and becomes a full-blown member of the community under study there will always be a tension between the role of observer and participant. As Bourdieu (1992: 19) points out:

> ... the relationship that is set up, here as elsewhere, between the observer and the observed is a particular case of the relationship between knowing and doing, interpreting and using, symbolic mastery and practical mastery, between logical logic, armed with all the accumulated instruments of objectification, and the universally pre-logical logic of practice.

This tension does not have to be a negative and can in fact be a very productive tension in terms of researchers and research participants gaining new insights into practice and theory.

Participants can also be active in research in various ways, from a collaboration with equal positions of power in terms of having control over the research process, to the other end of the spectrum where they are treated simply as respondents. Even in this case, they are still actively participating in the research process through their giving up of certain information in certain ways. The approach adopted will have implications for how the learning context is constructed through the research practices, the impact the research processes will have on the learning context and the understandings reached by those involved in the process. Sociocultural theories drawing on Vygotsky's dialectical approach to meaning and identity emphasize the importance of overcoming difference. An alternative dialogic perspective emphasizes the importance of difference as a prerequisite to participation (Wegerif 2008).

For instance, in the project discussed by Satchwell and Ivanič in the book, the methodology was broadly ethnographic. It sought to describe in as much detail as possible the literacy practices required for the study of particular curriculum areas, in becoming a college student, and those that learners manifest in the diverse contexts of their lives. This dimension was largely descriptive in the attempt to understand the culture and rituals of colleges and the artefacts through which literacy was mobilized. The aim was to obtain 'thick description' from the inside rather than merely act as observers from the outside. For this reason, university researchers partnered staff and students as members of the research team rather than them being simply respondents (Carmichael *et al.* 2007). The project was hermeneutic insofar as it recognized the recursive role of interpretation in the understanding of social practices, that is, the ways in which understanding is mobilized through the interrelationships between persons and artefacts and that these understandings help to shape future practices. The project sought to understand as well as describe literacy practices across a range of domains, but from within rather than from outside or above. However, as the researchers began to participate in and explore those domains and the flows within and across them, i.e. the learning contexts of participants, the participants also became active in the research context. This opened up a rich dialogic space in which to explore both theory and practice. We therefore see how researching learning contexts itself becomes a hybrid space of research *and* learning.

Complexity and dynamic systems theory, as discussed by Haggis in her chapter in this book, highlights how the ontological and epistemological foundations of the research process, when derived from an academic viewpoint, at times only serves to obscure the voices of participants rather than shed light on learning from the participants' point of view. She observes how in interpretive research there is often the imperative to do cross-sectional analysis of interview data in order to generate types or themes that emerge from the data. Haggis argues that this type of analysis derives from an idea of there being an underlying deep structure, which can be discovered by observing and analyzing the data in this manner to explain what is going on. Complexity theorists look at coemergence rather than causality. It rejects the commonsense notion that large changes in causes produce large changes in effects. It argues against reductionism and against reducing the whole to the parts. Space and time are not containers, but are 'internal' to the processes by which the physical world operates, helping to constitute the very powers of objects. Moreover, in a complex world there are no innocent methods; all involve forms of social practice that in some way or another are entangled with the patterns of the social or the physical.

For these reasons, Law and Urry (2002) conclude that research that uses observations taken at a single point in time–space will be representationally inadequate as they deal poorly with the fleeting, the distributed, the multiple, the sensory, the emotional and the kinesthetic. They urge for the development of methods that are sensitive to the complex and the elusive. Methods which can be more mobile and can find ways of knowing the slipperiness of 'units that are not', as they move in and beyond old categories (Law and Urry 2002: 9–10). How exactly we do this has yet to be formulated, however. It would involve being open to new ways of communicating, being and doing and not allowing entrenched forms of categorizing and recording to blind us to the new and emergent practices at the edges and spaces in between established communities and networks.

Haggis highlights the importance of the researcher being positioned within the system being studied, looking at histories and local interactions, rather than trying to climb high in order to get a 'broader view of the data'. She argues that this also implies a change in role. Instead of attempting to deduce underpinning or overarching principles, the researcher tries to define some of the interacting elements of the system, as well as perhaps the patterns and types of interaction which are taking place. A research design which combines the exploration of insiders' intuitive knowledge of their own social worlds with that of the outsider who needs to keep asking why, how, where and what questions in order to make sense of the naturalized objects, and practices which do the work of producing 'normal' members of the community (Bowker and Star 2000) can maybe go some way to uncovering the largely invisible boundaries and how they can be permeated by various objects, people and practices. At the same time maybe new spaces can be opened up for understanding learning contexts.

Conclusion

If we accept that the research process is going to impact on social practice and be a part of the shaping of learning contexts, then the ethical implications of how we carry out that research and what we do with it are even more important. A relational understanding of context means that when researching learning contexts it is necessary to follow the threads that form the pattern of the learning context. Each thread that is part of the woven cloth will have its own trajectory and be significant to some degree in terms of the overall pattern. By following these threads out of container-like contexts into the varying aspects of students' lives we can better understand the relationship between social practices in various domains and the formation of specifically learning contexts. Research methodologies that are formulated from a container view of context are likely to limit the ability to follow the threads and examine the relationships inherent in the combining of those threads. However, if we decide to follow some of these threads, we need to consider the ethical implications of our research methods carefully and also consider the implications of the inherent relations of power in the research relationships that develop and their impact on the findings that emerge. Any theoretical preconceptions will both make possible and limit the possible scope of a given methodology. It is important to be aware of this, of the co-emergence of research with the object of research, and be flexible in terms of an iterative process and allow our theoretical understanding to grow from the data and not limit our analysis unduly.

If we follow those threads right out of the classroom, the study/bedroom, the community centre or the workplace to the wider context of the national or global economic and social context and consider how the big picture connects up with the small place and vice versa, we also need to consider what role the researcher has betwixt and between various nodes along the way. Researchers occupy their own positions of relative power and powerlessness and can only operate within their own means. However, they do occupy the privileged position of being given time to engage in research activities, however they are funded or framed by the institutional contexts of which they are a part. Given the impact that research inevitably has on the learning contexts of which they become a part, it would seem evident that we should consider carefully how we want to impact on and influence those contexts. It is only by a careful and honest consideration of the performative nature of research that we can make the best use of the kind of resources we have in terms of time, money and the tools and practices of our trade. The theoretical orientations and their ontological assumptions play a powerful part in the shaping of research practices and their ethical implications. Phenomena that are not highly visible from one perspective may become visible from another perspective. So theoretical and practical implications of research need to be considered, along with their ethical dimensions, when investigating learning contexts.

The implications of a relational understanding of learning contexts for research stresses the importance of a reflexive consideration of the performative nature of research in terms of the methods used, the practices by which the research process is enacted and an uncovering of the often hidden ethical considerations informing and shaping the research process. Any assumption that researching learning contexts is a straightforward business is obviously challenged by the chapters in this book. The implications for research are profound, but not entirely clear.

References

Bowker, G. and Star, S. (2000) *Sorting Things Out: Classification and its Consequences*. Cambridge, MA: MIT Press.

Bourdieu, P. (1992) *The Logic of Practice*. Cambridge: Polity Press.

Biesta, G. (2006) 'Context and interaction: Pragmatism's contribution to understanding learning-in-context', a paper presented at the ESRC Teaching and Learning Research Programme Thematic Seminar Series, *Contexts, Communities, Networks: Mobilizing Learners' Resources and Relationships in Different Domains* – Seminar 4: Cultures, values, identities and power, Exeter, 22 February.

Carmichael, J., Edwards, R., Miller, K. and Smith, J. (2007) 'Researching literacy for learning in the vocational curriculum', in M. Osborne, M. Houston and N. Toman (eds) *The Pedagogy of Lifelong Learning*. Oxon: Routledge.

Draper, S. (2003) *The Hawthorne Effect: A Note*. Glasgow: University of Glasgow, Psychology.

Edwards, R. and Fowler, Z. (2007) 'Unsettling boundaries in making a space for research', *British Educational Research Journal*, 33, 1: 107–23.

Labov, W. (1966) *The Social Stratification of English in New York City*. Washington DC: Centre for Applied Linguistics.

Lankshear, C., Peters, M. and Knobel, M. (1996) 'Critical pedagogy and cyberspace', in H. Giroux, C. Lankshear, P. Mclaren and M. Peters (eds) *Counternarratives*. London: Routledge.

Law, J. (2002) 'Objects and spaces', *Theory, Culture and Society*, 19: 91–105.

Law, J. and Urry, J. (2002) *Enacting the Social*. Lancaster: University of Lancaster, Department of Sociology and Science Studies, www.comp.lancs.ac.uk/sociology/soc0099jlju.html

Pels, D., Hetherington, K. and Vandenberghe, F. (2002) 'The status of the object: Performances, Mediations, and Techniques', *Theory, Culture and Society*, 19: 1–21.

Wegerif, R. (2008), '*Research on educational dialogue*', *British Educational Research Journal*, 34, 3: 347–61.

Index